Why They Marched

WHY THEY MARCHED

Untold Stories of the Women Who Fought for the Right to Vote

SUSAN WARE

**The Belknap Press of
Harvard University Press**

CAMBRIDGE, MASSACHUSETTS
LONDON, ENGLAND
2019

First printing

LIBRARY OF CONGRESS CATALOGING-IN-PUBLICATION DATA

Names: Ware, Susan, 1950– author.

Title: Why they marched : untold stories of the women who fought for the right
   to vote / Susan Ware.

Description: Cambridge, Massachusetts : The Belknap Press of Harvard
   University Press, 2019. | Includes bibliographical references and index.

Identifiers: LCCN 2018039670 | ISBN 9780674986688 (alk. paper)

Subjects: LCSH: Women—Suffrage—United States—History. | Suffragists—
   United States—History.

Classification: LCC JK1896 .W37 2019 | DDC 324.6/23092273—dc23 LC record
   available at https://lccn.loc.gov/2018039670

To Anne Firor Scott,
born eight months after the ratification
of the Nineteenth Amendment and an
inspiration to women's historians ever since

Contents

Why They Marched

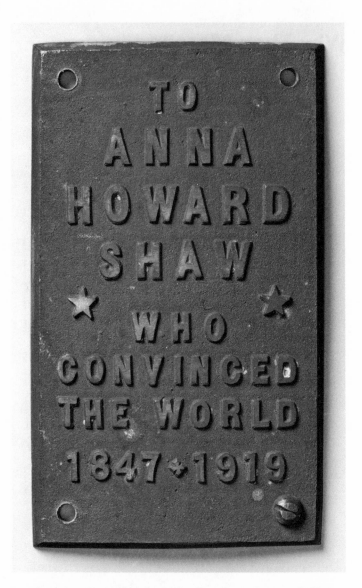

Tree plaque from Carrie Chapman Catt's suffrage forest. *Courtesy of Schlesinger Library, Radcliffe Institute, Harvard University.*

A Walk through Suffrage History

In THE SPRING OF 1919, just as suffrage leaders were facing the final, arduous process of winning ratification of the Nineteenth Amendment, Carrie Chapman Catt and her longtime companion and fellow suffragist Mary Garrett Hay bought a farm in Westchester county called Juniper Ledge. The estate in Briarcliff Manor, which featured a twenty-room house on seventeen acres of land, was an easy ninety-minute train ride from New York City. Hay disliked being so far away from the city, but Catt, who had served as president of the National American Woman Suffrage Association (NAWSA) since 1915, relished life in the country when she could tear herself away from suffrage politics: "I am in love with the place. It is isolated, quiet, restful, and gives promise of fun. There isn't much of any level land; God designed it for tired nerves not profit." Soon she came up with a creative use for the hilly terrain.[1]

Suffragists had a deep sense of history. They started collecting documents to chronicle their decades-long movement well before its ultimate conclusion was assured. In many ways they were our first women's historians. Juniper Ledge testified to that historical sense. Soon after moving in, Catt commissioned a series of twelve metal tree plaques to memorialize the giants of the

1

suffrage movement. Later that summer, she carefully installed them throughout the property. Taking a walk in the woods with Carrie Chapman Catt was like taking a course in suffrage history.

The placement of the plaques reflected both the lay of the land and Catt's estimation of her favorite foremothers. Starting out from a cow pasture, the path followed a lane towards a high rock above a small brook, which Catt conceived of as an altar. Right behind the altar were four majestic trees, with the one in the middle being especially noble. Catt chose that tree for the Susan B. Anthony plaque, which said simply "To Susan B. Anthony—Who Led the Way, 1820–1906." To her immediate right went the plaque for Anna Howard Shaw—"Who Convinced the World, 1847–1919." This plaque must have been especially poignant, since Shaw had just died that summer, exhausted by her wartime service on top of her years of suffrage activism. To Anthony's left was the plaque for her dear friend and lifelong collaborator, Elizabeth Cady Stanton—"The Fearless Defender of Her Sex, 1815–1902." Rounding out the altar was a plaque to Lillie Deveraux Blake—"Brave Champion of New York Women, 1835–1913." Not as well known as the trilogy of Anthony, Stanton, and Shaw, Lillie Deveraux Blake, the longtime president of the New York State Woman Suffrage Association, still earned pride of place in Catt's suffrage ramble.[2]

After leaving the altar and descending towards the brook, visitors next encountered plaques recognizing the international dimensions of the suffrage movement. First was Dr. Aletta Jacobs, "Who led the women of Holland to Political Liberty." Across the brook and back into the cow pasture was a parallel inscription to Millicent Garrett Fawcett, "Who led British women to Political Liberty," followed by Frau Minna Cauer, "Who led the way for Political Freedom for German Women." Those three leaders, with whom Catt had often collaborated during her years of international work, reminded those meandering in the woods that the suffrage struggle truly was a worldwide phenomenon.

Then it was back to suffragists who had toiled on American soil, starting with the abolitionist Abby Kelley, "Who Inspired Women to Break Their Silence." She was joined by two other towering figures of suffrage history: Lucy Stone, "Who Blazed a Trail," and Lucretia Mott, "Who said 'Truth for Authority not Authority for Truth.'" As part of this tableau, Catt chose for Angelina and Sarah Grimké twin trees "handsome and tall" which were joined at the base but separated into individual trunks higher up. The plaque for the Grimké sisters read, "Who Refused Taxation without Representation," a somewhat odd choice given that they were best known for their linkage of antislavery activism and women's rights. At least they were part of the pantheon.

One final spot was chosen with elaborate care. Behind the altar, a small group of pine trees formed a semi-circle. Here, on her own, Catt placed temperance leader Frances Willard, "The Woman of Widest Vision." Befitting someone whose motto was "Do Everything," the plaque saluted the breadth of Willard's vision, which linked temperance to a range of issues, including suffrage. It also gave another nod to the international dimensions of women's activism by recognizing Willard's leadership of the World Woman's Christian Temperance Union.

Catt's carefully curated mini-tour of suffrage history was not quite finished. A final plaque, commissioned by the recently formed League of Women Voters of New York City and added in 1922, celebrated none other than Catt herself. The inscription was in Latin—"dux femina facti," which roughly translates as "a woman who was leader of the exploit." No documentation exists to show where this plaque was placed—presumably not on the altar, but maybe across the brook with Abby Kelley or Lucy Stone? Or maybe Catt tucked it away off the beaten path, hesitant to take her place alongside the other suffrage pioneers. Truth be told, she deserved to be on the altar alongside Anthony, Stanton, and Shaw. Today, her plaque and eight others reside in the archives of the Arthur and Elizabeth Schlesinger Library on the History of Women in America at Radcliffe.[3]

There are many ways to tell the history of woman suffrage, but I want to follow Carrie Chapman Catt's lead and tell it through people, places, and objects. Too often, the necessity to cover the relentless chronological sweep from Seneca Falls in 1848 to the ratification of the Nineteenth Amendment in 1920 flattens the story, rendering it lifeless. Biography makes it come alive. To bring the story of the American woman suffrage movement to life, I have organized the narrative as a prosopography featuring nineteen discrete but overlapping biographical stories. This approach allows me to recapture the breadth and spirit of the movement through individual lives while providing an overview of the larger suffrage story.

As Carrie Chapman Catt's tree plaques suggest, things tell stories too. Along with photographs and illustrations, objects and artifacts bring another dimension to the history of the suffrage crusade. To make that connection explicit, in each biographical chapter, an object or image sets up the suffrage story that follows. Sojourner Truth's carte de visite, the commemorative pin given to Hazel Hunkins in 1919 by the National Woman's Party, Charlotte Perkins Gilman's death mask, and the 1909 *Washington Women's Cook Book* with "Votes for Women / Good Things to Eat" on its cover—all are characters in their own right in a book of suffrage stories.

The stories show the variety of places where the suffrage movement unfolded, starting with Carrie Chapman Catt's Juniper Ledge estate. Suffrage activism happened not only in church parlors, meeting rooms, and the halls of Congress, but also in graveyards on the outskirts of college campuses, on the steps of the Treasury Building in Washington, DC, at international conferences in Berlin and Budapest, and even on top of Mount Rainier. Few corners of the United States were untouched by suffrage activism. Especially after 1910, the suffrage movement was impossible to escape.

As charming as Carrie Chapman Catt's woodland tableau is, it provides an imperfect model for this project, which aims to probe more deeply into some of the more complex and hidden pockets of suffrage history than suffragists at the time were willing to acknowledge. Racism is an obvious place to start. Consistent with the deep-seated prejudices held by most white suffragists, Catt included no plaques to commemorate the thousands of African American women who participated in the struggle. Then there is Eurocentrism: the international suffragists honored in Catt's suffrage forest were all from western European countries, not from countries in South America, Asia, or Africa, which Catt condescendingly believed needed to look to First World women for guidance. Regional chauvinism was present as well: all the domestic suffragists were from the East Coast, with New York State heavily overrepresented. There was no one from California or the West and no one from the South, unless you count the Grimké sisters, who were born there but left because of their abhorrence of slavery. Finally, there is a clear personal snub: she commissioned no plaque for her rival Alice Paul, whose National Woman's Party caused much consternation for Catt and NAWSA in the final stages of the suffrage fight but whose militance was critical to the movement's ultimate victory.[4]

For too long, the history of woman suffrage has put forward a version that closely parallels Carrie Chapman Catt's suffrage forest: a top-heavy story dominated by a few iconic leaders, all white and native-born, and the national organizations they founded and led. Moving decisively away from that outdated approach uncovers a much broader, more diverse suffrage history waiting to be told. This new history shifts the frame of reference away from the national leadership to highlight the women—and occasionally the men— who made woman suffrage happen through actions large and small, courageous and quirky, in states and communities across the nation. Telling these suffrage stories captures the broad-based movement where it actually happened—on the ground.

Over the long durée of the suffrage campaign, women who had never before participated in politics suddenly found themselves doing things they never would have thought possible—filing law-suits, holding public protests, collecting signatures on petitions, lobbying members of Congress, marching in suffrage parades, and even risking arrest and imprisonment for the cause. Women may not have fundamentally changed politics when they began to exercise the franchise (does anyone ever hold men to that standard?) but many women's lives were profoundly altered by participation in the struggle to win the vote. This narrative captures those personal and political transformations.

Material culture is central to recreating and contextualizing women's suffrage experiences. History is not just made up of written documents and texts; objects and artifacts play key roles as well, especially in the creation of personal and group identities. This insight is particularly relevant for a social movement like suffrage, which came to embrace popular culture and public spectacle as a primary strategy to win support for its cause. Highlighting suffrage artifacts allows us to imagine how these messages were packaged, circulated, and received at the time, and demonstrates how innovative and politically savvy the women were who spearheaded the movement. Besides that larger cultural and political work, suffrage objects are especially evocative in connecting everyday lives with the broader movement. In many cases, they literally were "the things they carried."[5]

This diverse cast of characters, broadly defined to include both human actors and inanimate objects, hints at the richness of suffrage history waiting to be tapped. The stories cover the span of the suffrage struggle, but with a definite tilt towards the twentieth century. The profiles and objects from the West, South, and Midwest promise a more representative national story, and the inclusion of African American and working-class suffrage stories and artifacts reminds us that the movement was not only white and middle-class. The biographical line-up includes a best-selling writer who published a suffrage novel that tanked; a polygamist Mormon wife who was an avid suffragist; two prominent sisters who were on opposite sides of the suffrage divide; an artist who gave up her painting career to become a suffrage cartoonist; an African American activist who refused to march in a segregated suffrage parade; and fourteen more. With the exception of Susan B. Anthony, none of them held a top-tier leadership position. Instead, they represent the broad diversity of rank-and-file suffragism.

Focusing on individual suffragists does not mean sacrificing the larger picture—far from it. The lives of the characters overlap and connect in repeated but often serendipitous ways. In several instances, such as the 1913 suffrage parade in Washington, multiple characters were in the same place at the same time. Even though each story and its accompanying object can stand on its own, when read together, they provide a synthetic and surprisingly comprehensive history of the entire movement. If I have chosen my nineteen subjects and objects well, the whole truly will add up to more than the sum of its parts.

Eleanor Flexner titled her path-breaking 1959 survey of the suffrage movement *Century of Struggle.* Woman suffrage has been part of my life for almost half as long. As a twenty-year-old college student, I attended my first feminist demonstration on the historically significant date of August 26, 1970—the fiftieth anniversary of the Nineteenth Amendment. At Wellesley College, I wrote my senior thesis on the 1848 Seneca Falls Convention. I pursued my doctorate in women's history at Harvard, where my first seminar paper was on the local suffrage group in Cambridge, and my second on the feminist intellectual and suffragist Charlotte Perkins Gilman. While at Harvard, I was introduced to the treasures of the Schlesinger Library, beginning a lifelong association which this book gratefully acknowledges. I titled my first book about women in the New Deal *Beyond Suffrage,* and I joined the ranks of feminist historians pioneering the field of women's history. As the suffrage centennial approached, I wanted to return to where I had started.

But here I faced a larger challenge than I anticipated: how to make the fight for the vote come alive to modern readers? From my perspective as a historian, the woman suffrage movement stands out as one of the most significant and wide-ranging moments of political mobilization in all of American history. Among other outcomes, it produced the largest one-time increase in voters ever. As important as the goal of suffrage was, the struggle was always far broader than just the franchise, and it spoke to fundamental questions about women's roles in politics and modern life. Who gets to vote? When, and why? These give rise to further, profound questions about the relationship between citizenship and suffrage over time. If we think of suffragists as the voting rights activists of their day, we see how the suffrage movement fits into this larger story.

Yet most Americans dismiss the Nineteenth Amendment as a minor or inconsequential reform, in contrast to the antislavery and civil rights movements, which are presented as central to the ongoing struggle for equality and diversity in a democratic society. Why hasn't the suffrage movement won a similar place in the historical canon? This marginalization of woman suffrage does not hold up to scrutiny, historical or otherwise. If suffrage was such a minor reform, why did it generate such powerful and sustained opposition? Could it, perhaps, have been the threat of women acting out in public and demanding the right to hold and exercise power on an equal basis with men? As the historian Laurel Thatcher Ulrich once said in another context, "Well-behaved women seldom make history."[6] There is a direct line from the spectacles of the suffrage campaign to the sea of pink pussy hats worn at the Women's Marches held across the country—indeed around the world—in January 2017 to protest the inauguration of Donald Trump.

The suffrage campaign is especially important to the history of American feminism. Despite Winnifred Harper Cooley's often-quoted assertion that "All feminists are suffragists, but not all suffragists are feminists," suffragists *were* feminists, falling well within this definition provided by the historian Estelle Freedman: "Feminism is a belief that although women and men are inherently of equal worth, most societies privilege men as a group. As a result, social movements are necessary to achieve political equality between women and men, with the understanding that gender always intersects with other social hierarchies." In a story that stretches from the eighteenth century to the present and beyond, the suffrage movement is a key milestone in the longer feminist continuum, just as feminism is, and should be seen as, part of the broader struggles for equality and social justice.[7]

Suffragists' focus on gender consciousness brings them quite clearly into the feminist fold. As Nancy Cott argued in her influential book, *The Grounding of Modern Feminism*, "Feminism posits that women perceive themselves not only as a biological sex but (perhaps even more importantly) as a social group."[8] Suffragists were women ready and willing to say "we." Without that consciousness, there was no reason for them to join the suffrage movement. Alice Paul once suggested that some women are "born feminist"—she certainly was, and probably Susan B. Anthony was as well—but others take a slightly more meandering path to identification with women's issues. For many women, participation in the suffrage movement offered the equivalent of the 1960s "click" moment, when the powerful ideas of modern feminism hit home. And once that epiphany happened, there was no turning back. For more than seven decades, the suffrage movement provided a consciousness-raising vehicle for women (and a few far-sighted men) to work towards larger feminist goals. And that momentum continued in the postsuffrage era.[9]

In 1920 Oreola Williams Haskell published the book *Banner Bearers: Tales of the Suffrage Campaigns*, which in many ways provides the inspiration for this project. Comprised of a series of fictional sketches, "each embodying one special feature of the many-sided efforts to win the vote," the book tells the story through the eyes of ordinary, and often extraordinary, suffrage workers going about their daily business of the incredibly difficult task of winning the vote. Haskell puts human faces on the collective drama of broader social change. As she recreates the "hard application and intense living" of "the little world of the suffrage worker," she also highlights "its humor, its pathos and its passion," and especially the bonds of loyalty forged among suffragists who dedicated themselves to the cause. "Once of its circle," Haskell realizes, "life was forever deeper and different."[10]

Even though we are writing nearly a century apart, Haskell's goals and mine are remarkably similar: to recreate the passion and commitment that three generations of American women brought to the suffrage cause and to tell that story from the perspective of "those who have waged its battles and won its victories." That means bringing the story down to the personal level—to individual acts of courage and political defiance, to stories of quiet determination alongside displays of public spectacle. It also encompasses moments of fun and whimsy designed to buck up sagging spirits in the face of sustained opposition, in tandem with the rich trove of objects and memorabilia that connect suffragists' lives and times to our own. "May these pages seem like the diary they have never had time to write," Haskell hoped, "or like the portfolio of old photographs that, though faded, make the once vivid past live again."[11] At the very least, here are some fresh candidates for Carrie Chapman Catt's suffrage forest.

PART ONE

Claiming Citizenship

How can someone demand the vote without having that basic political right in the first place? That was the conundrum suffrage activists faced as they tried to convince men, especially male elected officials, to share the vote with them—without being able to use the vote as leverage. Suffragists intuitively knew that politics and political influence were about more than casting a ballot, and they devised creative ways to insert themselves directly into the political realm. Even if they could not vote, they could still perform the rituals of citizenship and civic participation that men enjoyed. All they had to do was present themselves as legitimate participants in the political process and act as if they were the fully vested citizens they aspired to become.

That task was made both harder and easier by the nation's experience after the Civil War. Reconstruction is fundamental to understanding the history of woman suffrage. The unimaginable had happened: a costly civil war ended slavery, and a new political order was in the making. What would be the relation between federal power and the role of the states? Who was an American citizen? What responsibilities went along with citizenship? The rights of newly freed slaves were central to the discussion about how to reconstitute the national state. In this fraught but pregnant political moment, women activists believed they might have a fighting chance to win those rights for women as well. In effect, they tried to insert gender alongside race in the national debate about citizenship.

When the Fifteenth Amendment was ratified in 1870, guaranteeing African American men—but not women of any race—the right to vote, that effort stalled, at least temporarily. Soon afterward, the political and moral imperatives that had provided support for a radical rethinking of the democratic promise in the wake of the Civil War weakened, then disappeared. But the unfinished business of Reconstruction continued to set the agendas for civil rights and women's rights for decades to come. The Civil War and its aftermath put questions of citizenship and human rights firmly on the national agenda, where they have remained ever since.

CHAPTER ONE

The Trial of Susan B. Anthony and the "Rochester Fifteen"

THE SENECA FALLS CONVENTION holds an iconic place in the history of woman suffrage, even though it was not, as is often asserted, the first convention ever held on the question of women's rights. On July 19 and 20, 1848, three hundred women and men gathered in the small upstate New York town of Seneca Falls. They came in response to a call issued by Elizabeth Cady Stanton, Lucretia Mott and Martha Coffin Wright—but not Susan B. Anthony, who would only join the movement two years later—to discuss "the social, civil and religious condition of woman." Acting as their wordsmith, Elizabeth Cady Stanton memorably turned the Declaration of Independence on its head by boldly asserting, in the preamble to the Declaration of Sentiments she drafted for the convention, that "all men and women are created equal." The only resolution to spark controversy was the call "to secure for themselves their sacred right to elective franchise."[1]

Why was the question of suffrage so fraught? Voting in the nineteenth century was very different from today. Instead of polling places being located in well-ordered settings such as schools, churches, or public buildings, ballots were cast at privately-owned structures, such as warehouses, livery stables, and saloons—literally places where no "respectable lady" would venture. Election days were rowdy and chaotic affairs, often featuring copious amounts of alcohol and incidents of physical intimidation, if not outright violence. No wonder women's demand for the vote was so hard to process—it struck at the core of nineteenth-century male political culture.

One of the first visual documents to refer to the 1848 Seneca Falls Convention was a color print captioned "Leaders of the Woman's Rights Convention Taking an Airing," published the same year by James S. Baillie, the owner of a lithography business in New York City. These women's rights advocates—none of whom seem to be literal portrayals of actual suffragists—may have been out "taking an airing," but this print was not going to win many converts to the cause. The print's main message can be summed up in one word: transgressive. All four women are dressed in outfits that depart from traditional female dress, including helmets and top hats. Instead of modestly riding side-saddle, they mount their steads like men, showing a shocking amount of leg (even a knee!) and featuring appendages that look more like hooves than dainty female feet. Everything seems topsy-turvy: a horse steals a bonnet, two of the women are disheveled, horses bolt out of control from under their riders. The print perfectly depicts a world turned upside down when women challenged their exclusion from politics and public life. And once women boldly—and bodily—entered the public sphere to claim the rights of citizenship for their sex, there was no turning back.

"Leaders of the Woman's Rights Convention Taking an Airing," color print by James S. Baillie, 1848. *Courtesy of Schlesinger Library, Radcliffe Institute, Harvard University.*

"WELL I HAVE BEEN & gone & done it!!—positively voted the Republican ticket—strait—this A.M. at 7 Oclock—& *swore my vote in at that.*" So Susan B. Anthony gloated to her friend and suffrage co-conspirator Elizabeth Cady Stanton in a letter from Rochester dated November 5, 1872. Fully aware of the publicity value of her attempt, she was prepared to go to jail for the cause and relished the legal fight to come. She even dared hope that women all around the country would spontaneously join her by going to the polls: "If only now *all the Woman* Suffrage *Women* would work to *this* end, of *enforcing the existing constitution*—supremacy of *national law* over state law—what strides we might make this very winter." It didn't work out quite as she planned, but Anthony turned her defiant act of voting into a public relations coup for the nascent suffrage movement.[2]

The immediate spur for her unprecedented act was an editorial in the *Rochester Democrat and Chronicle* the previous Friday urging voters to register: "Now register! Today and tomorrow are the only remaining opportunities. If you were not permitted to vote, you would fight for the right, undergo all privations for it, face death for it. You have it now at the cost of five minutes' time to be spent in seeking your place of registration and having your name entered.... Today and tomorrow are your only opportunities. Register now!" To modern eyes, this language seems remarkably ungendered—applicable to women as well as men, which is how Susan B. Anthony chose to read it. In fact, in 1872, the idea that women would take up the call to register to vote was so far-fetched that it never would have occurred to the editorial writers to limit the wording to men.[3]

Susan B. Anthony seized the moment. Gathering up her three sisters, the ensemble walked down to their local registration spot, a general store which also doubled as a barbershop, and asked to be allowed to register in advance of the upcoming election. They fully expected to be denied, and they planned to use that refusal to mount a legal challenge to their exclusion from the polls. To their surprise, the three local election inspectors, all relatively young, inexperienced, and clearly in over their heads, did not immediately turn them away. Susan B. Anthony pounced on their hesitation to read aloud from the text of the Fourteenth Amendment in support of her cause. Probably somewhat intimidated by being in the presence of one of Rochester's most famous public citizens, the two Republican inspectors agreed to enter the women's names on the voting rolls, overruling the objections of the sole Democratic official. Taking advantage of this unexpected turn of events, Anthony quickly got the word out that other women should register. That day and the next, approximately fifty women answered the call, setting the stage for the election-day drama.[4]

This was far from a spontaneous action. Susan B. Anthony had been contemplating a legal case to test federal and state voting regulations for several years. The post–Civil War political and legal landscape, specifically the Reconstruction-era amendments to the Constitution passed in response to the end of slavery, made such a test case possible, indeed necessary. Two aspects of these amendments had huge implications for the woman suffrage movement: the introduction of the modifier "male" when defining voters in the Fourteenth Amendment (1868) and the decision not to include "sex" alongside the prohibited categories of "race, color, or previous condition of servitude" in the Fifteenth Amendment (1870).[5]

Before the Civil War, the women's rights movement and abolitionism had been closely connected, but when the war ended, the old coalition linking race and gender split irrevocably. The dispute was about who had priority: African-American men facing new political terrain after slavery was abolished or white women, who also wanted to be included in the post–Civil War expansion of political liberties. Prominent reformers like Frederick Douglass and Wendell Phillips believed that this was "the Negro's hour," and that African American rights were the most pressing issue. Suffragists such as Lucy Stone, Henry Blackwell, and Julia Ward Howe had hoped for universal suffrage, but once the amendments were drafted, they supported ratification despite the exclusion of women. Susan B. Anthony and Elizabeth Cady Stanton adamantly refused to support the amendments, often employing racist language to imply that white women were just as deserving of the vote as African American men, if not more so. Even though African American women prominently participated in this debate, their rights and interests were often left out of the equation.

By 1869, the suffrage movement had split in two over this question, which was both strategic and philosophical. Stone, Blackwell, and Howe founded the Boston-based American Woman Suffrage Association, and the Stanton-Anthony wing set up the rival National Woman Suffrage Association, which was centered in New York. So heated were the underlying divisions that the two wings would not reunite until 1890, when the older generation of suffragists began to cede power to a rising generation that had not been so traumatically marked by the Reconstruction-era schism.

Even though the Fourteenth Amendment added new hurdles for the woman suffrage movement, as Elizabeth Cady Stanton had predicted in 1866—"If the word 'male' be inserted . . . it will take us a century at least to get it out"—in the short term, suffragists used the amendment to make a novel case for women's voting rights. Asserting that the Fourteenth Amendment conferred broad rights of citizenship without reference to gender, they argued that women already had the right to vote because it was a right of citizenship, one which states could not take away. If the courts had accepted that reasoning, then the next five decades of suffrage agitation would have been unnecessary.[6]

One of the first articulations of this intriguing idea came in 1869 from a St. Louis attorney named Francis Minor, whose wife Virginia was active in the Missouri woman suffrage movement. A widely circulated pamphlet making the Minors' case that women already had the right to vote and merely needed to exercise it spurred hundreds of direct actions at local polling places. By 1872, the National Woman Suffrage Association formally embraced this strategy, which it called the "New Departure." Now it only needed a test case to take to the Supreme Court. In fact, Susan B. Anthony expected such a test case to happen when she registered to vote in Rochester in 1872. When events proved different, she rose to the challenge and changed her strategy.

After Susan B. Anthony and fourteen other Rochester women committed the "crime" of casting ballots in their local Rochester wards on Tuesday, November 5, 1872, the legal wheels were set in motion. First, the local US commissioner invited the women to come into his office for an interview. Clearly enjoying the moment, Anthony "sent word to him that I had no social acquaintance with him and didn't wish to call on him. If he wanted to see me on official business he must come and see me." Two weeks later, a US marshal knocked on Anthony's door. He soon found himself sitting in the parlor making small talk with the formidable suffrage leader. Finally, the clearly embarrassed emissary admitted he was there to serve a warrant for her arrest. After asking permission to change her clothes (granted) and presenting her wrists for handcuffing (declined, and probably a wise decision), the marshal escorted Anthony and two of her sisters to the federal offices, paying their trolley fare as was the custom for all criminals facing arrest. They were not arrested, however, and they did not spend time in jail.[7]

The next day, all fifteen women appeared at a preliminary hearing, now represented by counsel, Henry R. Selden. The proceedings rehashed the events of the fateful day, including such comical questions as whether Anthony had dressed as a woman (no one had suggested the female voters were cross-dressing in order to vote), while Selden tried to establish that, because they believed they had a right to vote, the women had committed no crime. Various preliminary hearings continued into December and January. During this time, Anthony was technically under arrest and had refused to pay bail. Under more normal circumstances, this might have landed her in jail. But the authorities were unwilling to take her into custody. At the very least they seemed to assume she would stay put in Rochester. Instead, she defiantly set off on a trip to Washington, DC and New York City. Her lawyer posted her bail.

On Tuesday, January 21, 1873, a grand jury indicted Anthony. The other women of what today might be called "the Rochester Fifteen" were not indicted; the expectation was that Anthony's case was sufficient to address all the legal issues at stake. What crime had Anthony actually committed? Here the intricacies of state versus federal jurisdiction over voting came into play. Although it was not specifically mentioned in the indictment, she was charged with violating the Enforcement Act of 1870, a federal law designed to cut down on voter fraud in the post–Civil War South. But the law only applied to voting for federal offices, so even though Anthony had voted the straight Republican ticket, she was singled out only for voting for a representative to the US Congress. Her votes for local candidates, indeed for the President of the United States, were of no matter in the proceedings. The next step was a trial before an all-male jury. While awaiting trial, Anthony had the cheek to vote again in March, but since it was a local election, no charges were brought.[8]

In the months between her indictment and the trial, Susan B. Anthony took to the hustings, undertaking an extensive speaking tour in upstate New York to convince potential male jurors of the rightness of her cause. In effect, she was asking them to consider engaging in jury nullification. That is, even if she were guilty on the facts, they should find her not guilty because they believed the law she was charged under to be unconstitutional. This may sound like a longshot, but it was a known strategy. Northern juries in the 1850s occasionally refused to convict those who helped slaves to escape, because they disagreed with the highly punitive provisions of the Fugitive Slave Act of 1850. For a time Anthony's friend Matilda Joslyn Gage, a much more charismatic public speaker, joined her on the lecture circuit with a talk provocatively titled "The United States on Trial, Not Susan B. Anthony."[9]

Finally the trial—and the public venue in which Anthony so fervently desired to present her case—got underway in the Canandaigua courthouse, in June 1873. The presiding federal judge, Ward Hunt, had recently been appointed by President Ulysses S. Grant to the US Supreme Court. Like other Supreme Court justices, he also heard cases in a designated region—in his case, Western New York. Despite these credentials, Anthony was not impressed. "On the bench sat Judge Hunt, a small-brained, pale-faced, prim-looking man, enveloped in a faultless suit of black broadcloth, and a snowy white tie. This was the first criminal case he had been called on to try since his appointment, and with remarkable forethought, he had penned his decision before hearing it." She was not being sarcastic: that is exactly what happened.[10]

After the prosecution and defense had presented their cases, Judge Hunt turned to the jury and began to read from a prepared statement. Perhaps if the Fifteenth Amendment had included the word *sex*, he admitted, the argument might have had merit, but in his opinion the Fourteenth Amendment did not give women the right to vote. Therefore Anthony was in violation of the law. "Upon this evidence I suppose there is no question for the jury and that the jury should be directed to find a verdict of guilty." His instructions clearly violated the Sixth Amendment's guarantee of trial by jury. Some quick legal skirmishes by Anthony's lawyer failed to change the outcome, and the jurors were discharged without ever having a chance to discuss the case or be polled about their opinions. Writing later in her journal, Anthony called this "the greatest judicial outrage history ever recorded!"[11]

That was Judge Hunt's first mistake. The second was when he said at the sentencing hearing, "Has the prisoner anything to say why sentence shall not be pronounced?" Already standing as she awaited her fate, Anthony lashed out at the judge and the proceedings: "Yes, your honor, I have many things to say; for in your ordered verdict of guilty, you have trampled under foot every vital principle of our government. My natural rights, my civil rights, my political rights, my judicial rights, are all alike ignored." Despite the judge's repeated admonishment to sit down and stop talking, Anthony continued to press her case. "When I was brought before your honor for trial, I hoped for a broad and liberal interpretation of the Constitution and its recent amendments, that should declare all United States citizens under its protecting aegis. . . . But failing to get this justice—failing, even, to get a trial by a jury *not* of my peers—I ask not leniency at your hands—but rather the full rigors of the law." With that she finally sat down, only to be told to rise again while he pronounced her sentence: a fine of one hundred dollars and court costs. "I shall never pay a dollar of your unjust penalty," Anthony announced, and she never did.[12]

Although Anthony was thwarted in her desire to be handcuffed and hauled off to jail, she knew a good publicity moment when she saw one, and she began moving forward immediately with plans to circulate the transcript of the trial. (It isn't much of an exaggeration to say that reading the transcript today brings to mind a treatment for a play or even a Hollywood movie.) Published barely nine months after the conclusion of the trial, this "instant" book of more than two hundred pages let the transcript of the proceedings make the case both for the rightfulness of Anthony's argument and the wrongfulness of the trial that she received. Anthony raised enough money to print three thousand copies of the book for distribution to key allies and friends. The public could also buy the volume for fifty cents.

An editorial in the local *County Post* cogently summarized all that had happened: "If it is a mere question of who has got the best of it, Miss Anthony is still ahead; she has voted and the American Constitution has survived the shock. Fining her one hundred dollars does not rub out the fact that fourteen women voted, and went home, and the world jogged on as before." But even though the case was a public relations bonanza, it had little if any legal impact. Fulfilling suffragists' desire to win a definitive Supreme Court ruling was left to another test case working its way through the courts.[13]

The St. Louis attorney Francis Minor and his wife, who had raised the legal argument about women's voting rights being subsumed under citizenship back in 1869, pursued the legal case that Anthony originally thought would be hers. In October 1872, Virginia Minor sued Reese Happersett, the registrar who had rejected her application to register to vote, claiming that the Fourteenth Amendment guaranteed her right to vote even though the state constitution limited voting to males. Ironically, because married women in Missouri could not bring suit on their own behalf until 1889, her husband sued for them both. Their argument found no traction in the state courts, but the Supreme Court agreed to take the case because it addressed a constitutional question about federal versus state power. The case was argued in February 1875 and the decision announced seven weeks later. The unanimous outcome was definitive and devastating, handing the suffrage movement a defeat from which it took decades to recover.[14]

Chief Justice C. J. Waite began his opinion by restating the plaintiff's argument "that as a woman, born or naturalized in the United States and subject to the jurisdiction thereof, is a citizen of the United States and of the State in which she resides, she has the right of suffrage as one of the privileges and immunities of her citizenship, which the State cannot by its laws or constitution abridge." The court found this reasoning without merit, drawing a fundamental distinction between citizenship and voting rights. Women qualify as citizens, the court admitted, but the right to vote was not one of the "privileges or immunities of citizens of the United States" guaranteed by the Constitution. Here the court followed the country's long tradition, especially at the state and local levels, of imposing limitations on voting: property restrictions were widespread until the 1830s, and groups such as Native Americans, slaves, and Chinese immigrants, in addition to women, were barred from voting altogether in the nineteenth century. The Supreme Court was in no mood to condone universal suffrage for all citizens.[15]

Susan B. Anthony and Francis and Virginia Minor really thought they had found a creative legal strategy to enfranchise women, but *Minor v. Happersett* stopped the "New Departure" strategy dead in its tracks. As Anthony's co-counsel John Van Voorhis pointed out later, "if Miss Anthony had won her case on the merits, it would have revolutionized the suffrage of the country and enfranchised every woman in the United States." Unfortunately, the unanimous ruling was so definitive that legal recourse was no longer an option. It is always extremely difficult to get the Supreme Court to reverse itself on major decisions—it took fifty-eight years before *Brown v. Board of Education* set aside *Plessy v. Ferguson*'s separate-but-equal doctrine—and the conservative political and legal climate of the late nineteenth century made such a change in attitude highly unlikely.[16]

With legal challenges off the table, only two options remained to the suffrage movement. The first was to try to amend state constitutions to include female voters alongside male. The second was to work for a federal amendment to the Constitution that would ensure women's right to vote. Those two strategies basically defined the next half century of suffrage activism, with significant early victories at the state level, but a constitutional amendment still necessary at the end to ensure women's voting rights across the nation.

Susan B. Anthony relished a good fight, and she gave this one her all. The story of her attempt to vote and her defiance of the government prosecutors who tried to silence her added to her celebrity in nineteenth-century America. Indeed, the incident has become one of the most widely recognized deeds of her long and active life. She was always clear about her intent, which had implications far beyond a polling place in Rochester, New York. Challenged in one of the court proceedings as to whether she had presented herself as a female claiming the right to vote, she spiritedly replied, "I presented myself not as a female at all, sir. I presented myself as a citizen of the United States."[17] With her defiant act, Susan B. Anthony was claiming citizenship.

I SELL THE SHADOW TO SUPPORT THE SUBSTANCE.
SOJOURNER TRUTH.

Sojourner Truth's carte de visite, 1864. *Courtesy of Schlesinger Library, Radcliffe Institute, Harvard University.*

CHAPTER TWO

Sojourner Truth
Speaks Truth to Power

PHOTOGRAPHY HAS BEEN central to the creation of historical memory since the 1830s. By the late 1850s, a new photographic technique called cartes de visite had spread from France to the United States. The brainchild of André-Adolphe-Eugène Disdéri, a carte de visite was a thin albumen print attached to a heavy 2½-by-4-inch cardboard mount. It was created using a sliding plate holder and a camera with four lenses, which generated eight negatives each time a picture was taken; an added benefit was the possibility of printing more cards from the negatives at a later date. Originally conceived as an alternative to the calling card, the photographs were more typically shared as family mementoes. Up until this point, only the elite could afford to preserve their likenesses, mainly through commissioned portraits and paintings; even early photographic innovations such as the daguerreotype (invented in 1839) and the tintype were too costly for mass adoption. The relatively cheap cartes de visite brought the possibility of memorializing one's likeness for posterity to a far broader audience.

Soon America was in the grip of "cartomania." When photography studios sold cartes de visite of famous figures, they helped create a sense of common national purpose through the consumption of shared images. The wide circulation of Abraham Lincoln's image in the 1860 electoral campaign owes much to this new technology. When the Civil War broke out in 1861, the fad took on a somber tone as those who fought on both the Union and Confederate sides rushed to have photographic images taken for loved ones left behind. In turn, those family members posed for portraits that soldiers could take with them into battle, where the keepsakes were sometimes discovered tucked into a pocket or knapsack of a fallen volunteer. Thus did new technology interact with the most brutal of civil wars.

Women in the public sphere also embraced cartes de visite. Prominent writers and reformers such as Harriet Beecher Stowe, Julia Ward Howe, Clara Barton, and Victoria Woodhull authorized the distribution of their likenesses. Soon suffragists joined the trend, with cartes de visite representing some of the earliest examples of suffrage memorabilia. Sojourner Truth took this one step further and seized the possibilities of this new medium to position herself as one of the most widely recognized African American icons of her time.

SUSAN B. ANTHONY wasn't the only prominent American who attempted to vote in the 1872 election. In Battle Creek, Michigan, Sojourner Truth, an ex-slave, a woman, and a Battle Creek resident and property owner, presented herself to her local Board of Registration and demanded to be put on the voting rolls. After all, she had campaigned widely for Republican candidate Ulysses S. Grant—only half in jest, she vowed to move to Canada if Democratic candidate Horace Greeley was elected—and now she wanted to cast a ballot. Not surprisingly, she was refused. Even though she anticipated this outcome, she deliberately took the occasion to join hundreds of other women who were determined in 1872 to make a symbolic public claim to what they saw as a fundamental right of citizenship.[1]

Sojourner Truth was one of the most widely known African American women of the nineteenth century, rivaled only by the ex-slave Harriet Tubman, who was twenty years her junior. Her life shows the continuity between women's rights activism before and after the Civil War. Truth's antislavery feminism confirms the productive alliance between early women's rights activists and abolitionists, an alliance that was irrevocably damaged—with grave effects for both—by profound disagreements over the Fourteenth and Fifteenth Amendments in the late 1860s. Throughout her lifetime in the public eye, Sojourner Truth consistently refused to separate race from sex, insisting that black women's voices be heard in both freedom movements that affected their lives.

A good measure of Sojourner Truth's prominence can be traced to the widespread circulation of the cartes de visite which Truth sold at lectures and gatherings to support her career. As the biographer Nell Irvin Painter observed, "seizing on a new technology, Truth established what few nineteenth-century black women were able to prove: that she was present in her times. Her success in distributing her portraits plays no small role in her place in historical memory."[2]

Sojourner Truth deployed this new photographic medium in unique ways.[3] The first extant carte de visite bearing her image dates to 1861. Photographed before addressing a hostile pro-slavery crowd in Indiana, she wears what looks like a vaguely military get-up that includes a heavy shawl and a hooded hat. One historian aptly characterized the result as a "photograph of a woman all but overwhelmed by clothing and accessories." Truth later explained that the organizers of the event had specifically dressed her in that outfit, and she had gone along with some reluctance: "When I was dressed, I looked in the glass and was fairly frightened. Said I, 'It seems I am going to battle.'" Her talk was indeed interrupted at several points by hecklers and protestors, but she escaped physical violence.[4]

Two years later, she sat for a series of portraits in a style of dress and presentation more to her own liking. Dressed neatly according to standards of middle-class respectability, she wore a Quaker-style white cap and white shawl over her polka-dot dress and apron. She looks forthrightly through her eyeglasses into the camera, sometimes holding in her lap a carte de visite of her grandson who was serving in the Union Army. By 1864, her cartes de visite often featured a ball of yarn and her knitting, a symbol not of leisure but of industriousness and skill. These carefully staged portraits, which remained remarkably consistent for the rest of her life, suggest how deliberately she composed her own self-presentation.

Sojourner Truth's post-1864 cartes de visite feature another innovation: she copyrighted them in her own name. Instead of the photographer being given credit and control of the image, Sojourner Truth claimed all legal rights to distribute her likeness. In modern parlance, she controlled its intellectual property. At the time she applied for copyright protection, US law had not been updated to include photographs, although it soon was. Sojourner Truth seems to be the only person who ever copyrighted her own image on a carte de visite.[5]

Truth took it one step further. Starting in 1864, her cartes de visite featured not only the copyright and her name but also a caption: "I sell the shadow to support the substance." Shadow was a widely used term for the new medium of photography, so she was making a play on words. The "substance" it supported was her itinerant lifestyle as a preacher and women's rights activist. Selling these cartes de visite for thirty-five cents each (or three for a dollar) at her lectures and other public events, as well as through the mail, was her primary means of support. The wide circulation of her image—twenty-eight versions are extant, from at least fourteen different photographic sessions—increased her fame and celebrity.

Sojourner Truth found a novel way of "turning paper into value" in a way remarkably similar to the circulation of paper currency, which was becoming more widespread during the Civil War. As Oliver Wendell Holmes, Sr. said in 1863, "*card-portraits*, as everybody knows, have become the social currency, the sentimental 'green-backs' of civilization." Truth's image had value, and the public was willing to pay for it, thus providing her with a steady source of income. In the decades leading up to the Civil War, when the word *selling* was applied to African Americans, it most often referred to the trafficking of human slaves. Once freedom was assured, Truth turned that on its head by selling herself once again, but for her personal profit, not that of a slaveholder master.[6]

Sojourner Truth spent the first thirty years of her life in bondage. The exact date of her birth is unknown, but it was around 1797 and she was named Isabella. Her first language was Dutch. Over the first three decades of her life, she was the property of five owners. She married and bore five children, although the names of only four of them are known. Somewhat complicating the usual slavery story, her bondage occurred not in the South, but in Ulster County, New

York—a reminder of how ubiquitous the practice was in early-nineteenth-century America. Her freedom was linked to the passage of a New York State law in 1799 that began the process of gradual emancipation, with slavery to end completely in the state on July 4, 1827, the year she was freed.[7]

The enslaved part of her life concluded, the woman now known as Isabella Van Wagenen (after her last owner) became deeply involved in various religious and perfectionist communities in upstate New York and Massachusetts. In 1843 she took the name Sojourner Truth, which translates roughly as itinerant preacher. Inspired in part by the publication in 1845 of *Narrative of the Life of Frederick Douglass, An American Slave*, which sold 4,500 copies in less than six months, she began to dictate her own story. (Truth never learned to read or write, and she depended on others to take down her words and handle her correspondence.) The book appeared in 1850 as *Narrative of Sojourner Truth, A Northern Slave, Emancipated from Bodily Servitude by the State of New York, in 1828, with a Portrait.* The technology did not yet exist to include a photograph of the author, so it featured a tin engraving of her likeness, probably from a daguerreotype. Truth self-published the book, going into debt to pay for the plates, and then sold and distributed it during her travels. Priced relatively inexpensively at twenty-five cents a copy, the book went through several editions and was reprinted seven times.

As early as 1851, Sojourner Truth was already turning up on platforms speaking in support of women's rights. At a convention in Akron, Ohio, she made a powerful speech in which she announced, "I am a woman's rights" and declared that the sexes were equal: "I have as much muscle as any man, and can do as much work as any man. I have plowed and reaped and husked and chopped and moved, and can any man do more than that?" That contemporaneous rendition of her speech differs from Frances Dana Gage's more widely quoted 1863 version with its "Ar'n't I a Woman?" refrain, but either way, Truth was affirming that poor, black, and working women must be included in the discussion of women's rights. On the lecture circuit, she continued to face naysayers, including those who doubted whether she was actually a woman. At a 1858 gathering, she answered her critics by baring her breast, saying that "her breasts had suckled many a white babe, to the exclusion of her own offspring" and asking those who questioned her sex "if they, too, wished to suck!"[8]

While deeply committed to the abolitionist cause, Truth steered clear of formal politics in the 1850s. With the election of Abraham Lincoln and the outbreak of the Civil War, she became a dedicated Republican supporter. As the country debated the fate of freed slaves, hers was a unique voice: "I suppose I am about the only colored woman that goes about to speak for the rights of the colored woman." When the Civil War ended, she said forcefully of the broader women's cause, "We are now trying for liberty that requires no blood—that women shall have their rights, not rights from you. Give them what belongs to them."[9]

Sojourner Truth was right in the thick of the debates over the Fourteenth and Fifteenth Amendments, specifically whether the rights of freed African American men should take precedence over those of women, black and white. "There is a great stir about colored men getting their rights, but not a word about the colored women, and if colored men get their rights and no colored women get theirs, there will be a bad time about it," she predicted. Truth always supported universal suffrage and believed that, in many ways, black women needed suffrage even more than black men did, given their limited educational and job prospects. She also believed that the vote would encourage a measure of financial independence for African American women. As she said forcefully on another occasion, "if colored men get their rights, and not colored women theirs, you see the colored men will be masters over the women, and it will be just as bad as it was before."[10]

Truth never held a formal leadership role in the suffrage movement, but she was a frequent speaker at suffrage conventions, and was especially close to Elizabeth Cady Stanton and Susan B. Anthony. That friendship was strained by the disagreements over the Reconstruction Amendments, especially Stanton's defense of educational and property requirements for voting, her disparaging statements about whether black men were equipped to exercise the franchise wisely, and her support for Democratic candidates in 1868, anathema to a diehard Republican like Truth. Yet Truth tried very hard to find a middle ground as the former close alliance between abolitionists and women's rights activists strained and then snapped completely. Truth never wavered in her commitment to universal suffrage, but she pragmatically accepted the necessity of supporting the Fourteenth and Fifteenth Amendments.

In 1869, when the suffrage movement split in two, both sides had good reason to think they could count Sojourner Truth on their side. She initially sided with the Stanton-Anthony wing, despite her profound disagreements with their antiblack and anti-immigrant rhetoric, and she continued to hope that there might be a way to avoid a permanent break. By 1871, however, Truth found herself gravitating toward the American Woman Suffrage Association camp. Yet she retained enough personal ties to Stanton and Anthony to sign onto their "New Departure" campaign, which encouraged women to go to the polls in the 1872 presidential election—and she did so that November in Battle Creek, with determination and defiance.

When Elizabeth Cady Stanton, Susan B. Anthony, and Matilda Joslyn Gage wrote the first volumes of the *History of Woman Suffrage* in the early 1880s, Sojourner Truth was the only African American woman prominently included. Typical of the highly selective and often suspect choices of the authors, the Sojourner Truth who appeared in the official history only talked about women's rights; her longstanding commitments to universal suffrage and the civil rights of black men were downplayed or ignored. As Nell Painter aptly put it, "The Stanton-Anthony Truth tends first and last toward women."[11]

Stanton and Anthony did learn something fundamental from Sojourner Truth, at least indirectly: the importance of visual images. The early women's rights movement was the subject of vitriolic and sustained criticism, especially cartoons and caricatures like the 1848 "Leaders of the Woman's Rights Convention Taking an Airing" which mocked women for speaking out. The Bloomer costume with its short skirts and pantaloons, which several prominent suffragists adopted briefly in the 1850s, was an especially tempting target for mockery and disdain. To try to counter such negative portrayals, suffragists began to experiment with controlling their own images.

Suffragists in the post–Civil War era increasingly paid attention to their portrayal in the press, and they worked hard at presenting a positive, less threatening image to the American public. A daguerreotype of the eminently respectable Quaker activist Lucretia Mott became the basis for a carte de visite that circulated widely. Except for their different skin colors, there are strong similarities between Mott's self-presentation and Sojourner Truth's, especially their white bonnet caps and shawls. In 1870, Stanton and Anthony

Susan B. Anthony and Elizabeth Cady Stanton presented a united front when they sat for this joint portrait in 1870. Their close physical proximity and parallel uncompromising gazes suggest the strength of their personal and political bonds. *Courtesy of Schlesinger Library, Radcliffe Institute, Harvard University.*

got into the act, sitting for "pictures in all forms & positions" at a photography studio in New York, according to Anthony's diary. Twenty years later, they reprised the widely circulated dual format in another iconic pose, as they settled into what looked like (but wasn't) a sedate old age. As Elizabeth Cady Stanton exclaimed to the suffragist Olympia Brown, "We wish posterity to know that we were a remarkably fine looking body of women!!"[12]

Sojourner Truth continued to rely on the sale of her photographs until the very end of her life. Always concerned about her finances and saddled in old age with debt related to family responsibilities, she sat for three additional rounds of photographs in the early 1880s. At this point, Truth was more than eighty years old. Although she was not as active on the lecture circuit as she had been in the 1850s and 1860s, she remained a public presence and still needed to support herself. When it came time to place an order, she showed that she planned to stick around for quite a while by optimistically ordering two hundred cards, both cartes de visite and the larger 6½-by-4½-inch cabinet cards that were coming into use.

These final images of Truth differ somewhat from the earlier ones. For one thing, she no longer wore glasses or held her knitting in her lap. Perhaps at her advanced age, her vision was clouded by cataracts, and arthritis prevented her from holding the knitting needles. She still aimed to convey middle-class respectability in her dress, head covering, and shawl, but now she was often shown standing, rather than sitting. And the backdrops of some of her photographs were more ornate, cluttered with bric-a-brac and "stuff," reflecting a different aesthetic from the earlier days of photographic portraiture. Yet the power of her gaze was just as strong as ever. Sojourner Truth the itinerant preacher was bearing witness right up to her death in 1883.

Sojourner Truth spoke truth to power, literally and symbolically, in her person and with her image. Truth lectured on suffrage platforms and participated in suffrage debates from the 1850s to the 1880s, claiming a place in the wider national discussion about the rights of both newly freed slaves and women. Her presence served as a challenge to the racism which was so deeply embedded in the white suffrage movement. African American women believed they had just as strong a right to full citizenship as white women, and they acted on that conviction. They were there from the start, and they made a difference.

Woman's Exponent.

VOL. I.   SALT LAKE CITY, UTAH, JUNE 1, 1872.   NO. 1.

NEWS AND VIEWS.

Women are now admitted to fifty American colleges.

Rev. De Witt Talmage is pronounced a success as a sensation preacher.

Theodore Tilton says the best brains in northern New York are wearing white hats. They might wear chapeaux of a more objectionable color.

Daniel W. Voorhees in one day destroyed the political record of a life-time, and that was when he became henchman to a judge with an ecclesiastical mission.

An Alabama editor writes "United State," and refuses to write "United States"—a straw to show how Southern sentiment runs. What a state he must be in?

The season of scattering intellectual filth has set in over the country. It occurs quadrennially a few months before the Presidential election.

Dr. Newman failed to become a Bishop at the Methodist General Conference, and Dr. Newman mourns this second great defeat. He has remembrances of Salt Lake in connection with the previous one.

Great outcry is raised against the much marrying of the Latter-day Saints. The tendency of the age is to disregard marriage altogether, but there seems no indication of a desire to have the race die out.

The "Alabama" muddle like "confusion worse confounded" becomes worse mixed the more it is stirred. It stretches itself over the path of time, and "like a wounded snake drags its slow length along." The country has become heartily sick of it.

Some Eastern journals head their Utah news with "Deseret." With keen appreciation of the coming and inevitable, they accept the mellifluous name chosen for the region wrested by that industry which "the honey bee" represents, from the barren wilds of nature.

George Francis Train sends us a bundle of Train Ligres. The compliment is appreciated, but the act is like sweetness wasted. We can vote, but not for "the next President of America." Utah has not become Deseret yet, nor can it participate in Presidential making.

The last week of May, 1872, will be memorable in American annals as the first time since the first ordinance of secession was passed in the South, that both houses of Congress had their full list of members. Statesmanship can retain a complete Federal legislature, but the article has grown somewhat scarce.

To pardon the worst class of criminals on condition that they emigrate to the United States, is growing in favor with European monarchies. Germany and Greece so far have done the largest business in this line, the latest batch of villains thus disposed of being the Marathon murderers from Greece. Orders have been forwarded by President Grant to New Orleans, to which port it is understood they have been sent, to prevent their landing. They should be captured, ironed, returned to Athens with Uncle Samuel's compliments, and a bill for direct and "consequential" damages presented.

News comes from France that trailing dresses for street wear are going out of fashion. So many absurd and ridiculous fashions come from Paris that the wonder is thinking American women do not, with honest republican spirit, reject them entirely. This latter one, however, is so sensible that its immediate adoption will be an evidence of good sense wisely directed.

The anti-Mormon bill of Judge Bingham seems to have fared no better in the judiciary committee of the House of Representatives than the one to which Mr. Voorhees stood sponsor. It is gratifying to think that a majority of that committee yet respect the antiquated and once revered instrument still occasionally referred to as the Constitution.

Rev. James Freeman Clark claims "that if it is an advantage to vote, women ought to have it; if a disadvantage men ought not to be obliged to bear a stigma." Speaking from experience we feel safe in affirming that the Reverend gentleman is right, and we hope for a time when this immunity may be universally enjoyed by our pure-minded and light-loving sisters. We don't presume that those belonging to the opposite class care anything about it.

Mrs. Carrie F. Young, editor of the "Pacific Journal of Health," has been lecturing in Idaho on Temperance and Woman Suffrage. The editor of the "Idaho World" was not present, but did not regret his absence. He says, "We feel a most decided repugnance to the exhibition of a woman upon the rostrum, advocating such degrading theories as 'woman suffrage' and other cognate subjects." He omits to state whether "Temperance" is one of the "degrading theories" to which he refers.

Force is ever the argument of a bad cause. The principles which cannot be overcome except by the exercise of physical power, present a front that arrests the attention of thinking minds. Where argument fails and force is employed to overcome an opponent, the power of the principles to which opposition is made is admitted. Will those who urge repressive legislation against the people of Utah think of it? Witness the Voorhees bill as an illustration.

A notable event, as a result of the late terrible Franco-German war, is the opening of the German University in Strasbourg, which takes place June 1st—to-day. That famous city on the Rhine, after a siege memorable in the annals of warfare, passed into the hands of the Germans, and now they take the surest means to permanently consolidate their power, by establishing there one of those seats of learning for which Germany has become enviably famous.

Miss Susan B. Anthony, it is said, declared before the Cincinnati Convention met, that if it gave her cause "the cold shoulder," she would go to Philadelphia and pledge the ballots of the women of America to U. S. Grant. As the women of America are yet without ballots, and as it is very questionable, if they had them, whether they would authorize any single individual to pledge them for any candidate, the supposition is fair that Miss Anthony possesses too much good sense to have made any such declaration.

Rev. Mr. Peirce, a Methodist clergyman who has made Salt Lake his headquarters for some time, in lecturing east proposed the extinction of polygamy by the introduction here of vast quantities of expensive millinery goods, and by inducing "Gentile" women to dress in gorgeous style that "Mormon" women might imitate them and run up such heavy dry goods bills that it would be impossible for a man to support more than one wife, if even one. Mr. Peirce, no doubt, preaches modesty and humility occasionally, by way of variety; now he recommends the encouragement of pride, vanity and extravagance to accomplish his "Christian" designs. The course he advises has been largely followed in many places, has tenanted brothels, aided to fill prisons, broken up families, hurled women of reputation and position down to degradation and infamy, and has met heavy denunciations from inspired men whom Mr. Peirce professes to revere. He would steal the livery of evil to serve religion in. There is not much of this reverend gentleman, and what little there is must be either very silly or very wicked.

The editor of "The Present Age" has been to a church and heard an orthodox sermon, in which the preacher took occasion to say that all religions are "isms," including Mahometanism, Mormonism and Spiritualism, rested their claims for being true upon miracles. The "Age" is a Spiritualist and denies that his "ism" bases its claims to be true upon miracles. Latter-day Saints deny that Mormonism bases any claim for credence in it on miracles; the reverse is the truth. The "Age" defines a miracle to be "the setting aside for the time being of a natural law to meet an unexpected emergency." Had he said a miracle was the bringing into operation of certain natural laws not generally understood or comprehended, he would have been nearer correct. When somebody can tell how a natural law may be set aside, except by the operation of some other natural law, his definition, which is the generally received one, may be entitled to more consideration. We imagine the working of the overland telegraph is as great a miracle to the Cheyenne Indians as any recorded miracle that the "Age" or the orthodox minister can quote.

Mrs. Laura De Force Gordon attended the Cincinnati Convention and claimed a seat as a delegate from California. Her claim was treated with hisses and laughter. She took a position in front of the stand and endeavored to speak, but her voice was drowned by a tumultuous discord. Her persistence in receiving her with hisses and uproarious laughter, was disgraceful. The Liberal Republicans assembled in Cincinnati for a general work of purification and reform, evidently stood greatly in need of general reform themselves, in the matter of manners as well as in politics. Mrs. Gordon was as much entitled to a seat in that Convention as Carl Schurz himself, for we have yet to learn that the call for it specified that "male" Republicans only were admissible.

A new periodical in London is called "The Ladies."

First issue of the *Woman's Exponent* (June 1, 1872). *Courtesy of Brigham Young University Special Collections.*

CHAPTER THREE

Sister-Wives and Suffragists

THE SAME YEAR that Susan B. Anthony and Sojourner Truth attempted to register to vote, a newspaper called the *Woman's Exponent* began publication in the territory of Utah. Although not an official organ of the Church of Jesus Christ of Latter-day Saints (LDS)—the official name of the religion as distinct from its popular designation as *Mormon*—it was closely linked to the church. Conceived of as the voice of Utah's women, and for many years the rare women's publication west of the Mississippi, the eight-page, semimonthly periodical contained editorials, letters, articles, and poetry of interest to its predominantly female Mormon readers. From the very beginning, Emmeline B. Wells was a regular contributor.

Utah plays a special role in the history of woman suffrage. When it became a territory in 1870, women in this overwhelmingly Mormon settlement received the right to vote alongside men, making them among the tiny minority of nineteenth-century American women able to exercise the franchise. Mormon women were proud of their status as voters, and they took their rights of citizenship seriously. The inaugural issue of the *Woman's Exponent*, published on June 1, 1872, prominently mentioned Susan B. Anthony on the first page. 41

That front page also mentioned in passing the "great outcry" raised against "the much marrying of the Latter-day Saints," a reference to the controversial practice of celestial (or plural) marriage. The *Woman's Exponent* was no antipolygamy screed. Its editors and readers unapologetically supported the right to practice polygamy, placing it in the same category as other women's "rights" such as suffrage. Wells, who would be its editor for more than thirty-five years, was herself a plural wife. Hopes that Mormon women might use the vote to outlaw plural marriage proved totally unrealistic.

The "Mormon Question," as it was widely called at the time, posed complicated challenges for the woman suffrage movement, which had to decide whether to embrace or disown polygamous Mormon women voters. More fundamentally, the constitutional question of whether Mormons should be legally allowed to practice polygamy went to the heart of the relation between law, morality, and religion in nineteenth-century America. As suffragists debated their relationship to Mormon women, they found themselves at the center of one of the most far-reaching political and legal questions of their times.

THE CALL for a mass meeting on Saturday, May 6, 1886, appeared in the leading Salt Lake City newspapers five days before the event was to be held. Addressed to "the ladies of the Church of Jesus Christ of Latter-day Saints," it boldly stated its purpose: "to protest against the indignities and insults heaped upon their sex" and "also against the disfranchisement of those who are innocent of breaking any law." Having been voters since Utah became a territory in 1870, Mormon women now faced the prospect of being formally barred from the polls. Even more troubling, federal authorities had stepped up their campaign against polygamy, catching plural wives (the term preferred by Latter-day Saints) in the legal snare along with their polygamous husbands. Mormon women, deeply involved in political and religious life, were highly respected members of their communities, and they were not afraid to take a public stand in support of polygamy. In 1870, leading Mormon women staged an "indignation meeting" to protest congressional attempts to outlaw the practice. Now sixteen years later, they gathered to protest once again.[1]

The weather on the day of the mass meeting was "propitious," and an eager crowd assembled in the portico and on the steps of the Salt Lake Theater. When the doors opened, nearly two thousand women—and a smattering of men—filled the theater to capacity. It was one of the largest gatherings of its kind ever convened in Utah Territory. This was no fringe group. The stage was filled with a cross-section of well-connected Mormon women, many of whom were married to leading figures in the church. After an opening prayer and a sampling of hymns sung by the Tabernacle Choir, fifteen women spoke to the assembled crowd. Nine additional talks, which could not be delivered because of time constraints, were later published along with correspondence from leaders who had been unable to attend in *"Mormon" Women's Protest: An Appeal for Freedom, Justice and Equal Rights.*

The use of the colloquial term for their religion in the pamphlet title suggests that participants were well aware that their real audience was not the several thousand women jammed into the theater but the country as a whole, especially representatives in Washington, DC who held power over territorial affairs. A second intended audience was the national suffrage movement, which had a strong interest in protecting Utah women's right to vote, even if suffrage leaders disagreed about the controversial issue of polygamy. The fact that woman suffrage, polygamy, and statehood were all intertwined reveals how complicated a seemingly straightforward issue like votes for women could be.[2]

The story of Mormon women's politicization starts long before Utah women received the vote in 1870.[3] The prophet Joseph Smith founded the Church of Jesus Christ of Latter-day Saints in upstate New York in 1830. From the start, his small band of followers faced distrust and persecution from the surrounding communities. Within ten years, they were forced to relocate to Nauvoo, Illinois. After Joseph Smith's death in Nauvoo in 1844, Brigham Young led the followers to the arid desert of Utah, where they set about building a new society (Zion) from scratch. Already controversial as a new religion, the Mormons faced even more negative scrutiny after the church doctrine of celestial or plural marriage was officially announced in 1852, confirming the already widespread practice. Polygamy soon drew the attention of federal authorities, which passed various laws to challenge the practice, beginning in the 1860s. These laws proved unenforceable where Mormons were a firmly entrenched majority, but the issue became too politicized to disappear quietly.

Opposition to polygamy rested on both moral and legal grounds. In 1856, the Republican Party called slavery and polygamy the "twin relics of barbarism." Once the Civil War settled the question of slavery, polygamy remained as a heinous moral stain on the country. Opponents could not imagine that women would willingly enter into such relationships—something Mormon women heartily disputed—and concluded they must have been coerced. Such marital despotism, which the popular press often compared to heathen harems, was presented as antithetical to monogamous Christian morality based on consent.[4]

Even if polygamy was seen as morally abhorrent, how to challenge it legally was a conundrum, because the regulation of domestic relations was traditionally a local or state concern. Furthermore, Mormons insisted the practice was a religious duty protected by the First Amendment. Polygamy in Utah thus presented a two-pronged challenge to the American legal system: Did the protection of religious freedom include the protection of polygamy? And in a federal system, which vested broad powers in local and state sovereignty, under what mandate could the federal government intercede in domestic affairs? As a constitutional conflict loomed, public antipathy towards polygamy hardened.

The 1886 mass meeting was a last-ditch attempt by Mormon women to mobilize national public opinion in support of the increasingly isolated and beleaguered Mormon minority. Nearly all of the speakers at the meeting were plural wives, and they presented themselves as upstanding community members who willingly accepted the tenets of celestial marriage as part of their religious faith.[5] While it is clear that individual women often struggled with the daily challenges of family life with their sister-wives, they were not ashamed of the practice, and they publicly spoke in its favor. The women's case for polygamy emphasized that it freed them from male lust while guaranteeing that all women would have the opportunity to marry and enjoy secure homes and respectable social positions. Turning public perceptions on their head, Mormons always claimed the high moral ground.[6]

At the mass meeting, Mormon women strongly challenged the widespread view that they were mere pawns of religious leaders or slaves to their husbands. "Hand in hand with Celestial Marriage is the elevation of women," asserted Dr. Romania Pratt, a graduate of the Woman's Medical College in Philadelphia and a plural wife. Dr. Ellis R. Shipp, another path-breaking female physician, concurred: "We are accused of being down-trodden and oppressed. *We deny the charge!*" As Mrs. Elizabeth Howard put it, "These are women that any nation should be proud of."[7]

Mormon women were especially proud of what they had done with the vote, which Dr. Ellen Ferguson, answering another common charge, asserted had been deployed without "coercion or priestly dictation." (Ferguson, an English immigrant who was probably the first woman physician in Utah, was the rare monogamist on the platform.) Demonstrating solidarity with their non-Mormon sisters, speakers found it especially galling that pending legislation would strip all Utah women, not just Mormons, of the vote. Needless to say, Mormon women hoped this threat would galvanize leaders of the national movement to intervene.[8]

The greatest indignation, however, was reserved for the federal authorities who were actively hunting down known polygamists and compelling their wives to testify against them, contravening long-standing common-law spousal protections. To Mormon women, these inquisitions, which included extremely intimate questions about the timing of sexual relations and the paternity of children, bordered on prurient intrusions into a private sphere no man should enter—certainly not law officials "who watch around our dooryards, peer into our bedroom windows, ply little children with questions about their parents, and, when hunting their human prey, burst into people's domiciles and terrorize the innocent." This affront to the dignity of their womanhood troubled them just as much as the loss of the vote did.[9]

Emmeline Wells was not able to attend the protest meeting, but she sent a carefully crafted letter of support from Chicago, calling the impending disfranchisement of Utah women "an act of despotism" and reminding the assembled sisters of the "greater liberty" and "equality of sex" of women in the Mormon Church.[10] Because of her stature in the community and her frequent interactions with eastern suffragists, Wells was chosen along with Ellen Ferguson to journey to Washington, DC to present the Mormon women's memorial to President Grover Cleveland, members of Congress, and other federal officials. Their appeal fell on deaf ears, as the Congress soon after passed the Edmunds-Tucker Act of 1887, which disfranchised all Utah women and confiscated Church property in an attempt to end polygamy. Even though she was now voteless after proudly exercising that right since 1870, Emmeline Wells was still a suffragist, and she redoubled her efforts to win back the vote for all her Utah sisters, not just the Mormon ones.

The decades-long suffrage activism of Emmeline Wells provides a window into the complex interplay between suffrage and polygamy in Utah and the nation at large. Born Emmeline Blanchard Woodward in Petersham, Massachusetts in 1828, she converted at the age of fourteen after her mother joined the church. The next year she married the son of a local Mormon leader. The young couple joined the exodus to Nauvoo in 1844, and, in a short space of time, she gave birth to a son who died and her teenage husband abandoned her. In 1845, she became the plural wife of Bishop Newel Whitney, who was thirty-three years her senior. In what seems to have been a loving and supportive relationship, she had two daughters with him before he died in 1850. By then she was living in Salt Lake City.[11]

In 1852, she entered into another plural marriage (her husband's seventh and final) with Daniel H. Wells, a counselor to Brigham Young and later the mayor of Salt Lake City, with whom she had three additional daughters. This marriage gave her social standing and allowed her to embark on something approaching a public career. Her first position was as the private secretary to Eliza R. Snow, a plural wife of founder Joseph Smith who, after his death, became a plural wife of his successor Brigham Young. Snow was president of the Relief Society, the most influential leadership role available to women in the Mormon community.

When the *Woman's Exponent* was founded in 1872, Wells became a regular contributor. In 1877, she took over as editor, a position she held until the periodical ceased publication in 1914. The masthead of the *Woman's Exponent* stated "The Rights of the Women of Zion, and the Rights of the Women of all Nations," and Wells's goals for the publication were similarly expansive: Mormon women "should be the best-informed of any women on the face of the earth, not only upon our own principles and doctrines but on all general subjects." In turn, her editorship of the publication enhanced her national stature, providing an important credential when she dealt with eastern suffragists.[12]

When territorial Utah women unexpectedly won the vote in 1870, the two national suffrage organizations took note. The groups had recently split over whether to support universal manhood suffrage or focus on securing the ballot for women; Mormon women and polygamy became another issue fundamentally dividing the two groups.

Since the vast majority of Utah voters were Mormons, it proved impossible to separate the issue of polygamy from suffrage. Lucy Stone and her more conservative American Woman Suffrage Association (AWSA) distanced themselves completely from polygamous Mormon women, while Elizabeth Cady Stanton and Susan B. Anthony took a different tack, welcoming them into the fold of the National Woman Suffrage Association (NWSA). Thus began a complicated tango within the suffrage movement lasting two decades, with one wing gingerly acknowledging Mormon women as allies while the other emphatically refused to have anything to do with them.

Curious about the recent turn of events in Utah, Elizabeth Cady Stanton and Susan B. Anthony took advantage of the newly opened transcontinental railroad in 1871 to visit Salt Lake City on their way to California. During their weeklong stay, they juggled rival Mormon factions while also showing their support for Utah's newest voters. Stanton's views on topics such as birth control proved too radical for the Mormons, but Anthony became a much admired figure despite her personal abhorrence of polygamy. She earned this respect with her willingness to work with Mormon woman suffragists on their own terms, regardless of their status as plural wives. If they supported woman suffrage, that was all that mattered. Stanton's and Anthony's openness to a variety of differing viewpoints was a clear contrast to the AWSA's more cautious approach, but it had its costs. The hot-button issue of polygamy increasingly became a liability that threatened to outweigh the benefits of embracing these newly enfranchised voters.[13]

In the 1870s, however, things were a bit more fluid. This worked to the benefit of Mormon woman suffragists, who wanted to enhance their legitimacy through affiliation with the national movement and challenge the unflattering stereotypes of Mormon women held by many American citizens. They also hoped to build political support for eventual statehood, which would keep woman suffrage intact. In 1877, Emmeline Wells took the lead in organizing Utah women in support of a proposed sixteenth amendment (woman suffrage) to the Constitution by collecting thousands of petition signatures as well as securing financial support from the LDS leadership. Her activism earned her a spot as a representative of Utah on the NWSA board. She was the first Mormon so recognized. In 1879, she and Zina Young Williams, Brigham Young's daughter, journeyed to Washington, DC, where Wells addressed NWSA's national convention.

But such prominence on the national stage was short-lived. The political climate, never very supportive, turned more sharply against polygamy after a definitive Supreme Court decision in 1879 ruled that Mormons did not have a constitutional right to practice a form of marriage expressly prohibited by Congress as a violation of public morality. The Edmunds Act of 1882 offered more sanctions against the practice in the territory, a process completed by the Edmunds-Tucker Act of 1887. As early as 1884, even the NWSA was distancing itself from Mormon women, focusing instead on trying to keep the ballot for non-Mormon and non-polygamous women. That year, Emmeline Wells was quietly dropped from the NWSA national masthead.

For the Mormon community, 1890 was a "year of shocks." Mormon leaders, desirous of statehood and the legitimacy it would convey, recognized the futility of fighting for the right to practice polygamy, and they officially renounced the practice. (Whether it would continue informally was another matter.) Among other things, removing the issue of polygamy in Utah helped pave the way for Susan B. Anthony's initiatives to reunite the two wings of the suffrage movement, and in 1890, the National American Woman Suffrage Association (NAWSA) was formed.[14]

Even before the formal abandonment of polygamy, Mormon suffragists quietly began to put forward only monogamous (or "innocent") women as delegates to national conventions. For example, Emily Richards, the monogamist wife of a prominent Mormon lawyer based in Washington, DC, was chosen to address the inaugural gathering of the International Council of Women in the nation's capital in 1888, while Emmeline Wells sat the conference out. And in January 1889, when the Utah Woman Suffrage Association was formed, an informal understanding that no one who had "ever been in plural marriage" could hold a leadership position sidelined Wells. While she realized the political necessity of the decision, it was undoubtedly painful.[15]

When Wyoming officially became a state in 1890, it provided the first star for the suffrage flag, followed by Colorado in 1893 and then Utah and Idaho in 1896. When Utah's suffragists attended the 1896 NAWSA convention, they were welcomed as heroes. But only four Utah women made the trip. The day the delegation left for Washington, Emmeline Wells could "scarcely believe" that she was not going with them. In the end, despite all she had done to make woman suffrage a reality, she could not raise the necessary funds to pay her way.[16]

In retrospect, participation in the national suffrage movement in the 1880s and 1890s represented a high point of political activism among Mormon women. Their twin goals of suffrage and statehood achieved, Mormon women moved warily into electoral and partisan politics, but they found the terrain challenging. Other newly enfranchised female voters across the country shared the sentiment. As the first generation of Utah Mormons died out, and as more time elapsed since the heroic early efforts of both sexes to make the Utah experiment viable, Mormon women's activity in national politics continued, at least through the Progressive era, but with diminishing support from the LDS leadership for their participation in active public roles. This conservative thrust greatly intensified as the rest of the twentieth century unfolded, and Mormon women's activism on behalf of the vote was quickly forgotten.

The centennial of the Nineteenth Amendment offers a chance to write these Mormon women back into history. Mormon suffragists were highly politicized actors. They knew how to organize mass meetings, gather petitions, raise money, and lobby politicians and church leaders. Far from the popular image of downtrodden women degraded by polygamy, these proud and committed suffragists saw no conflict between their religious beliefs and their activism on behalf of their sex. In fact, they felt privileged to be part of a community which took women so seriously. Mormon women deserve to be part of suffrage history both on their own merits and also because their peculiar situation helps explain the wide divisions that kept the national suffrage movement divided until 1890.

While suffrage leaders consciously distanced themselves from their earlier controversial associations as they maneuvered the movement into the political mainstream after 1890, the lingering effects of the battle played out in national political life. The antisuffrage movement recycled ideas from the antipolygamy campaign, especially the argument that giving women the vote was an attack on traditional marriage and the family. There are strong parallels between the antipolygamy campaign and the efforts to restrict Chinese immigration. The language describing Chinese prostitutes as degraded and akin to slaves, for instance, was very similar to earlier descriptions of Mormon women under polygamy, putting both groups on the outside as "others." In legislation like the Dawes Act of 1887, which mandated a system of land allotment based on individual families rather than tribes, Native Americans were pressured, as Mormons had been, to conform to Protestant views of marriage and family life. Far from an interesting anomaly in the suffrage story, polygamy remains a surprisingly central aspect of late-nineteenth-century political history.

Emmeline Wells's contributions to Mormon life and the suffrage movement were far from over when polygamy officially ended. Widowed in 1891—and thus technically no longer a plural wife—she attended the 1891 NAWSA convention as a delegate-at-large. In 1899, Wells delivered a speech to the International Council of Women in London on "The History and Purposes of the Mormon Relief Society," and the next year she and other Mormon suffragists presented Susan B. Anthony with a bolt of black silk brocade made in Utah for her eightieth birthday. In 1910, Wells became the fifth president of the Relief Society, the prestigious welfare and relief organization most closely associated with women's empowerment in the church. When she turned ninety, she was celebrated with a festive event at the Hotel Utah, and two years later, more than a thousand people attended her ninety-second birthday party.

Emmeline Wells didn't have to wait for the passage of the Nineteenth Amendment to cast her first vote. Except for a short interval, she had been voting regularly since 1870, making her one of the longest-voting women of her era. But she managed to live to see the Nineteenth Amendment's adoption. She died in 1921 at age ninety-three, after a lifetime of activism on behalf of women and her Mormon faith, a gentle but forceful reminder that those two causes have not always been in fundamental opposition.

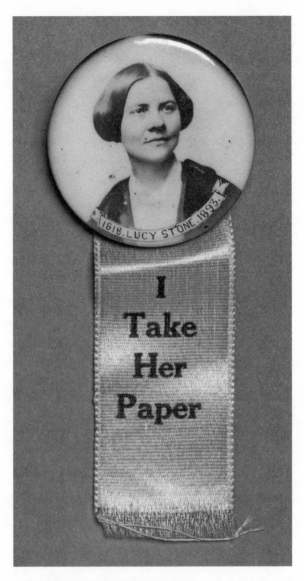

Woman's Journal button with portrait of Lucy Stone (1818–1893).
Courtesy of Schlesinger Library, Radcliffe Institute, Harvard University.

CHAPTER FOUR

Alice Stone Blackwell and the Armenian Crisis of the 1890s

WINNING THE VOTE for women drew on the energies and talents of three generations of activists: the "founding mothers" who began the movement in the 1840s and 1850s, a middle generation who joined up in the 1880s and 1890s, and a final cohort who propelled the movement to victory in the first two decades of the twentieth century. Sometimes the passing of the torch from generation to generation was a literal transition from mother to daughter. Elizabeth Cady Stanton passed on her passion for women's rights to her daughter, Harriot Stanton Blatch, who became a significant suffragist in her own right, especially in New York State. Alice Stone Blackwell had an even stronger family legacy: both of her parents, Lucy Stone and Henry Browne Blackwell, were lifelong reformers and women's rights activists.

Nowhere is this family connection clearer than in the *Woman's Journal*, the weekly suffrage organ edited by the wife-and-husband team and later taken over by their precocious only child. Established in Boston in 1870 as "a weekly paper devoted to the interests of woman, to her educational, industrial, legal and political equality, and especially to her right of suffrage," the

Woman's Journal (as would the *Woman's Exponent* two years later in Utah) had an influence that far outstripped its limited subscription base. For most of its history, the publication remained independent of the major suffrage organizations, which meant it received no outside funding, despite its vital role in connecting individual suffragists with news of the wider women's movement. Instead, it depended on subscriptions and donations to keep itself afloat—a constant battle.[1]

Because of its precarious financial status, the *Woman's Journal* was always looking for ways to increase subscriptions. One promotion offered a button featuring Lucy Stone's portrait attached to a bright yellow ribbon. There was no need to explain "I take her paper"—the association would have been self-evident to supporters. Distributed some time after Stone's death in 1893, this 1.3 × 3.25 inch portrait is based on an image from 1855, when she was thirty-seven and recently married. Wearing this badge would have been a fine way to demonstrate public allegiance to the cause.

Alice Stone Blackwell probably had an additional motive for commissioning this keepsake beyond building support for the *Woman's Journal*: ensuring that her mother received her proper due as a suffrage pioneer. She had no intention of letting Elizabeth Cady Stanton's and Susan B. Anthony's legacies overshadow her mother's.

WHAT IS THE ARMENIAN GENOCIDE doing in a book of suffrage stories? Throughout the 1890s, Alice Stone Blackwell prominently featured coverage of the deepening crisis in Armenia on the front pages of the *Woman's Journal*. Blackwell's advocacy was part of a nationwide engagement with what became America's first international human rights crusade. Given Boston's long abolitionist tradition, it is not surprising that its concerned citizens took the lead. At its epicenter were women associated with the woman suffrage movement, most notably Alice Stone Blackwell, Julia Ward Howe, and Isabel Barrows. Women's rights and human rights went hand in hand.[2]

Nineteenth-century Americans had long felt a strong connection to Armenians, the largest Christian Aryan minority living under Ottoman Turkish rule. Concentrated in a mountainous region in western Asia near Mount Ararat—often represented as the site of the original Garden of Eden—Armenians endured the role of a persecuted religious minority at the hands of successive waves of conquerors. The most recent conquerors, the Ottoman Turks, had sacked Constantinople, the seat of the Byzantine Empire, in 1453. As the Turks consolidated their rule over the succeeding centuries, Armenians found themselves legally designated as "infidels" by their Muslim overlords. When Armenians began to agitate for more rights for non-Muslim minorities in the 1890s, they came up against one of the worst despots the world had ever seen. Sultan Abdul Hamid II, "the bloody Sultan," decided that the way to deal with the Armenian problem was to annihilate its population. Between 1894 and 1896, approximately two hundred thousand Armenians were killed—half massacred by the Sultan's troops and henchmen, the other half dead from disease and famine.

This campaign of state-sponsored terror, which would be taken to even more extreme ends in the Armenian Genocide of 1915, provoked the first international human rights crusade to address the misery and suffering inflicted on the Armenian minority. Spear-headed by the Boston-based United Friends of Armenia as well as the National Armenian Relief Committee, groups raised massive amounts of money in the United States and Europe to bring humanitarian relief and medical supplies to devastated Armenian communities. In 1896, Clara Barton, the founder of the American Red Cross (and the person who likely introduced the phrase "starving Armenians" into the American lexicon), led the first international mission of that organization to Turkey. That year, Congress passed the Cullom Resolution condemning the Sultan for the massacres, "the first international human rights resolution in American history."[3]

Alice Stone Blackwell was right in the middle of this growing global crisis.[4] Born in 1857, Alice grew up in a household suffused by suffrage and reform. She spent her early life in New Jersey before moving to the Boston area in 1869, where her parents bought a seventeen-room home in Dorchester, a fifteen-minute trolley ride into town. A diary she kept at age fifteen was dotted with references to luminaries in her close family network, including Julia Ward Howe, Wendell Phillips, Stephen Foster, Louisa May Alcott, and Frederick Douglass. One guest who failed to impress was Susan B. Anthony, who took notice of her "in quite an embarrassing way": "I don't much like Miss A. She strikes me as being tall, sharp, dictatorial, conceited, pugnacious & selfish." The only word of praise she managed was that Anthony was undoubtedly "plucky."[5]

The Stone-Blackwell family's relocation to Boston coincided with the split in the suffrage movement. In 1868, Elizabeth Cady Stanton and Susan B. Anthony had started a newspaper called *The Revolution* ("Women their rights and nothing less; men their rights and nothing more"), but it only lasted for two years. The Boston-based American Woman Suffrage Association, led by Stone, Blackwell, and

Julia Ward Howe, deemed this an auspicious moment to establish their own newspaper. The *Woman's Journal* debuted on January 8, 1870 and remained in print for six decades, never missing a weekly issue.[6]

Lucy Stone had naively thought that running the newspaper might be a good way to combine her childrearing responsibilities with ongoing suffrage advocacy, but the *Woman's Journal* quickly turned into more than a full time job. (Emmeline Wells discovered the same thing when she helmed the *Woman's Exponent*.) Perhaps it was inevitable that Alice Stone Blackwell would be drawn into its maw. As early as 1879, she confided her concerns about her mother's burdens to a cousin: "It is a heavy load for poor Mamma—the Journal every week, the general supervision of the suffrage cause in Massachusetts, and the care of this big place, indoors and out," including "keeping an absentminded daughter clothed and in running order." As a teenager, she made frequent trips to the journal's offices on Tremont Place and handled routine chores related to its printing and production. When she graduated from Boston University in 1881, one of only two women in her class, she was already serving as an editor, a position she formally assumed in 1884.[7]

Lucy Stone, Henry Blackwell, and Alice Stone Blackwell did not draw salaries for their service to the *Woman's Journal*. Luckily, Alice found the task quite congenial: "I can't think of any line of work open to me that I should like so well." In 1888, she took on added responsibility for the *Woman's Column*, a subscription service of suffrage news that she oversaw until 1904. And like her mother, she participated in the broader suffrage movement both nationally and locally. Blackwell played an especially critical role in the reconciliation of the two rival suffrage organizations in 1890, and she served as recording secretary for the National American Woman Suffrage Association for the next twenty years.[8]

Alice Stone Blackwell's personal introduction to the Armenian cause came through Isabel Chapin Barrows, a pioneering female doctor who had studied at the Woman's Medical College of the New York Infirmary for Women and Children, an institution which Alice's aunt, Dr. Elizabeth Blackwell, had founded. In 1881, she and her husband Samuel June Barrows moved to Boston, where he served as minister of the First Unitarian Church in Dorchester and later edited the *Christian Register*, the weekly organ of the Unitarian Church. The couple quickly became deeply enmeshed in the cosmopolitan Boston reform community. They grew so close to the Stone-Blackwell family that Alice called her Aunt Isabel and signed her letters "your loving niece."

In the winter of 1893, Isabel Barrows and her daughter Mabel met three Armenian students at the boarding house in Leipzig, Germany, where they were staying while traveling abroad. The students first caught their attention by politely rising when the women took their seats at dinner, a courtesy that German students had failed to extend. From them, the visitors learned of the terrible conditions in Armenia, where the Sultan was intensifying his persecution of the Christian minority. Isabel Barrows was especially impressed by a theology student named Ohannes Chatschumian, whom she invited to come to the United States to represent the Armenian Church at the World's Congress of Religions, held in conjunction with the World's Columbian Exposition in the summer of 1893 in Chicago. Afterwards, the Barrows invited him to visit their camp at Lake Memphremagog, on the Quebec-Vermont border. As she had been many other summers, Alice Stone Blackwell was one of the other guests.[9]

Although she was at first "foolishly repelled by his foreign aspect," Alice and Ohannes soon took to each other. Chores at the camp were shared between the sexes, and one night, while doing the dishes after supper, Ohannes told her about the battle of Avarair, an iconic fifth-century struggle in which Armenian warriors valiantly but unsuccessfully resisted a Persian onslaught. Alice spoke no Armenian, and Ohannes hadn't learned much English, but they connected nonetheless. Sensing their personal and literary connections, Isabel Barrows suggested they try to translate some Armenian poems into English verse together. By the end of the summer the two were inseparable—and also the subject of a certain amount of friendly ribbing from their friends.[10]

Short and chubby, with a mat of curly hair, Ohannes Chatschumian was a charismatic character and a gifted advocate for the Armenian cause, especially after he picked up English, which he did quickly. With the support of Isabel and June Barrows, he applied to the Harvard Divinity School for the 1893–1894 academic year. When making his case to the dean, Isabel pointed out that he was so "accustomed to simple living that he could subsist on what most Harvard students waste." Alice also wrote a letter of recommendation, noting his "real avidity for knowledge" and "lovable disposition," as well as his ability to read fourteen languages by the age of twenty-four. His application was accepted, and he spent a fruitful year studying at Harvard. Alice and Ohannes continued to work on their translations of Armenian poetry throughout the year, and they participated in so many meetings and events that Alice later apologized to her family for inflicting "so much of my Armenio-mania on you."[11]

At the end of his time at Harvard, Ohannes returned to Leipzig to finish his degree. Alice continued to work on the volume of poems, which was published under her name in February 1896, featuring a dark green cover with a colorful coat of arms depicting historically significant Armenian symbols, such as Noah's Ark and Mount Ararat.[12] Alice knew little more than the Armenian alphabet, so she relied on rough translations into French and English by her Armenian friends, which she then rendered into English verse without trying to match their original meter. Alice was as captivated by the poems' beauty as she was by Ohannes's passion for his cause, and she wanted American readers to experience it first hand. As she explained in her preface to the volume, "as the beauty of the Armenian girl is often conspicuous even in rags, so it is hoped that the beauty of some of these Armenian poems may be visible even through the poverty of their English dress."[13]

Alice Stone Blackwell had a clear political purpose in publishing the poems: "that the sympathy already felt for the Armenians in their martyrdom at the hands of the Turks would be deepened by an acquaintance with the temper and genius of the people, as shown in their poetry."[14] No more than two Armenian poems had previously been translated into English, so these sixty poems fulfilled the goal of bringing them to a wider audience. Blackwell later collaborated on volumes of poetry in translation from Yiddish, Russian, Hungarian, and Spanish. In 1917, she published an expanded version of *Armenian Poems* to raise funds for Armenian refugees displaced by the 1915 genocide, when close to 1.5 million Armenians (between half and two-thirds of the population) perished in a state-sponsored campaign of extermination that is still denied by the Turkish government.

Ohannes Chatschumian never had a chance to see the volume of poetry he inspired. His health, never robust, declined after he returned to Germany, where he grew increasingly weak from consumption. He died in Leipzig on May 16, 1896, at the age of twenty-seven. In his letters to friends and benefactors in Boston, he had tried to downplay his condition but when it became clear that he was gravely ill, Isabel Barrows and Alice Stone Blackwell rushed to book passage to Germany to see him. When their boat docked in Le Havre, they received the news that he had died days before. Instead of visiting the young man with whom Alice had formed a deep bond, and whom Isabel Barrows considered practically a son, the two women oversaw his burial arrangements and the disposition of his few belongings.[15]

Later in life. Alice Stone Blackwell told her suffrage compatriot Edna Stantial that "if Ohannes had lived they no doubt would have been married." The two definitely had a brief romance—the only "real affection" Alice ever admitted towards a man in her entire life.[16] It is unclear whether a marriage was seriously considered, but it seems there was no formal engagement or even informal understanding when Ohannes returned to Leipzig in the fall of 1894. Lucy Stone had just died the year before, and Alice would not likely have deserted her father and all her family connections to take up an uncertain residence abroad. She must also have worried that the *Woman's Journal* might not survive without her steady editorial hand.

Other factors undercut the potential marriage. In addition to the large gap in their ages—when they met, she was thirty-seven to his twenty-four—Alice had previously exhibited a strong pattern of crushes on other women dating to her school days. She also considered herself "betrothed" to Kitty Barry, the adopted daughter of her aunt Elizabeth Blackwell, with whom she would share a home at the end of her life. So perhaps marriage wasn't exactly in the cards, but the romantic spark was undeniable, if brief.[17]

Without question, Ohannes Chatschumian's exposure of the horrors and tragedy of Armenian history to Alice Stone Blackwell had a major impact on her editorship of the *Woman's Journal*. The weekly paper provided prominent and in-depth coverage of the Armenian conflict, averaging one or two articles in every issue at the height of the crisis in 1895 and 1896. Practically the entire issue of April 6, 1895 was devoted to Armenia. As editor, Blackwell ran a range of stories and eyewitness accounts that brought the genocide home to her American readers. The coverage included historical sketches, poems (often translated by Blackwell herself), book reviews—Frederick Davis Greene's *The Armenian Crisis in Turkey* got especially prominent attention—and appeals for funds. Alice Stone Blackwell even introduced a resolution on Armenia at her father's seventieth birthday celebration—and then wrote up the event for the paper.[18]

The *Woman's Journal* coverage looks remarkably modern. It focused on civilian casualties and systematic damage to the institutions that bound communities together, such as churches and other charitable organizations. Especially striking was its emphasis on the massacres' toll on Armenian women. In a two-part article on "The Women of Armenia," Ohannes Chatschumian mentioned the "barbarous" custom of picking out Christian girls for Muslim harems in Turkey and how girls sometimes disfigured themselves "to escape the lascivious search of the soldiers."[19] Repeated references to how women had been "outraged to death"—a euphemism for rape—as well as brutally killed or maimed demonstrated a sensitivity to how women civilians were targeted victims in civil wars.[20] The focus on the violation and sexual subjugation of women simultaneously played into the trope of the superiority of Western civilization over the supposedly barbarous and backward customs of the offending Turks. Since civilization was coded as white and Christian, this stance further reinforced the denigration of Muslims and their religion. Ohannes Chatschumian likely realized that readers of the *Woman's Journal* would respond affirmatively to stories of the Armenian horrors when they were framed through the Western imperial gaze.[21]

For both Alice Stone Blackwell and Ohannes Chatschumian, as well as for many suffragists, there was a clear connection between women's rights and human rights. "For me there is no distinction between the freedom of Armenia and the entire freedom of women," Ohannes wrote to Isabel Barrows. "These both kinds of freedom rest on the same principle." In "An Armenian View of the Woman Question," one of the last pieces he published before his death, he wrote, "We see that women have now come to an understanding of their condition, and they are asking for their human rights."[22]

Making those connections had a lifelong effect on Alice Stone Blackwell's progressive politics. "Talking on religious matters (& many other matters) with Ohannes gave me such a sense of the solidarity of mankind as I never had before," she told Isabel Barrows.[23] Blackwell remained active in various Friends of Armenia groups and gave generously to the cause, despite her meager financial resources. She also acted as an informal employment agency for Armenian refugees who managed to get to the Boston area, especially nearby Watertown, where a vibrant Armenian community grew up and still exists.

The passage of the Nineteenth Amendment and the absorption of the Armenian Republic into the Soviet Union in 1922 did not diminish Alice Stone Blackwell's engagement with broader political crusades. No longer serving as editor of the *Woman's Journal* after NAWSA took it over in 1917, she threw her support behind the newly organized League of Women Voters. In addition to her ongoing involvement with the Armenian community, she worked with the American Friends of Russian Freedom and collaborated with Catherine Breshkovsky on her autobiography and a collection of her letters. An early supporter of the American Civil Liberties Union, she was very active in the Sacco and Vanzetti case, which roiled Boston and the nation in the 1920s. In 1934, she received the annual Ford Hall Forum medal for the citizen of Greater Boston who made the most notable contributions to the public weal.

In what qualifies as a painful historical irony, Alice Stone Blackwell's strong links to the Armenian community contributed to a last, sad chapter in her life, although one that ultimately had a happy ending. During the depths of the Great Depression, she lost all her savings after investing them with an old friend and trusted business agent, who was Armenian. When Maud Wood Park heard of Blackwell's near-destitute situation, she put together a committee to raise funds for an annuity. Alice Stone Blackwell's stature in the feminist community was so iconic that Park was able to recruit Carrie Chapman Catt and Eleanor Roosevelt to join her as national co-chairs. Their successful appeal raised over $17,000 from 1,300 contributors, enough to provide Blackwell with $1,500 a year, until her death in 1950.[24]

Throughout her long and productive life, Alice Stone Blackwell always strove to live up to her mother's deathbed admonition to "make the world better." She drew strength from her brief but incredibly rich relationship with Ohannes Chatschumian—"a young man from the heart of Asia" whose ideas were "so much like those of our best thinkers here."[25] A full century before Hillary Rodham Clinton stood before the United Nations International Women's Conference in Beijing in 1995 to proclaim that "human rights are women's rights, and women's rights are human rights," Alice Stone Blackwell was already hard at work trying to make the world live up to that very same ideal.

CHAPTER FIVE

Charlotte Perkins Gilman Finds Her Voice

In 1932, Charlotte Perkins Gilman learned she had inoperable breast cancer. She was not afraid of dying, but having watched her own mother endure a long and painful death from the same disease, she dreaded being incapacitated. She quietly began to stockpile chloroform so she could end her life when she chose. The sudden death of her husband in 1934 spurred a decision to leave the East Coast for Pasadena, where her only daughter lived. Knowing that time was short, she splurged on a cross-country airplane ticket on the Lindbergh Line, her "last 'fling.'"[1]

On August 17, 1935, having said goodbye to friends and family over the past weeks and months, Gilman went upstairs to her bedroom and peacefully took her own life. "Human life consists in mutual service," she explained in the note she left behind. "But when all usefulness is over, when one is assured of unavoidable and imminent death, it is the simplest of human rights to choose a quick and easy death in place of a slow and horrible one." In her case, "I have preferred chloroform to cancer."[2]

As far as we know, Gilman did not request that a death mask be made after her passing, but her daughter decided to commission what was in effect one last portrait. In ancient times, death

67

masks were thought to preserve the soul; in the pre-modern and modern eras, death masks became a way to preserve an image of a well-known person. Beethoven, Napoleon Bonaparte, Henry VII, Ulysses S. Grant, and Richard Wagner are among the noted personages for whom death masks survive. Still popular into the twentieth century, but now usually intended as treasured family mementoes, death masks went beyond photography to capture the departed's final visage in three dimensions. Seeing Charlotte Perkins Gilman's actual death mask in the vault of the Schlesinger Library is an experience both haunting and profoundly moving.[3]

Within hours of Gilman's death, the family physician carefully layered wet plaster bandages on her face and allowed them to dry. The next day, a local sculptor named Sherry Peticolas cast the death mask from that mold. Gilman's body was then cremated—in her view, "such a clean sweet natural redistribution of things!"—and her ashes were scattered in the San Gabriel mountains. "There was an air of peaceful triumph in her quiet figure," her daughter recalled. "She had carried out her plan in all details as she had wished."[4] Charlotte Perkins Gilman left life very much on her own terms.

It may seem odd to preface this story of the leading feminist intellectual of her day with the end of her life, but how Charlotte Perkins Gilman chose to die was perfectly consistent with her philosophy of *living*, a term she preferred to *life* because of its connotations of growth and change.[5] The suffrage movement was very much part of that living, although far from the only component. Gilman is

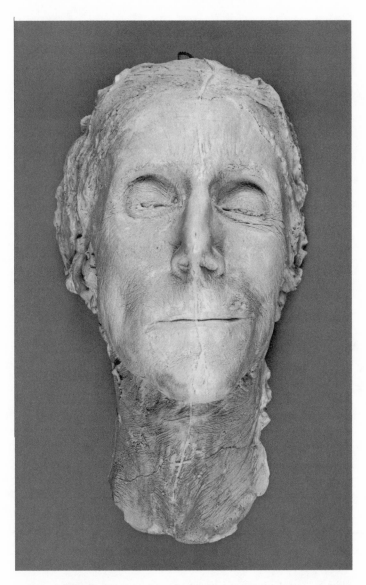

Charlotte Perkins Gilman's death mask. *Courtesy of Schlesinger Library, Radcliffe Institute, Harvard University.*

often cast as an indifferent suffragist, but her suffrage career stretched for more than thirty years and involved a wide range of contributions to the cause. Proselytizing for the vote helped Charlotte Perkins Gilman find her voice and gave her a platform. She in turn used her celebrity and keen mind to build popular support for the cause.[6]

In some ways, she could claim such public authority as her birthright: after all, she was a proud member of the Beecher clan, whose members, male and female, dominated nineteenth-century intellectual life. But her family circumstances were far more challenging than her venerable lineage would lead one to expect. She was born Charlotte Anna Perkins in Hartford, in 1860. Her parents separated when she was young and she was raised in pinched financial circumstances by her mother, whose life she called "one of the most painfully thwarted I have ever known." She struggled with depression her entire life and despaired that marriage, women's conventional lot, would end her hopes for a full and productive life. "I am not the combining sort," she warned a prospective suitor. "I *don't* combine, and I don't want to."[7]

Despites those doubts, she married the struggling artist Charles Walter Stetson in 1884. The challenges of that marriage, followed by the birth of their daughter Katharine the next year, caused a breakdown that she described in these wrenching terms: "Here was a charming home; a loving and devoted husband; an exquisite baby, healthy, intelligent, and good; a highly competent mother to run things; a wholly satisfactory servant—and I lay all day on the lounge and cried." Next came the hospitalization for a rest cure under the supervision of the noted psychologist S. Weir Mitchell, which she later recounted in the haunting semi-autobiographical 1892 story "The Yellow Wallpaper." The Stetsons separated in 1888—"It was not a choice between going and staying, but between going, sane, and staying, insane"—and Charlotte and Katharine moved to California. The couple divorced in 1894, and with Charlotte's blessing, Walter married Grace Channing, her best friend, and Katharine went to live with them. Charlotte's unconventional approach to the fraught questions of divorce and child custody caused a scandal which would trail her for the rest of her life.[8]

She was determined to put that behind her, as she confided to her diary just after she turned thirty: "[M]ade a wrong marriage— lots of people do. Am heavily damaged, but not dead. May live a long time. It is intellectually conceivable that I may recover strength enough to do some part of my work. I will assume this to be true, and act on it." Three years later, she set much loftier goals for the rest of her life: "Probably forty years' time before me. Desired to accomplish in that time—the utmost attainable advance of the human race."[9]

She rebounded quickly by throwing herself into the vibrant Progressive reform climate in California in the 1890s. In that decade, she produced "a surprising output of work, some of my best," which laid the foundation for her lecturing and writing career. A gifted public speaker (a trait she attributed to her Beecher heritage), she lectured extensively to the Nationalist Clubs in California inspired by Edward Bellamy's utopian novel *Looking Backward* (1888).[10] She also found her voice as a writer: her poem "Similar Cases" was published to great acclaim in 1890, and three years later, it was included in her first volume of poetry, *In This Our World*. Her schedule kept her constantly on the road, but this "at large" lifestyle of "never having a settled home, but always feeling perfectly at home anywhere" strangely suited her. Unfortunately, the income from her lecturing and writing barely paid the bills, and she often found herself mired in debt.[11]

In 1898, she published her masterwork, *Women and Economics: The Economic Factor between Men and Women as a Factor in Social*

Evolution, which argued for women's economic independence and critiqued institutions such as the family and marriage for isolating women and preventing their participation in broader (that is, human rather than sex-specific) social developments. Preventing women's social participation not only stunted their growth, it also acted, in her understanding of hereditarian evolution, to retard the development of the human race as a whole. She was especially caustic about society's propensity for excessive sex distinction between men and women: "There is no female mind. The brain is not an organ of sex. As well speak of a female liver." Despite her damning dissection of contemporary gender roles, she concluded *Women and Economics* on this optimistic note: "When the mother of the race is free, we shall have a better world, by the easy right of birth and by the calm, slow, friendly forces of social evolution."[12]

While she was developing the ideas for *Women and Economics*, she fell in love with her first cousin Houghton Gilman, who worked as a patent lawyer in New York City. Their marriage in 1900 finally allowed her to strike a satisfying balance between her personal life and her public work—precisely the issue she wrote *Women and Economics* to address. "If this were a novel, now, here's the happy ending," she wrote in her autobiography, perhaps a bit too glibly. She always remained much more comfortable living in the public realm than dealing with private emotions.[13]

Gilman's suffrage activism continued as the new century began: "To help [suffrage] is a clear duty. To oppose it is to stand ridiculous and wrong to future history." She had long enjoyed a close relationship with Alice Stone Blackwell and the Boston-based *Woman's Journal*, and had contributed her first poem to the paper in 1884. From 1904 to 1905, she served as the newspaper's associate editor, although her ideas proved a bit too broadminded for the readership, and she and Blackwell mutually severed the relationship after a year. One thing the two women continued to share was an abiding concern for the human rights violations in Armenia.[14]

Several years later, Gilman teamed up with Harriot Stanton Blatch in the Equality League of Self-Supporting Women in New York City, a cross-class suffrage alliance unified by the ideals of economic independence she had expounded in *Women and Economics*. Gilman attended the sixtieth anniversary celebration of the Seneca Falls Convention in 1908 and campaigned in 1911 for California's successful state suffrage referendum. That year, she published a small volume of suffrage songs and verses. But she never lost sight of her vision of suffrage as part of a larger struggle for human progress in which women would play a leading role. As a suffragist once said to her with grudging admiration, "After all I think you will do our cause more good than harm, because what you ask is so much worse than what we ask that they will grant our demands in order to escape yours."[15]

In the midst of her ongoing suffrage advocacy, Gilman continued to publish widely in leading journals, magazines, and newspapers: over two thousand works of non-fiction over the course of her career, in addition to 675 pieces of fiction and almost five hundred poems.[16] But as her experience at the *Woman's Journal* showed, she chafed at editors' attempts to tone down her unconventional and often controversial ideas. Gilman's desire to have the freedom to say what she wanted without editorial interference led her to take the unusual step of founding her own monthly magazine, the *Forerunner*, in 1909, and serving as its sole writer, editor, and publisher. "What makes you so lazy?" joked one subscriber. "*Why don't you set the type?*"[17]

The *Forerunner* proved the vehicle for some of Gilman's sharpest suffrage commentary. She especially delighted in exposing the backward, reactionary thinking that dominated antisuffrage ideology, calling out male opponents as "masculist" and sneering at "Women Who Won't Move Forward." As the biographer Judith Allen observed, "in her war on the Antis, Gilman rose to her rhetorical best, loyal to and fiercely defensive of her fellow women, certain of the contribution a female electorate could make to Progressive social reforms."[18]

This debunking of antisuffrage misogyny was especially effective in plays like "Something to Vote For" which appeared in the *Forerunner* in 1911. This fifty-minute parlor theatrical, performed with a small cast of characters and minimal stage requirements, featured victims, villains, unsung heroes, and even a little romance in a plot about a women's club and a campaign for pure milk. When it was revealed that a local businessman had tried to bribe the milk inspector, the club president discarded her earlier opposition to suffrage and enthusiastically signed on to the cause: "Rich or poor, we are all helpless together unless we wake up to the danger and protect ourselves. . . . I'm willing to vote now! I'm glad to vote now! I've got something to vote for!" Although the mass epiphany was something only a die-hard suffrage propagandist could imagine (*"Clubwomen all rise and wave their handkerchiefs, with cries of 'Aye!' 'Aye!"* as the curtain falls), the play's wide topical sweep made the case that suffrage was intricately bound up in larger questions of Progressive reform. In the end, pure milk and votes for women both win.[19]

Gilman later calculated that the amount of material she generated for the *Forerunner* "equaled four books a year, books of thirty-six thousand words," a pace she kept up for almost seven years. Many of her best-known novels, including *What Diantha Did* (1910), *The Crux* (1911), *Moving the Mountain* (1911), and *Herland* (1915) first appeared in its pages. Gilman relished not having to pitch or tailor her ideas to unenlightened or picky editors, but relying primarily on the *Forerunner* to spread her ideas had the contrary effect of removing her voice from the public debates of her day. One biographer compared it to playing solitaire. Individual subscriptions never came close to covering the cost of this huge undertaking, and Gilman reluctantly shut the magazine down in 1916.[20]

In the 1910s, Charlotte Perkins Gilman was in the thick of the heady early days of modern feminism. Here is how she defined the term: "Feminism is a term applied to what was previously known as 'The Woman's Movement,' and still earlier, as 'Women's Rights.' That Movement, in its largest sense, consists in the development of human qualities and functions among women; in their entering upon social relationships, instead of remaining, as has been almost universally the case, restricted to the sexual and domestic." While generally "individual and unconscious," feminism was also "increasingly conscious and organized." Gilman was especially excited about the prospects for the future: "The latest and highest form of Feminism has great promise for the world. It postulates womanhood free, strong, clean and conscious of its power and duty." That definition sounds to modern ears like a close approximation of Gilman's own philosophy, but she always preferred to call herself a humanist rather than a feminist.[21]

This is where Charlotte Perkins Gilman, the suffrage movement, and the larger history of feminism intersect. Starting with Mary Wollstonecraft, John Stuart Mill, and Margaret Fuller, the question of woman's status and women's rights had long been debated and discussed. The word *feminist* was a more modern construction, derived from the French *feminisme* of the 1880s but not widely deployed in the United States until the second decade of the twentieth century. That decade was also the height of suffrage

WHAT IS FEMINISM?
COME AND FIND OUT

FIRST FEMINIST MASS MEETING
at the PEOPLE'S INSTITUTE, Cooper Union
Tuesday Evening, February 17th, 1914, at 8 o'clock, P. M.

Subject: "WHAT FEMINISM MEANS TO ME."

Ten-Minute Speeches by

ROSE YOUNG	GEORGE CREEL
JESSE LYNCH WILLIAMS	MRS. FRANK COTHREN
HENRIETTA RODMAN	FLOYD DELL
GEORGE MIDDLETON	CRYSTAL EASTMAN BENEDICT
FRANCES PERKINS	EDWIN BJORKMAN
WILL IRWIN	MAX EASTMAN

Chairman, MARIE JENNEY HOWE.

SECOND FEMINIST MASS MEETING
at the PEOPLES' INSTITUTE, Cooper Union
Friday, February 20th, 1914, at 8 o'clock, P. M.

Subject: "BREAKING INTO THE HUMAN RACE."

The Right to Work.—
RHETA CHILDE DORR

The Right of the Mother to Her Profession.—
BEATRICE FORBES-ROBERTSON-HALE.

The Right to Her Convictions.—
MARY SHAW.

The Right to Her Name.—
FOLA LA FOLLETTE.

The Right to Organize.—
ROSE SCHNEIDERMAN.

The Right to Ignore Fashion.—
NINA WILCOX PUTNAM.

The Right to Specialize in Home Industries.—
CHARLOTTE PERKINS GILMAN.

Chairman, MARIE JENNEY HOWE.

ADMISSION FREE. **NO COLLECTION.**

This handbill from 1914 poses a question—What is feminism?—that is still being debated today. Charlotte Perkins Gilman was one of the speakers who attempted to answer it for the Cooper Union audience. *Courtesy of the New York Historical Society.*

advocacy, and the two movements were closely intertwined. Those who self-consciously adopted the feminist label often embraced a broader commitment to economic independence and sexual emancipation than suffrage's more narrow demand for the vote, an issue which functioned as the lowest common denominator around which politically active women could converge. But taking the long view, both suffragists and feminists were marching in the same general direction.[22]

The best example of contemporary feminism was a group called Heterodoxy, founded in 1912 by twenty-five charter members, including Charlotte Perkins Gilman, which met every other Saturday in Greenwich Village. Described as "women who did things and did them openly," Heterodoxy's members included self-described modern women such as Inez Haynes Irwin, Zona Gale, Fola La Follette, Crystal Eastman, and Elsie Clews Parsons. All subscribed to Marie Jenney Howe's vision for the club: "We intend to be ourselves, not just our little female selves, but our whole big human selves." The club brought together like-minded women, most of whom were a generation younger than Gilman, to talk about the challenges of the liberated lives they envisioned for themselves and, by extension, all women. These were heady discussions.[23]

Some of them, such as two panels held at Cooper Union in New York City in 1914, took place in public. "What is Feminism? Come and Find Out" read the handbill. The first program featured twelve speakers, including six men, on the topic "What Feminism Means to Me." The subject of the second mass meeting was "Breaking into the Human Race."[24] At both events, many of the speakers had ties to Heterodoxy, the suffrage movement, or both, including Marie Jenney Howe, the journalist Rheta Childe Dorr, the labor activist Rose Schneiderman, and the actress Fola LaFollette. Charlotte Perkins

Gilman spoke at the second meeting on "The Right to Specialize in Home Industries," an expansion of her ideas in *Women and Economics* and its sequel *Human Work* (1904). The event drew extensive coverage, even in conservative antisuffrage papers like the *New York Times*, which headlined its article "Feminists Ask Equal Chance: Leaders in Movement Discuss 'Breaking into the Human Race' at Cooper Union: Wants Sex Fences Cut Down."[25]

That spring, Gilman also offered two subscription lecture series. The first, "The Larger Feminism," drew audiences of between fifty and two hundred people to its weekly sessions. The second was called "Studies in Masculism." The writer George Middleton, the husband of Fola LaFollette, left this recollection of the series: "She presented her facts in chiseled prose but, like all feminists I know, with devastating humor. She herself was a mistress of sarcasm, amusing as her lectures were peppered with ridicule and irony." Not all in the audience were so entranced. Clara Savage Littledale, a journalist at the *New York Evening Post* and recent Vassar graduate, confided to her diary: "She has a lovely face but a harsh voice and I didn't like her especially." A month later at another session, Littledale was still not a fan: "Sore throat, curse, and Charlotte Perkins Gilman. It made for a very nervy morning."[26]

Charlotte Perkins Gilman did not play an active role in the suffrage movement's final push to victory. By then, her fame was beginning to wane, a process which continued until her death in 1935. Gilman was rediscovered and celebrated in the early days of women's history in the 1970s and 1980s, but she holds a more vexed place in feminist history today. Her ideas about how sexual characteristics could be passed on to future generations have been discredited by genetics, and she has been taken to task for her anti-immigrant, pro-eugenics stance at the end of her life. Even her classic story "The Yellow Wallpaper" has been reinterpreted as a deeply racist text.[27]

Yet Gilman deserves a place in both the suffrage and feminist pantheons. From the 1890s until the 1920s, she was the most widely known feminist public intellectual of her day—"the high priestess of feminism."[28] She used her public renown to engage audiences in discussions of the most pressing issues of the day, not just those limited to women. Always looking forward, always in motion, she crafted a life that allowed her to share her far-reaching ideas with public audiences across the country and, indeed, around the world.

Once Charlotte Perkins Gilman found her voice, she used it to promote woman suffrage, but like many suffragists, her conception was far broader than just the vote. Her 1893 poem "She Who Is to Come" captures that ideal well. That the poem became such a beloved anthem for several generations of suffragists suggests how broadly shared Gilman's capacious vision was:

A woman—in so far as she beholdeth
Her one Beloved's face;
A mother—with a great heart that enfoldeth
The children of the Race;
A body, free and strong, with that high beauty
That comes of perfect use, is built thereof;
A mind where Reason ruleth over Duty,
And Justice reigns with Love;
A self-poised, royal soul, brave, wise, and tender,
No longer blind and dumb;
A Human Being, of an unknown splendor,
Is she who is to come![29]

PART TWO

The Personal Is Political

Wʜɪʟᴇ ᴡᴏᴍᴀɴ ѕᴜꜰꜰʀᴀɢᴇ is often seen primarily as a political movement devoted to enacting a legislative goal, the suffrage cause was not something that its participants could turn off at the end of the day when the picket signs were put away and the last meeting adjourned. Once a woman became a suffragist, it changed her relationships with her family of origin and with the significant others in her life, especially husbands and partners, but also friends and professional colleagues as well. It potentially affected her political party identification, her livelihood, which organizations she belonged to, and where she lived and traveled. Participating in suffrage events even affected how she dressed. The personal and the political were two sides of the same coin.

Signing on to the woman suffrage campaign often changed how women thought of themselves. In the day-to-day work of this broad and diverse movement, budding suffragists suddenly found themselves doing unexpected and often daring things. It took courage to stand up publicly for the cause, but suffragists did not have to go it alone: they enjoyed the camaraderie of being part of a movement they all knew was bigger than themselves. Oreola Williams Haskell called this "the romance" of the woman suffrage cause.[1] That, as much as the actual goal of winning the vote, was often what made the drudgery and hard work worthwhile.

By virtue of declaring their support for suffrage in the first place, suffragists took themselves outside the bounds of what was considered acceptable behavior for women at the time. The woman suffrage campaign provided a place where it was okay to be different, okay to be an outlier in regard to accepted gender norms and in other ways too. The suffrage movement gave women a space to combine meaningful work with satisfying personal relationships, including a broad range of alternative lifestyles. Suffragists participated in companionate marriages, with both husband and wife signed on to the cause; in deep friendships with other women that turned into lifelong partnerships; as "New Women" experimenting with and claiming sexual prerogatives usually reserved for men; and independently, as single women without the constraints of marriage. Viewed in this way, suffragists turn out to be a much more interesting group than their somewhat dour public reputation gives them credit for.

CHAPTER SIX

The Shadow of the Confederacy

NEW ORLEANS was a popular spot for conventions in 1903. In May, tens of thousands of former Confederate soldiers and their families from all over the South descended on the city for the annual gathering of the United Confederate Veterans, an organization formed in that same city in 1889. One of them was Alexander Green Beauchamp, a veteran from Mississippi who had served under General Nathan Bedford Forrest before being taken prisoner by Union forces at the battle of Selma on April 2, 1865. His badge identifying the outfit with which he served became a treasured family memento. It arrived at the Schlesinger Library by way of marriage: Beauchamp's grandson Joseph Howorth married Lucy Somerville, a fellow lawyer and the daughter of Nellie Nugent Somerville, a noted Mississippi suffragist and NAWSA official.

In an odd quirk of history, Nellie Nugent Somerville had likely been in New Orleans just two months earlier than Beauchamp, attending the National American Woman Suffrage Association convention in March. The gathering, orchestrated by the Louisiana suffragists (and rabid white supremacists) Kate and Jean Gordon, was profoundly shaped by its southern setting. It was only the second time that the national convention was held in the South; Atlanta in 1895 had been the first.

Bowing to local prejudice, African American women were barred from all convention proceedings. Worse still, NAWSA adopted an official policy statement in New Orleans that allowed individual state organizations to determine their own standards for membership and "the terms upon which the extension of suffrage to women shall be requested." In other words, NAWSA caved to prevailing racism by endorsing a states' rights policy that gave southern suffrage groups free rein to exclude African American women. NAWSA's new policy also emboldened southern suffragists to deploy arguments that bolstered white supremacy and the exclusion of African Americans from public life, such as claiming that enfranchising white women would offset the votes of African American men. It was not the suffrage movement's finest hour.

Juxtaposing these two conventions—the United Confederate Veterans and NAWSA—held in the same year in the same southern city reminds us of how deeply and powerfully the legacy of the Civil War shaped southern politics and public life even fifty years after Appomattox. For many southerners, the war never really ended; upholding the "lost cause" was an ongoing source of pride and civic duty. That was the unfriendly terrain on which white southern suffragists labored.

WHEN MARY JOHNSTON's suffrage novel *Hagar* appeared in 1913, it caused quite a stir. Set in a small backwater of rural Virginia, it offered a fictional account of scenes that could have played out in

Confederate Army reunion pin and ribbon, 1903. *Courtesy of Schlesinger Library, Radcliffe Institute, Harvard University.*

actual households across the South. The chapter "A Difference of Opinion" opens with a character named Colonel Ashendyne discovering a letter stamped "Votes for Women." "How do you happen to get letters like that?" he challenges his granddaughter Hagar.

"Why not?" she replies. "I propose presently actively to work for it myself."

Her grandfather reacts to that statement with "apoplectic silence," leaving her grandmother to put into words what both are thinking: "Women Righters and Abolitionists!—doing their best to drench the country with blood, kill our people and bring the carpetbaggers upon us!" Then comes an ultimatum from the family patriarch: "Either you retire from such a position and such activities, or you cease to be granddaughter of mine."[1]

What was a New Woman—and a southern one at that—to do? At first Hagar feels trapped, but "then she realized she was not trapped, and she smiled." She is a successful writer—"good for something more than ten thousand a year"—and she is economically independent. She doesn't have to go along with her family's conservative ideas about woman's place in southern society. She could instead embrace her "Fourth Dimension": "inner freedom, ability to work, personal independence, courage and sense of humour and a sanguine mind, breadth and height of vision, tenderness and hope." Within days, Hagar is on her way back to New York City.[2]

Totally forgotten today, Mary Johnston was one of the country's most popular turn-of-the-century writers, often mentioned in the same breath as Sir Walter Scott and Tolstoy. *To Have and To Hold*, a historical romance set in colonial Jamestown, was the nation's bestselling novel in 1900, selling close to half a million copies. Johnston followed it with a string of historical novels, including two deeply researched bestsellers about Virginia in the Civil War: *The*

Long Roll (1911) and *Cease Firing* (1912). Margaret Mitchell, no slouch herself when it came to writing about the conflict, later confessed, "I felt so childish and presumptuous for even trying to write about that period when she had done it so beautifully, so powerfully— better than anyone can ever do it, no matter how hard they try." Alas, Johnston's suffrage novel failed to capture the reading public's attention, and it did not earn back its $10,000 advance.[3]

"No stronger characters did the long struggle produce than those great-souled Southern suffragists. They had need to be great of soul." That assessment by Carrie Chapman Catt and Nettie Shuler certainly applies to Mary Johnston. She was born in 1870 in the small town of Buchanan, Virginia, "a Southern aristocrat, raised in a climate of reverence for the Confederacy." She was the oldest of John William Johnston's and Elizabeth Dixon Alexander Johnson's six children. John William Johnston was a railroad executive who had been a major in the Confederate artillery; his family tree included Joseph E. Johnston, a Confederate general under whom Elizabeth's father served at Vicksburg. "We lived in a veritable battle cloud, an atmosphere of war stories, of continued reference to the men and the deeds of that gigantic struggle," Mary Johnston wrote, and she drew on that family history as inspiration and background for several of her novels.[4] She even made her father an actual character in *Cease Firing.*

Johnston's twenties were a combination of crisis and opportunity. When she was nineteen, her mother died, and Mary assumed responsibility for her younger siblings. The next year, she accompanied her father on a European tour. This pattern of exposure to ideas and people outside the South influenced both her personality and her writing, as did her father's financial reverses in 1895. "We were living comfortably in an easy Southern fashion in New York," she remembered. "In a week all was changed. There was a sharp need of retrenchment and even when retrenchment was accomplished, need remained." Without telling anyone of her plans, she began writing the historical novel which became *Prisoners of Hope*, a love story / political intrigue set in mid-seventeenth century Virginia that Houghton Mifflin published to positive reviews in 1898.[5]

The launch of Johnston's literary career coincided with a revival of popular interest in large-scale historical romances and adventures. Her next book, *To Have and To Hold*, set in Jamestown in 1622, recounted a love story, between a recent settler and a disguised lady-in-waiting, in the midst of an Indian uprising. The prestigious *Atlantic Monthly* published the chapters serially from June 1899 to March 1900—quite an accomplishment for an author's second book. The serialization created such a buzz that sixty thousand advance copies of the book were sold, and it sold 135,000 more in the first week after publication. That burst of sales earned Johnston a sizeable $50,000, and additional sales would increase her take to $70,000. *To Have and To Hold* remains Johnston's best-known work.

In the first decade of the twentieth century, the author the *New York Times* referred to as a "high-bred aristocratic girl of the South" found both critical success and a large popular audience for her novels, including *Audrey* (1902), a melodrama which took place in eighteenth-century Virginia, and *Lewis Rand* (1908), a tale of ambition and intrigue set in the early republic. Her first nine books earned over $200,000, which allowed her to support herself and take care of her family after her father's death in 1905. In 1911, Johnston, who never married, bought forty acres of land in the resort area of Bath County, Virginia, outside the town of Warm Springs. She commissioned a grand twenty-room Italian Renaissance house with a Colonial Revival interior, as well as cottages for two of her sisters, who also never married. Johnston lived at Three Hills for the rest of her life.[6]

Mary Johnston first expressed public support for the suffrage movement in a 1909 newspaper interview. Such an endorsement from a well-known literary celebrity was quite a boost for the cause. Three weeks later, she, her friend and fellow writer Ellen Glasgow, and the social activist Lila Meade Valentine—"some of the best people of Virginia"—founded the Equal Suffrage League of Virginia, based in Richmond. Reflecting how retarded suffrage activism was in the South as compared to the nation at large, the Equal Suffrage League marked the first viable suffrage association in the state.[7]

For the next six years, Johnston was actively involved in the suffrage cause. With her impeccable southern pedigree always proudly on display, she wrote articles, gave speeches, and lobbied and testified before the Virginia legislature. She even took elocution lessons to improve her public speaking, a meaningful commitment for a writer who had not previously associated herself with any political causes. In addition to her suffrage advocacy, she also expressed support for the labor movement and privately identified as a socialist. She declined, however, to speak publicly for those causes, for fear of damaging support for suffrage, which was already controversial enough in her native state.

Mary Johnston laid out her emerging ideology in an April 1910 article in the *Atlantic Monthly*. She called the movement "The Woman's War"—a telling phrase from someone so steeped in Confederate history—and noted at the outset the difficulties it faced in her state. "Virginia, if the dearest of states, is also the most conservative. Her men are chivalric, her women domestic. . . . She makes progress, too, but her eyes are apt to turn to the past." Such conservatism explained "the shock of surprise, or more or less indignant incredulity" that greeted the Richmond women's decision to ask for the vote. As Johnston noted, "in the South we are not used to woman's speaking—not, certainly, on the present subject."[8]

When Johnston published that piece, she was deeply immersed in the research for her Civil War novels, which would come out in 1911 and 1912. When a reporter trying to find an angle from the publicity-shy author asked her if she was going to write a book on suffrage, she demurred, but clearly it was on her mind. Yet a narrative set in the present—a first for her—and dedicated to a controversial idea posed quite different challenges than her earlier historical novels had.[9]

The eponymously named *Hagar* tells the story of Hagar Ashendyne, a product of the Old South who grows up to be a New Woman. Just as memories of the Civil War shaped southern life, so does the novel reflect the legacy of slave life on the plantation, albeit indirectly. Hagar's ancestral home, Gilead Balm, draws its name from the well-known Negro spiritual "There is a balm in Gilead." More pointedly, the main character shares a name with a Biblical character who has long been associated with the suffering of enslaved women. Hagar is the Egyptian slave of Sarah, who offers her to her husband Abraham as his concubine. Later Hagar and her son Ishmael are cast out, wandering in the wilderness until God comes to their rescue. These biblical allusions were well known to Johnston's readers.[10]

Hagar is twelve and already something of a free spirit when the novel begins. She has a decidedly unconventional family situation. Her artist father is roaming around Europe, having left his bedridden wife Maria at home with his parents at their Virginia plantation. Maria suffers from nervous prostration and soon dies. Hagar eventually reunites with her father, whose second marriage

Edmonia Lewis, the first woman of mixed African American and
Native American heritage to win acclaim as a sculptor, created
this white marble statue of the enslaved woman Hagar in 1866.
Mary Johnston also drew inspiration from that biblical character as
the name of the white protagonist of her suffrage novel. *Smithsonian
American Art Museum, Washington, DC / Art Resource, NY.*

to a wealthy widow ends with the widow's drowning and his being left a cripple. The two of them spend much of her twenties traveling throughout Europe and South America together.

By now Hagar has become a successful novelist. Her travels bring her into contact with new people and new ideas, and she embraces a far broader view of women's roles than she had been brought up with in the conservative South. At the very top of her list is a commitment to women's economic independence, a key factor in her desire to become a writer. While she never abandons her roots in Gilead Balm, she feels most at home living on her own in New York City, where she gets involved in the socialist movement, settlement work, and the suffrage movement. That involvement sets up the "difference of opinion" confrontation with her kinfolk back home, but she does not back down. Having rejected various suitors along the way, at the end she meets a bridge builder named John Fay, who accepts her as the liberated woman she is and still wants to marry her. She in turn surprises him—and the reader—by saying she would like to have children. The novel ends with them walking hand-in-hand back from a beach where they have almost drowned in a storm.

For a work that is usually referred to as a suffrage novel, *Hagar* doesn't really devote much plot time to the issue—only the last seventy-five pages of an almost four-hundred-page book. But the novel is very much in the spirit of the wide range of pro-suffrage literature—short stories, plays, poetry, novellas, autobiographies, and journalistic sketches, as well as novels—produced over the course of the long struggle. The novel most readily associated in the popular mind with women's rights was Henry James's *The Bostonians* (1886), with its hostile portrait of Verena Tarrant, Olive Chancellor, and Basil Ransom, but far more sympathetic treatments appeared in novels such as Edna Ferber's *Fanny Herself* (1917), Gertrude Atherton's *Julia France and Her Times* (1912), Zona Gale's *Mothers to Men* (1911), and Alice Duer Miller's *Are Women People?* (1915). Popular literary works proved a handy way to broadcast the ideas of the suffrage movement to a general audience.[11]

Like Oreola Williams Haskell's *Banner Bearers*, what mainly comes through in Johnston's novel is Hagar's unequivocal belief in the justice of the cause and her delight at sharing the camaraderie of the movement dedicated to winning it. In the end, *Hagar* is as much a general plea for women's emancipation as a suffrage tract. In order for women like Hagar to grow and prosper, the old values of the South must give way to more modern views that include political equality and much more.

Johnston's evolutionary approach to social progress clearly owes a large debt to Charlotte Perkins Gilman's *Women and Economics* (1898). In fact, Gilman and Johnston were friends. Gilman's description of Johnston's doubleness perfectly captures how the writer used the façade of a genteel southern lady to slip powerful ideas by her often unsuspecting audience. "You fascinating person," Gilman wrote her friend. "You always make me think of an eagle, delicately masquerading as a thrush—so soft and gentle and kind—and with big *sweepingness* in back of it all." Gilman was especially impressed by what Johnston had accomplished in *Hagar:* "I feel as if, having established your high reputation in historical novels, you were now doing far better and bigger work. People won't like it as well, of course, but keep on."[12]

Like all of Johnston's novels, *Hagar* was widely reviewed, but critics were split. While some cheered her decision to write a present-day story dealing with contemporary issues, many more found the result little more than unsatisfying propaganda. For example, Helen

Bullis's review in the *New York Times* called it "a very pleasant story" but noted that it began to "sag" when if left Hagar's childhood. The reviewer gave Johnston credit for her convincing depiction of suffrage as hard work, "but we would remind Miss Johnston that it is not novel writing. The novel reader 'must be shown'—he resents being told." Literary criticism ever since has generally agreed that this book was not among her best. But when it's read as a window on the New Southern Woman circa 1913, the book has much to offer.[13]

Hagar and Mary Johnston offer an interesting perspective on the southern suffrage movement, which encountered steep resistance throughout its duration. So revered was the cultural ideal of the southern lady, the embodiment of the region's hierarchical and patriarchal way of life rooted in slavery and its aftermath, that any attempt to change gender roles was seen as a threat to southern womanhood, the home, and white supremacy. To the vast majority of southerners, suffrage advocacy was yet another dangerous idea promoted by outsiders—that is, northerners—in a region still smarting from the Civil War and the Reconstruction experiment that followed.[14]

Despite such odds, a determined cadre of southern suffragists began to speak up. Like Mary Johnston, many of them traced their pedigrees to the southern elite. "The truth was," according to the historian Marjorie Spruill Wheeler, "only southern women of Johnston's type, rearing, and environment could violate social convention so thoroughly and get away with it, and thus, with very few exceptions, the leaders of the southern suffrage movement were drawn from the region's social and economic elite." Imbued with a strong sense of *noblesse oblige*, they were dismayed by the politicians who dominated the South when Reconstruction ended.

Women like Laura Clay of Kentucky, Kate Gordon of Louisiana, Belle Kearney and Nellie Nugent Somerville of Mississippi, and Rebecca Latimer Felton of Georgia wanted to raise the standards of public life, and they quickly realized they needed the ballot to have an impact. But although suffrage organizations appeared throughout the South, and although southern suffragists played significant roles in NAWSA, especially in the 1890s, every suffrage campaign in a southern state was defeated.[15]

Southern suffrage was always very much tied up with race. Even after the end of Reconstruction in 1877, southerners feared that the federal government might enforce the Fourteenth and Fifteenth Amendments more aggressively. This fear provided an opening wedge, albeit a racist one, for the suffrage movement to take root in the 1890s: enfranchising white women, they argued, would offset votes by black men. By the turn of the century, however, southern states had figured out how to keep black voters from the polls through other means, so this argument became less compelling. For the first decade of the twentieth century, the movement went dormant.

Starting around 1909, things picked up again in various southern states. Since black men had been effectively disfranchised by then, there was less need to portray woman suffrage as a cornerstone of white supremacy. But a new challenge appeared as the national movement increasingly coalesced around a federal amendment. Southern states' rights advocates recoiled, dismayed at the prospect of the federal government intervening yet again in what they saw as a state and local matter. In the end, most southern suffragists drifted towards support of NAWSA's "Winning Plan," but support for a federal amendment was still an uphill battle. Only four southern states (Texas, Arkansas, Kentucky, and Tennessee) voted to ratify the Nineteenth Amendment. Virginia didn't officially do so until 1952.

Much attention has focused on the racism of southern suffragists and their strategies, and there is no denying that race was often explicitly deployed in ways harmful to African American rights. Such explicit playing of the race card goes beyond the generalized racism that plagued the entire movement. Much of the worst race baiting occurred in the 1890s, and it was much less prevalent after 1910. Suffrage leaders in the various states displayed a definite range of attitudes on race and white supremacy. On the one extreme was Kate Gordon of Louisiana, who was one of the most egregious at playing the race card. Belle Kearney of Mississippi, who gave the keynote address at the 1903 convention, was also outspoken in her defense of Anglo-Saxon purity.[16]

At the other end of the spectrum was Mary Johnston, who showed—within the limits of being a white southern woman of a certain class and mindset—much more restraint when it came to questions of race, both in terms of her suffrage advocacy and her writing. Johnston's novels are relatively free of demeaning stereotypes and portrayals of black southern folk, yet this support only went so far: Johnston never publicly spoke out against the widespread disfranchisement of black voters. Only after suffrage was won did Johnston tackle touchy subjects like slavery or lynching in her writing.[17]

Even so, Johnston brought an unusual sensibility about race to her suffrage work. When contemplating the question of property qualifications for voting, she cautioned, "I think that as women we should be most prayerfully careful lest, in the future, that women—whether colored women or white women who are merely poor, should be able to say that we had betrayed their interests and excluded them from freedom." When Kate Gordon's antiblack rhetoric became too toxic in the Southern States Woman Suffrage Council, a group dedicated to pushing for state suffrage amendments rather than a federal amendment, Johnston quietly resigned in 1915. She did not participate in the final push for suffrage, or the ratification battle. Instead, she turned her attention back to her writing.[18]

Hagar marked something of a turning point for Mary Johnston. In addition to her newfound political engagement, she also became increasingly interested in mysticism, which she incorporated in her later novels. Each time she changed her style and focus, however, she lost more readers than she added, which affected both her popularity and her earning power. When she tried to rekindle her old affinity for historical adventure in the 1920s, she found herself preaching to an increasingly small core of dedicated followers in changed literary times. Her books never again became bestsellers.

Mary Johnston always took the long view, about both her writing and her advocacy for women's emancipation. "I am an educated and intelligent woman, and I cannot understand how it is possible for an intelligent woman not be interested in a question of such worldwide importance not only to the women but to the race, a reform so necessary and vital. The race cannot be emancipated until all its members are emancipated," she told the *New York Times* in 1911. Even though suffrage was a hard sell in her native South, Johnston was sure it would prevail. "The Southern woman has pride,—Oh she has pride! . . . [and] when it comes to her aid, she will become a suffragist."[19]

Ballot box from a special primary held in Chicago and Cicero, Illinois on April 9, 1912. *Courtesy of Chicago History Museum.*

CHAPTER SEVEN

Ida Wells-Barnett and the Alpha Suffrage Club

WHEN MALE VOTERS in Cook County, Illinois showed up at the polls on April 9, 1912, they were handed a special suffrage ballot in addition to the official primary slate. Its charge was straightforward: were they for or against the extension of suffrage to women? Election officials were instructed to place the suffrage ballots in a special ballot box and keep a separate tally, which was to be counted immediately after the polls closed, before any other ballots were tallied. One of those distinctive ballot boxes now resides in the collection of the Chicago History Museum.

The Chicago Political Equality League was the driving force behind this initiative. Founded as an offshoot of the elite Chicago Woman's Club in 1894, the league counted prominent clubwomen such as Ellen Henrotin and Catherine Waugh McCullough among its early members. Later, its membership expanded to include the Hull House founder Jane Addams, the African American activist Ida Wells-Barnett, Margaret Haley of the local teachers' union, and the public school superintendent Ella Flagg Young. After an unsuccessful attempt to include municipal suffrage in a proposed city charter in 1907, Chicago suffragists mobilized again to put the question on the April 1912 primary ballot, distributing "Vote Yes" fliers to wards and pre-cincts throughout the city. Asking men to "look at BOTH sides of this Question," they hoped such suffrage literature would con-vince skeptical voters to "play fair" and check the top box on the ballot. Alas, the men of Chicago—or at least the minority who voted in the primary—defeated the referendum.[1]

Illinois suffragists did not have to wait long to erase that set-back. In 1913, the state legislature extended presidential suf-frage, as well as the right to vote in many municipal races, to women. Primarily the brainchild of Grace Wilbur Trout, this brilliant strategy meant that instead of having to convince unsympathetic male voters, the suffragists only had to win the support of a majority of the state legislature for what seemed like (but wasn't) a limited goal. It was still not an easy task, but the politically savvy suffragists were clearly up to it. It had an immediate political impact, especially in cities like Chicago where citizens of both sexes, including a large number of Afri-can American women, could now vote.

IN THE FIRST SIX MONTHS OF 1913, Illinois was a hotbed of suf-frage activism, and Ida Wells-Barnett wanted to make sure that African American women were part of the action. Despite being a longtime member of the Illinois Women's Suffrage Association, she had not previously been able to drum up much interest on the question within Chicago's growing black community. But now that the Illinois legislature was considering the law to grant presi-dential and municipal suffrage to women, things were different. "When I saw that we were likely to have a restricted suffrage," Wells-

Barnett recalled, "and the white women of the organization were working like beavers to bring it about, I made another effort to get our women interested." On January 30, 1913 she founded the Alpha Suffrage Club, the first African American suffrage organization in Chicago. Two months later, at a march timed to protest President Woodrow Wilson's inauguration, she challenged the racism of the white-led national movement head on—and she prevailed.[2]

Even though African Americans at the time were overwhelmingly associated with the Republican Party, the Alpha Suffrage Club was nonpartisan. Its primary goal was to educate African American women about the duties and responsibilities of citizenship and voting. As Wells-Barnett admitted, the club often started from scratch: "If the white women were backward in political matters, our own women were even more so." The goal was to make African American women feel more comfortable in the realm of politics and then to "use the vote for the advantage of ourselves and our race."[3]

One of the Alpha Suffrage Club's first tasks was to raise money to send its president to Washington, DC for the suffrage demonstration Alice Paul was planning on March 3, 1913, to coincide with Woodrow Wilson's inauguration. Ida Wells-Barnett was one of more than sixty Illinois suffragists who made the trip—so many that the *Chicago Tribune* sent a reporter and photographer to cover the story.

Once the Illinois delegation arrived in the nation's capital and began to practice their drill formation for the parade, Grace Wilbur Trout, the president of the Illinois Equal Suffrage Association, informed the delegation that the leaders of the National American Woman Suffrage Association had advised them "to keep our delegation entirely white" because many women, especially those from southern states, would not march otherwise. Instead blacks were to be relegated to a separate section at the end of parade. "We should like to have Mrs. Barnett march with us," Trout told the assembled Illinois suffragists, but "if the national association has decided it is unwise to include the colored women, I think we should abide by its decision."[4]

This stunning declaration caused a "murmur of excitement . . . around the room," according to the reporter, "and those standing near the colored woman kept an embarrassed silence." Virginia Brooks, a white woman who, along with Belle Squire, had affiliated with the Alpha Suffrage Club at its founding, quickly spoke up, pointing out that "we have come down here to march for equal rights," and it would be undemocratic to exclude Wells-Barnett on the basis of race. "If women of other states lack moral courage," Brooks said, "we should show them that we are not afraid of public opinion. We should stand by our principles. If we do not the parade will be a farce."[5]

Then Ida Wells-Barnett spoke, her voice trembling with emotion and two tears rolling down her check, according to the sympathetic but somewhat patronizing *Chicago Tribune* account. "If the Illinois women do not take a stand now in this great democratic parade then the colored women are lost," she argued forcefully. When a white member of the delegation said in ignorance, "If I were a colored woman, I should be willing to march with the other women of my race," it provoked a pointed response from Wells-Barnett. "There is a difference . . . which you probably do not see. I shall not march with the colored women. Either I go with you or not at all. I am not taking this stand because I personally wish for recognition. I am doing it for the future benefit of my whole race." Grace Trout seemed swayed by these sentiments, and she agreed to take the matter up again with the national leaders, but to no avail. Although Trout personally disagreed, she said she would abide by their wishes. Wells-Barnett would have none of it. "When I was asked to come down here, I was asked to march with the other women of our state, and I intend to do so or not take part in the parade at all."[6]

When the Illinois delegation set out down Pennsylvania Avenue, four abreast and decked out in white dresses, "jaunty turbans," and suffrage sashes, Ida Wells-Barnett was nowhere to be seen. Most of the delegates assumed she was either marching with the other black women or had decided to skip the parade entirely. The *Tribune* reporter on the scene was a first-hand witness to what happened next: "Suddenly from the crowd on the sidewalk Mrs. Barnett walked calmly out to the delegation and assumed her place at the side of Mrs. Squire," her white ally. No one questioned or challenged her, and she finished the parade as part of the Illinois delegation without incident. A photograph of Wells-Barnett, Squire, and Brooks ran on page five of the *Chicago Tribune* on March 5.[7]

When Ida Wells-Barnett returned to Chicago after her momentous trip to Washington, she heard from Catherine Waugh McCullough, a leading white suffragist, who had read the accounts in the newspapers and wrote Wells-Barnett with her unqualified support for her stand. "As I told Mrs. Squire and Miss Brooks," wrote McCullough, "it only required that our women should be as firm in standing up for their principles as the Southern women are for their prejudices." As a token of their budding friendship, Ida Wells-Barnett invited McCullough to the first annual dinner of the Alpha Suffrage Club held the following November.[8]

Ida Wells-Barnett was no stranger to controversy.[9] Born a slave in Holly Springs, Mississippi during the upheavals of the Civil War, she spent the rest of her life fighting for full citizenship, both as an African American and a woman. After a yellow fever epidemic killed her parents and a younger sibling in 1878, she dropped out of school and became a teacher to support her family, even though she was only sixteen years old. Seeking broader opportunities, she relocated to Memphis, where she became a journalist.

Ida B. Wells's first experience with challenging discrimination came in 1883, when she was forcibly evicted from the "ladies" car on a Chesapeake & Ohio train and forced to relocate to the much less commodious "colored" car. Indignant at her treatment, she sued the railroad company, claiming she was entitled to ride in the ladies' car because she had purchased a full-fare ticket specifically designated for it. She won an initial settlement from the railroad company, but it was later overturned. Confirming the deteriorating climate for African American rights, the Supreme Court upheld the practice of Jim Crow segregation in *Plessy v. Ferguson* in 1896.

Ida B. Wells is best known for her antilynching activism. Her epiphany occurred in 1892 in Memphis, where she had become part owner of a newspaper called the *Memphis Free Speech*. When three black men were lynched by a white mob, Wells exposed the real reason for the racial violence in her pamphlet *Southern Horrors: Lynch Law in All Its Phases*: successful black shopkeepers posed an economic threat to white businessmen. She also challenged the claim that black men were lynched because they raped white women, pointing out that some white women voluntarily engaged in sexual relations with black men. In retaliation for such inflammatory statements, the office of her newspaper was trashed, and she was basically run out of town. Several years later, she relocated to Chicago, where she married the lawyer Ferdinand Barnett and had four children. She lived in Chicago for the rest of her life.

Antilynching was but one of the many crusades for justice that Ida Wells-Barnett (as she was now known) took on. In 1893, she publicly challenged the organizers of the World's Columbian Exposition in Chicago for excluding the contributions of African Americans. In 1894, she attacked the temperance leader Frances Willard for making racist statements about black men's moral character and demanded, without success, that the Woman's Christian Temperance Union make antilynching part of its broad reform agenda. In 1910, she organized the Women's Second Ward Republican Club on Chicago's South Side, "to assist the men in getting better laws for the race and having representation in everything which tends to the uplift of the city and government." She also founded a South Side settlement house called the Negro Fellowship League. Three years later, she founded the Alpha Suffrage Club.[10]

A lot was happening on the political front in 1913. The Illinois legislature passed the Presidential and Municipal Suffrage Bill in June, making Illinois the first state east of the Mississippi to allow women to vote. Ida Wells-Barnett and her nine-year-old daughter Alfreda proudly marched in the victory parade with none of the bigoted second-guessing that had marred the Washington, DC march. African American women in Chicago's Second Ward began gearing up for the primary in February 1914. The increasing number of African American migrants from the South, combined with the potential addition of newly enfranchised black women voters, created an unprecedented opportunity to act as a force in Chicago's electoral politics. Activists set their sights on the battle for alderman, a local political position which carried far more power than its lowly title might imply. Their goal: to elect a "race man" to represent the increasingly black Second Ward.[11]

The Alpha Suffrage Club threw itself into block-by-block canvassing to register new voters. It was surprisingly difficult work—according to Wells-Barnett, "men jeered at them and told them they ought to be at home taking care of babies"—but it produced dramatic results. These efforts added 7,290 new female voters in the Second Ward to the 16,327 male voters already registered—more than enough for politicians to take notice. But multiple candidates, white and black, competed for electoral loyalty.[12]

Ida Wells-Barnett soon learned how tricky navigating partisan politics could be when she and the Alpha Suffrage Club endorsed William Randolph Cowan, the Independent candidate. Despite three thousand women casting ballots, Cowan lost the primary. Looking ahead, Republican leaders were concerned that if the club continued to back independent candidates, the black vote would be divided, and a Democrat might win. They proposed a deal: there would probably be a vacancy for alderman in 1915, and the Republican machine was willing to back a black candidate, Oscar DePriest. But that race got complicated when two other black candidates declared their intentions to run, all competing for the support of the Alpha Suffrage Club. In the end, DePriest won the primary and went on to defeat three white opponents in the general election to become Chicago's first black Alderman. Women's votes were crucial to his victory, accounting for more than one-third of the ballots cast for him.

In 1915, newly politicized African American women voters found themselves drawn into the campaign for Chicago's mayor. Seeking to secure the increasingly important black vote, the Republican candidate William Hale "Big Bill" Thompson won the support of Ida Wells-Barnett and her husband, who began actively campaigning on his behalf. But several months later, another candidate entered the primary—Judge Harry Olson, the very man who in 1913 had secured a patronage appointment for Ida Wells-Barnett as an adult probation officer in the municipal court. She felt she had no choice but to switch her support to him, no matter how slim his chances. Thompson prevailed in the general election, which cost Wells-Barnett her job. Adding to the sting, Thompson reneged on his offer to secure a judgeship for Ferdinand Barnett. Ida Wells-Barnett learned firsthand that political maneuvering could come at a personal cost.

Women like Wells-Barnett were not only in politics to get patronage or other rewards, however. They fervently believed that political engagement was a key tool for African American women to improve conditions for their communities and for their race. As a flier for an Alpha Suffrage Club meeting stated, "If the colored women do not take advantage of the franchise they may only blame themselves when they are left out of everything." In many ways, black women could make the case that they needed the ballot even more than white women did, because of the dual discrimination they faced from racism and sexism. Sojourner Truth had made that same point decades earlier in the aftermath of the Civil War.[13]

The vote took on an almost sacred role for African Americans in these years, precisely because of the systematic disfranchisement of black men that had been occurring in the South since Reconstruction. If blacks could not vote in the South, then black voters in the North and West, both men and newly enfranchised women, might be able to use their votes to help their southern brethren. How? By voting the Republican ticket as a counterweight to Democratic Party control of the solid South, with the hope—albeit a distant one—of encouraging an activist federal government to take a larger role in protecting African Americans' rights, as it had during Reconstruction's brief heyday. This sentiment was graphically represented in a May 1916 cartoon in *The Crisis*, the magazine of the recently founded National Association for the Advancement of Colored People. Titled "Women to the Rescue!" it showed an African American woman defending her race against Jim Crow laws and segregation by wielding a bat representing the federal constitution.[14]

The fortunes of African American suffrage and woman suffrage were closely connected, even as they were on different trajectories. Geography mattered, as the ability to vote increasingly became determined by region more than gender or race: "The disfranchised, both men and women, resided in the South; the enfranchised, including women, lived outside that region." As African American men's access to the ballot declined due to Jim Crow restrictions, women's access expanded. The earliest suffrage victories occurred exclusively in the West, which resulted in the enfranchisement of women who were almost exclusively white. Only when more urban states like Illinois and later New York joined the suffrage bandwagon did black women benefit. But the deeply embedded racism of the suffrage movement meant that its leadership was unwilling and unable to embrace black women voters on an equal basis. Far too often, as the 1913 suffrage parade demonstrated, expediency prevailed, with southern support being deemed far more important than African American women's aspirations for the vote.[15]

Organized white women's lack of interest in the voting rights of African Americans continued in the postsuffrage era, when both the League of Women Voters and the National Woman's Party consciously defined black voting rights as a matter of race, not gender, and thus not of primary concern to their political agendas. In many ways, the passage of the 1965 Voting Rights Act, not the Nineteenth Amendment, was the culmination of black women's long struggle for the vote.[16]

Ida Wells-Barnett's crusade for justice did not end with woman suffrage. She continued to play an active role in Republican Party politics in the 1920s, campaigning for Herbert Hoover in 1928 and providing strong support for a white candidate, Ruth Hanna McCormick, in two elections: her successful run in 1928 for congressman-at-large from Illinois and her unsuccessful attempt in 1930 to be the first woman elected to the Senate. While the main priority of the Alpha Suffrage Club remained political education and the election of the best "race men" to represent Chicago's growing African American community, in the 1920s, Ida Wells-Barnett began to encourage women to run for political office themselves rather than just relying on men. Following her own advice, she ran for the state senate in Illinois in 1930, but finished a distant fourth. As she said with evident disappointment, "few women responded as I had hoped."[17]

At the time of her death the following year, Ida Wells-Barnett was working on an autobiography which ends, literally, in mid-sentence.[18] While the manuscript contains a full description of the Alpha Suffrage Club's political activities in the 1910s, it failed to mention the 1913 suffrage parade. Perhaps she planned to include it in later revisions, or perhaps it didn't loom that large in her memory. But for generations since, Ida Wells-Barnett's courageous defiance of suffrage leaders who told her, to use a metaphor from the civil rights movement, to move to the back of the bus has served as an iconic emblem of the deeply embedded racism and prejudice that marred what was supposed to be a movement for democracy and full citizenship.

"Votes for Women" suffrage button. *Courtesy of Schlesinger Library, Radcliffe Institute, Harvard University.*

CHAPTER EIGHT

Two Sisters

THE HEIGHT OF the suffrage movement coincided with what has been called "The Golden Age of Campaign Buttons." The 1896 presidential election was the first in which inexpensive celluloid buttons were widely used, and they have been prominent parts of political campaigns ever since. Like cartes de visites, new technology made this innovation possible. Not only did the buttons offer a novel way to publicly proclaim one's political views, they also were nifty souvenirs suitable for collecting.[1]

Suffragists were always looking for new ways to spread their message, and the popularity of buttons—and the fact that they were cheap and easy to produce—meant that they were quickly added to the suffrage arsenal. During the 1917 New York State referendum, suffragists distributed more than a million buttons to citizens across the state. Most suffrage buttons were fairly small—just five-eighths of an inch, much smaller than ones today—which called for simple messages. "Votes for Women," "Ballots for Both," and "I'm a Voter" were some of the most popular.

Suffragists were encouraged to wear buttons and badges to provoke discussion from curious strangers and to demonstrate their allegiance to the cause. "Show your colors all day long," exhorted the California suffragist Alice Park, who amassed an extensive collection of her own. Park emphasized the symbiotic relationship between the self-confidence it took to wear a suffrage button in public and the broader gains for the movement as a whole: "Until women have the courage of their convictions, how can they expect to win recognition and approval?" Ironically, this public "showing of the colors" often led suffragists to have to give away their suffrage buttons when prospective supporters asked where they could get one of their own.[2]

Soon antisuffragists got into the act, not willing to cede public display to their more flamboyant suffragist sisters. Realizing the importance of branding, "antis" countered suffragists' purple, gold, and white color scheme by choosing red to identify their cause. The red rose, often worn in lapels or corsages, quickly became their most recognizable symbol. For those occasions when red roses wouldn't do, the antisuffrage movement offered its own array of buttons. Usually deploying a striking combination of red, black, and white, these buttons stated their platform so boldly that often one word did the trick: "No."

THE SISTERS WERE BORN in New York City in the 1860s, into a prominent Jewish family that traced its American roots through eight generations to the eighteenth century. One married her much older first cousin at age seventeen. She became active in civic and philanthropic work, and her name is especially linked to the Consumers' League, an organization that tried to harness consumer power to improve conditions for the workers who produced the goods that elite women purchased. The other wanted to be a writer and took classes at Columbia College, despite being precluded from registering for a degree because of her sex. She too married an older man, and she played a prominent role in the founding of Barnard College, which opened its doors in 1889. She also wrote several novels and twenty-six plays, including *The Dominant Sex* (1911). But while one was a prominent suffragist, the other was a vocal opponent.

Both Maud Nathan and Annie Nathan Meyer seemed destined to end up in the pro-suffrage camp, but in the end, the sisters took different routes. This twist of fate introduces a new element into the history of the suffrage movement: women who actively campaigned against their own enfranchisement. It doesn't take too much historical imagination to grasp why men might have opposed suffrage: they liked things the way they were and remained unsympathetic to changes in traditional gender roles. Women who took this stand are more of a puzzle, but their motives and tactics deserve consideration alongside those of the eventual winners. Making that point through the life choices of two sisters brings abstract arguments into the more concrete, daily realm. Not surprisingly, both personal and ideological factors were at work.

Maud and Annie Nathan had a privileged upbringing, but it was not without its emotional and economic challenges. They proudly traced their heritage on both sides of their family to Sephardic Jewish roots—the "nearest approach to royalty in the United States," as Annie put it. Their parents, Robert Weeks Nathan and Annie Augusta Florance, were part of the established, well-connected uptown Jewish elite who actively participated in the full range of New York City's cultural and social life; the extended family included the poet Emma Lazarus and future Supreme Court justice Benjamin Cardozo. The four Nathan children paired off by age, not sex: Maud, the older daughter, was closest to her older brother, whereas Annie, who was five years younger, threw in her lot with the younger brother. Emotional distance, not affinity, was always the rule between the sisters.[3]

In 1875, Mr. Nathan's business reverses upended the family, forcing them to relocate to Green Bay, Wisconsin, where they were one of the few Jewish families. The children enjoyed their new surroundings, but the move was especially hard for their mother, who had to leave everything she loved in New York to start over in the Midwest. She also had to deal with her husband's frequent dalliances and the marital instability they created, which led her to make several suicide attempts and develop a serious drug dependency. After her husband returned to New York, she took her children to Chicago, but she became increasingly distraught and had to be hospitalized in 1878. At age sixteen, Maud shepherded her two younger siblings back to New York on the train to live with their grandparents. A month later, they learned of their mother's death.

This event crystalized the rivalry between Maud and Annie that would later play itself out in the suffrage context. According to Annie's account, Maud hogged the limelight with her grieving and shut Annie out, making her feel neglected and lost. "Smarting at the injustice," Annie later wrote, "her little sister crept unnoticed into a corner and watched with burning jealous eyes the incredible fuss made over her." This discrepancy was even harder to bear because Annie was convinced she was her mother's favorite. "The seeds of jealousy were planted then and there—a jealousy of my sister which was largely responsible for spoiling our relations for many years."[4]

Maud reacted to her mother's death in part by accepting her first cousin's marriage proposal. Frederick Nathan was the son of her father's brother and almost eighteen years older than Maud. They married in 1880, when Maud was seventeen, and set off on a sixteen-month honeymoon in Europe. When they returned to set up housekeeping, Maud Nathan—like Eleanor Roosevelt, she had no need to change her name—was not yet nineteen years old. It took six years before she conceived a child, and her beloved daughter Annette Florance was born in 1886. Tragically, Annette died at the age of nine. The reformer Josephine Shaw Lowell encouraged Maud Nathan to channel her grief into civic and reform work, which led to her decades-long association with the Consumers' League, the work for which she is best known. From there, suffrage was a logical next step.

Annie was only eleven when her mother died. Because her older sister soon left to marry, she charted her own path through adolescence. Largely self-taught, Annie and six friends convened a group called the Seven Wise Women to study women writers, using Margaret Fuller's conversations as their model. But Annie wanted more formal education, so she enrolled in the Collegiate Course offered to women at Columbia, despite her father's steadfast insistence that no man would want to marry an educated woman. She proved him wrong when, at age twenty, she married Dr. Alfred Meyer, a prominent physician thirteen years her senior.

Annie's marriage caused her to drop out of the Columbia program, but it did not lessen her interest in higher education for women. Soon, she was spearheading the campaign for the establishment of Barnard College, which opened its doors to female students in 1889. For the rest of her life, Annie Nathan Meyer bitterly resented that she was not given proper credit for her role in founding Barnard, her proudest achievement. She always suspected that the slight was in large part because she was Jewish, and historians agree.[5]

At this point, the similarities between the two sisters far outweighed their differences. Like her older sister, Annie had entered into a very rewarding and long-lived marriage to an older man. Like her older sister, Annie took a long time to conceive, bearing her only child, Margaret, in 1895. More importantly, at a time when opportunities for elite women were extremely restricted, both sisters shared a sense of restlessness and ambition that caused them to expand their aspirations far beyond marriage and the domestic sphere. Maud called this "my restless spirit which reached out for broader contacts"; later, she realized that her "latent feminism" propelled her to work with the Consumers' League and the woman suffrage movement.[6] Annie too identified with women who were "heart-hungry" and "brain-famished," and once captioned a youthful picture of herself, "Listen, honestly, Get Out."[7] But as the twentieth century dawned, the two sisters found themselves on opposite sides of the suffrage divide.

Maud Nathan offered this somewhat bemused account of how suffrage became taboo within her intimate family circle. Both her brothers were adamantly opposed to the idea ("My older brother was so irascible when the subject was mentioned he refused to discuss it"), as was her cousin, Benjamin Cardozo. But it was her sister's choice that confounded her:

My sister, Annie Nathan Meyer, who had been instrumental in founding Barnard College, for the higher education of women, who had gone to Denver, Colorado, to attend a convention of the Association for the Advancement of Women, who had addressed the Parliament of Religions in Chicago, who was one of the first women in New York to ride a bicycle—at a time when it was considered most unwomanly to make herself so conspicuous—

who, in brief, stood for everything that claimed to be progressive, took her stand on the opposite side and joined the group of anti-suffragists!

Never especially close to her older sister, and nursing simmering resentments since their mother's death, Annie apparently relished the chance for a public feud. A lifelong gadfly, she could accomplish two goals at once: goad her older sister and make trenchant comments about women's status designed to keep herself very much in the public eye.[8]

"The fighting Nathan sisters," as they were soon referred to in the press, offer a contrasting set of viewpoints. Maud Nathan was first drawn to the suffrage cause for a simple reason: "I became convinced that legislators would never give consideration to the women's point of view, so long as we women had no political status."[9] Her involvement with the Consumers' League made her especially attuned to working women's concerns, and, like Charlotte Perkins Gilman, she frequently linked political and economic independence. Like most suffragists, she gravitated towards a vision of modern women's lives that moved far beyond the domestic realm, stressing that the vote was an important tool for women's civic engagement. "Bestowing upon women the responsibility of citizenship broadens them, makes them more companionable as wives, enables them the better to teach their sons and daughters, by example as well as precept, the true meaning of patriotism and the duties incumbent upon citizens of a democracy."[10]

Maud Nathan quickly became one of the most sought-after suffrage leaders in New York. A charismatic speaker, she appeared on suffrage platforms several times a week, often accompanied by her husband, who was also an avid suffragist.[11] Her speeches were closely covered by major newspapers, and she employed a clipping service to collect and carefully preserve her press notices and articles in scrapbooks. One of the most revealing clippings described a mock suffrage debate in 1911. Nathan, playing the "anti" side, had dressed in a hoop skirt and shawl reminiscent of the style sixty years earlier. As one of the New York papers observed, "Mrs. Nathan, of course, is known far and wide as one of the most able and ardent supporters of the suffrage cause, and the way she took the opposite side in the burlesque debate was really an effective argument for giving women the ballot."[12] And, no doubt, a not-so-subtle jab at her younger sister.

Like Maud, Annie Nathan Meyer was an effective speaker, but she preferred to stir things up with her pen. By one count, she published over 350 letters to editors in her lifetime, as well as numerous articles, many of which were carefully collated by her clipping service.[13] (One wonders if she and Maud kept score of who got more press.) Her antisuffrage platform focused on several themes. She often complained that suffragists made unrealistic claims about what women would do with their votes, and she challenged the idea that women would vote as a bloc. She liked to point out that many of the advances in women's lives since the nineteenth century had been driven by women who were at best lukewarm about suffrage, if not actively opposed to it: "This confusion of the suffrage movement with every movement that made for advance goes merrily on, and few take the trouble to stop it." She also disparaged the suffrage movement for what she saw as its anti-male stance, despite their attempts to round up "all the contented wives they could muster." As she noted with a certain smugness, the suffragists were "very angry" when she accused them of sex antagonism.[14]

While Annie Nathan Meyer clearly enjoyed poking fun at suffragists, including her sister, this disagreement was about more than
sibling rivalry. Women's antisuffrage arguments were grounded in a
clear—and to many citizens at the time, convincing—political philosophy that proved quite resonant with early-twentieth-century
audiences.[15]

Far from consigning women to the domestic sphere, as their
opponents often implied they did, antisuffragist women encouraged a broad range of activities in the public sphere. "We believe
that women according to their leisure, opportunities, and experience should take part increasingly in civic and municipal affairs
as they always have done in charitable, philanthropic and educational activities," argued Josephine Dodge of the National Organization Opposed to Woman Suffrage in 1916, "and we believe that
this can best be done without the ballot, as a non-partisan body of
disinterested workers."[16] Theirs was an antipolitics stand, therefore,
not an anti-public-engagement stand. Traditional partisan politics,
especially in states with entrenched political machines, were seen
as dirty and unappealing. Why would women want to sink to that
level? Moreover, to vote meant to declare allegiance to a political
party, thereby foregoing the disinterestedness that many women
felt was key to their success in the public realm. More than anything
else, this commitment to nonpartisanship was at the root of many
female antisuffragists' opposition to the vote. This stance may seem
naïve or misguided, but it's worth noting that the League of Women
Voters adopted this same approach in the postsuffrage era.

The organized antisuffrage movement, beginning with the
founding of the Massachusetts Association Opposed to Further
Extension of Suffrage for Women in 1882 and the New York State
Association Opposed to Woman Suffrage in 1895, grew into a

formidable political presence. By 1900, there were additional groups in Illinois, California, South Dakota, Washington, and Oregon; eleven years later, when the National Association Opposed to Woman Suffrage opened a headquarters in New York City, over two hundred thousand committed antisuffragists belonged to over twenty-five state organizations. Well-known public figures like the muckraking journalist Ida Tarbell, noted for her exposé of John D. Rockefeller and Standard Oil, added their support. The very fact that so many women were saying they didn't want the vote was a powerful weapon in the battle for public opinion.[17]

As with the Nathan sisters, the pro- and antisuffrage movements had both strong similarities as well as differences. Both employed traditional forms of political persuasion, such as speeches, pamphlets, and public forums, to build their cases, and both drew their leadership from elite white middle- and upper-class women. (If there was such a thing as a female African American antisuffragist, she was a lonely character indeed.) And yet the antisuffrage movement was unable to stop the momentum of the campaign for votes for women. Once the suffrage movement took to the streets with its parades, street-corner sermonizing, and other displays of public spectacle, it became a topic of vital national interest that no American could ignore. And once politicians began to realize the risk of antagonizing future voters by their continued opposition, they too got on board. As Harriot Stanton Blatch later observed, "if both sides had agreed to stay at home and argue pleasantly and pray, the antis would have won out."[18]

America's impending entry into the war in Europe and a change in leadership in the antisuffrage movement help explain the shifting fortunes of the two codependent movements. New York State had always been a stronghold of antisuffrage sentiment, and the

National Association Opposed to Woman Suffrage played a key role in preventing the passage of a suffrage amendment in that state in 1915. By the time of the second referendum just two years later, many female antisuffragists were already deeply involved in patriotic war work, where they found themselves increasingly working under the leadership (if not domination) of men. For members of an organization like the New York State Association Opposed to Woman Suffrage, which didn't even allow men to join until 1914, this was a major shift.[19]

As men began to dominate the antisuffrage movement after 1917, the focus of the campaign shifted as well. Antiradical, antisocialist rhetoric had been nonexistent in the early years of antisuffragism, but as wartime hysteria gripped the country, feminism, socialism, and woman suffrage were increasingly portrayed as enemies of the state. There is a direct line between the final years of the antisuffrage movement and the emergence of a conservative women's agenda in the 1920s. Right-wing patriotic groups like the Woman Patriots dedicated themselves to fighting anything considered un-American and unpatriotic, with Progressive women reformers, many of them former suffragists, coming under special attack. And so the battle continued.[20]

Making the link between the last gasp of antisuffragism and the emergence of right-wing activism in the postsuffrage era is important for understanding the larger story of conservative women in twentieth-century America. Not all politically engaged women, then or now, support a liberal or progressive agenda. A telling example is Phyllis Schlafly, whose Eagle Forum mobilized a core of grass-roots activists in the 1970s to stop the Equal Rights Amendment dead in its tracks. Like the antisuffragists, the Eagle Forum understood the political resonance of women saying they were quite happy with the rights they had. Of course while the suffragists prevailed, the ERA supporters did not, but the antis were among the conservative women of their day, a reminder that not all women think or vote alike.

That, of course, was precisely the point that Annie Nathan Meyer made over and over. She could not abide the claims that women would end prostitution, vote in prohibition, or stop war—because she knew that those claims would be impossible to implement, even if women did vote as a bloc. Starting around 1912, she devoted less time to her antisuffrage activism and more time to her writing. After New York State women won the vote in 1917, she rashly suggested in a letter to the *New York Times* that women refrain from going to the polls, but quickly recanted. While she did eventually join the League of Women Voters, she still considered herself an anti when she published her autobiography in 1951: "While I think that giving women the vote has done no good, I am perfectly ready to admit that neither has it brought about the dreadful results that the extremists prophesied. I am quite convinced that I was correct in my conviction that women would never vote as a sex. They vote—as they should—as individuals, swayed by all sorts of varying influences."[21] In many ways she was right, even if she overstated how often the suffrage movement resorted to the grandiose claims she despised.

Towards the end of their lives, some of the animosity between the two sisters faded. Still, nothing could bridge their suffrage divide, which was rooted as much in temperament as in ideology. At base, woman suffrage was a forward-looking movement. In the end, that is one reason why Maud Nathan's side, not Annie Nathan Meyer's, prevailed.

CHAPTER NINE

Claiborne Catlin's Suffrage Pilgrimage

PROBABLY THE MOST iconic image of the American woman suffrage movement is Inez Milholland astride a white horse. Born into a privileged New York family, Milholland, a graduate of Vassar (1908) and the New York University School of Law (1912), led many of the early suffrage parades, including the 1913 counter-inauguration procession in Washington, DC pictured here. Newspapers were fascinated by her: "No suffrage parade was complete without Inez Milholland," concluded the *New York Sun*, "for with her tall figure and free step, her rich brown hair, blue eyes, fair skin and well cut features, she was an ideal figure of the typical American woman." And yet her horse, whose name was Gray Dawn, rarely received any attention at all. This is a surprising omission, because horses are *everywhere* in the suffrage campaign.[1]

In 1910, there were twenty-four million horses in the United States, approximately one for every 3.8 Americans. Offering cheap and efficient short-term transport for goods and people, horses functioned as "living machines," literally providing "horse-power" in a variety of contexts, including agriculture, public transportation, and conspicuous consumption (for instance,

123

liveried chauffeurs ferrying the upper classes around town in fancy horse-drawn carriages). Horses also added to the public health hazards of modern urban life by the copious amounts of manure and urine they deposited on city streets.

By the 1910s, the popularity of electric and internal combustion automobiles was challenging the preponderance of horses in cities and on farms. While it seems a foregone conclusion in retrospect that cars would and should replace horses, for several decades, they coexisted fairly well. But as the number of automobiles on the road increased dramatically—from 459,000 in 1910 to 1.7 million just four years later—the balance began to shift.

These are precisely the years when the suffrage movement took to the streets with its suffrage parades and other pageants. While automobiles were often featured as novelties, horses were ubiquitous, pulling floats and serving as trusty mounts for parade marshals and other dignitaries. When Inez Milholland was surrounded by hostile bystanders in Washington in 1913, she simply spurred her horse (she was an expert equestrian) and rode straight in to the rowdy crowd, which was eventually subdued by the arrival of the US Cavalry—on horseback, of course.

Suffrage spectacles bore more than a passing resemblance to military parades, so women confidently riding horses like military leaders made a powerful political statement. Harriot Stanton Blatch deemed such iconography far superior to the take-away from automobile-driven suffragists. "Riding in a car did not demonstrate courage," she complained, and "it did not show discipline." Turning the tables, when President Wilson wanted to slip past the suffragists picketing the White House,

Inez Milholland leads the 1913 suffrage parade in Washington, DC. *Courtesy of Schlesinger Library, Radcliffe Institute, Harvard University.*

a car—not a horse-drawn carriage—was his preferred mode of escape.[2]

Occasionally, horses moved beyond supporting roles to become leading characters in their own right. That certainly applies to the horses Claiborne Catlin rode on her suffrage pilgrimage across Massachusetts in 1914.

CLAIBORNE CATLIN was at her wit's end. "The General"—Susan Fitzgerald of the Massachusetts Political Equality Union—had put her in charge of advertising an upcoming meeting featuring the noted national suffragist Anna Howard Shaw at Boston's Tremont Temple in the spring of 1914. After several weeks of ceaseless effort, she had been unable to get a shred of free publicity, a necessity for the cash-strapped movement. So worn out that she had literally collapsed on a table at suffrage headquarters, she suddenly had an inspiration. "I had remembered how Inez Milholland had ridden horseback for suffrage in New York—not so long ago. I could ride. Why not try that." She borrowed a horse, adorned it with two plac- ards advertising the event, and with some trepidation set out down Washington Street on a rainy day. "Then something happened. I found myself telling those crowds of umbrellas which pressed against both stirrups *why* I was there. And as I did it, I began to realize that they were listening to me, who had hardly raised her voice on the subject before, as if I were Anna Shaw herself."[3]

For three days, the crowds and reporters faithfully followed Catlin around as she rode up and down the streets of Newspaper Row. Local merchants offered her food and drinks. More impor- tantly, she garnered gobs of free publicity for the upcoming event, which went on to be a sold-out success. "And that is how I got the idea of campaigning on horseback for suffrage that summer."[4]

In the 1910s, after decades of steady, plodding work that had produced very little concrete success, suffrage organizations throughout the country were stirring to life, and the Massachusetts movement was no different. The suffrage parade held in downtown Boston on Beacon Street in 1913 was symptomatic of this new infu- sion of energy and ideas as women literally took to the streets to press their cause. A state referendum on the issue was scheduled for 1915, further energizing suffragists' efforts. Eastern states with strong political machines, active Catholic churches, and many recent immigrant voters were among the most challenging turfs for suffragists, but Massachusetts women were undaunted. They believed in their cause, and they believed its time had come. Claiborne Catlin was one of those legions of women.[5]

What kind of a woman would embark on such a quixotic and, for a woman traveling alone, potentially dangerous journey as riding a horse across Massachusetts for suffrage? Little is known about Claiborne Catlin's background and upbringing. She was born Mary Augustine Claiborne Grasty in Baltimore, Maryland in 1881, although her ancestors hailed from Virginia. At a fairly young age—too young, she later realized—she married Joseph Albert Catlin. Four years later, he was dead of typhoid, and his childless widow set off for New York City, where she enrolled in the New York School of Philanthropy. Her coursework exposed her to the horrors of slum life, and she became a suffragist in order to challenge the status quo: "Voting now seemed the most important thing in the world to me." She worked for a time doing settlement work in New York, studied eugenics with Dr. Charles Davenport at Cold Spring Harbor on Long Island, and was a staff member at a psychological clinic at the University of Pennsylvania. By 1914, she had landed in Boston, where she plunged into the local suffrage movement and hatched her plan to tour the state on horseback to win converts to the cause.[6]

At first, she thought she would have to raise a substantial chunk of money to cover her expenses, but after talking with a potential supporter she dramatically changed her plans. "I came out completely convinced that money was *not* necessary; indeed, to go without money was the only way I really should, or could do it." This meant that she would rely on the kindness and generosity of strangers, mainly sympathetic women but occasionally men, not all of whom considered themselves suffragists, to cover all expenses

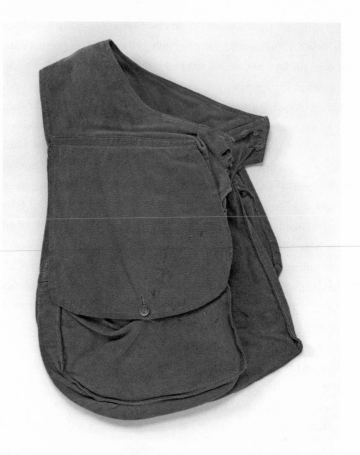

Claiborne Catlin packed light. Everything she needed for her four-month suffrage pilgrimage had to fit in these brown canvas saddlebags. *Courtesy of Schlesinger Library, Radcliffe Institute, Harvard University.*

for lodging and food for her and her horse, for an estimated four months. "Woman to Urge Cause in Saddle—Mrs. Catlin, Suffragist, Will Tour State on Horseback—Starts Penniless" read the headline in the *Boston Herald* on June 30, 1914.[7]

Not only was she penniless, but she also traveled light. Her traveling clothes consisted of a khaki jacket and divided skirt donated by Filene's department store, supplemented by a matching khaki hat, brown riding gloves, one seersucker waist, a change of underwear, a yellow slicker for protection against the rain, plus toiletries, a fountain pen, and a road map. (Needless to say, she became quite adept at washing out her laundry, something she had always left to servants in the past.) She carried a riding crop and a small bag to pass around for collections when she spoke. All her personal effects, as well as a parcel of leaflets and a horse blanket, had to fit into a pair of saddlebags fashioned by a Marshfield suffragist. The final touch was a shoulder strap of three ribbons in the suffrage colors of white, green, and gold, which said "Votes for Women."

While the Boston papers hailed her as "very gay about her trip, and very enthusiastic," astute reporters noted an undercurrent of doubt. "Tell me," Catlin said to one, "you don't think I shall starve, do you?" Or as she confided later in her memoir of the journey, "they shoot dogs that are gun-shy. Someone ought to shoot me."[8]

True to her "no money" pledge, Catlin first had to raise enough money for a train ticket to pick up her first horse, a black mare named Trixie. (She would ride six in all.) She accomplished this by organizing a spontaneous suffrage meeting under the Lincoln statue at Park Square in downtown Boston, which netted $1.98 in collections, enough to pay her fare to nearby Mansfield. She left there with a flotilla of suffragists, reporters, and photographers, taking comfort in the parting words of the groom who had helped her get to know her mount: "I don't mind telling yuh, that for a gurl your size, yore all right!" Then she headed south toward Cape Cod, where she would spend most of the summer taking advantage of the crowds of tourists and vacationers.[9]

Two weeks later she had an encounter with a benefactor that literally changed the course of her adventure. A well-dressed woman identified only as Mrs. Lilian Snow came by in a fancy motor car—a clear sign of affluence and female independence in 1914—called out, "You're a great looking suffragette," and invited her home.[10] Not only did she pamper her guest with a warm bath and clean linens, she lent her a fresh horse, the incomparable Diana whom Catlin rode for the next six weeks as she traversed the Cape. Ironically, Snow was a confirmed "anti" who was not the least bit interested in woman suffrage. But she was quite captivated by Catlin ("I do believe in you, little lady"), admiring both her attractive personality and her novel mode of disseminating propaganda.[11]

Catlin soon settled into a routine. She would give as many as three talks a day, usually at town squares or outside postoffices— anyplace a crowd might be drawn on short notice by a traveling suffragist on a horse. She would talk for a half hour or so, take up a collection, and ride on to her next destination. When she was ready to stop, she would seek out a farmhouse with a stable so that Diana could be fed and bedded down for the night; when passing through towns, she often sought out a blacksmith to cobble her horse. Very often, the smiths did this for free, and she rarely had to pay for lodging, usually staying in private homes rather than inns. Only once was she forced to camp out for the night in the rain. Luckily, she had oats for Diana, but she herself went hungry that night. It was the only meal she missed her entire trip.

Often bedraggled after a day on the road, Catlin must have been quite a sight when she went around to the kitchen door to ask for lodgings. As she recounted one encounter with a woman reputed to be a suffrage supporter, "I found myself wondering quite sympathetically, as I watched her embarrassment, what I should have done, in her place, if without warning, I had been asked to take into my castle, a female tramp, who, in the name of suffrage, had

dropped at my door and cheerfully demanded food and shelter."
That night she was directed to a nearby boarding house.[12]

Catlin's stump speech offered three main arguments for suffrage. First, it was a matter of justice. Women were taxed without
representation—shouldn't they have a say in how their tax money
was spent? Second, women needed the vote for protection—of
their homes, their families, and their womanly values. The vote
was especially important to women industrial workers to regulate
the conditions under which they labored. And thirdly, for development: how could women develop into responsible public citizens
if they remained voteless? Her overarching goal was to encourage
"the responsibility of public housekeeping." Women knew a great
deal about human life because they produced it, and men knew a
great deal about matters of property and business. "We want laws
to which both contribute what they know for the welfare of their
country."[13]

As much as pushing specific arguments, Catlin hoped that her
willingness to take risks and make sacrifices for the cause would
win support and respect from male voters, as well as their wives,
who were often the ones who went out of their way to help her.
"When the men see that we are willing to give up comfort and
pleasure for the vote they will become interested in the matter
themselves. Gameness always counts."[14]

Even though local newspaper coverage praised Catlin for her
effective speaking voice and arguments, reporters were absolutely
fixated by the appearance of the "horseback suffragette." Words like
pretty and *vivacious* dot the stories. Confounding many people's
expectations of what a suffragist would look like, the thirty-two-
year-old Catlin was quite slight, and her youth and vigor made
a dramatic impression on her audiences. Her appearance also

won over some doubting conservatives, who initially judged her horseback proselytizing a stunt and called her an "adventuress." When shown her picture, one naysayer changed her mind: "Why, she's a little thing. I thought she must be an Amazon."[15]

Even more than her arguments or pleasing personality, the powerful novelty of seeing an expert female rider enter town astride a horse—no side saddle for her—won converts for the cause. A description of a West Dennis suffrage meeting in July attended by about a hundred people captures this well: "Presently, in the most dramatic way, Mrs. Catlin came riding up the street from under the shade of trees—a brave young figure—on a spirited horse, sitting like a Calvary figure. She reined up in front of the people, faced up and began." She talked for half an hour "in her beautiful voice" giving a "good straight suffrage argument. . . . Truly, she was thrilling. She looked like a Jeanne d'Arc. I think everyone was fascinated, moved by her girlish fervor." Then when she had finished, she wheeled her horse around "and rode swiftly away into the night." The observer concluded, "I cannot tell you what a unique, captivating incident it was!"[16]

Claiming public space was often a problem for a single woman and her horse stumping for suffrage. When she took over a venue like a town square or a bandstand, her speech was occasionally— and sometimes deliberately—drowned out by brass bands who thought they had a stronger claim to public spaces. Once, she and Diana were pelted by apples thrown from a speeding car. The horse probably appreciated the apples, but the rider definitely did not.

Luckily, her benefactors far outnumbered her adversaries. She would never forget small kindnesses like a "knight in overalls" who took Diana off to a stable and sent her to a restaurant, where she was instructed to eat as much as she wanted on his coin, or the woman who had spent time on the road herself and knew how hard it was for a woman alone, who offered her a place to come back to if she became sick. The kindnesses extended to her horses were likewise indelible, as when a reporter in Weymouth left a dollar and this note: "Buy Diana another oat."[17]

Her suffrage pilgrimage afforded her intimate glimpses of women's lives in their homes. One woman was so cowed by her overbearing husband that she did not offer her guest dinner, causing Catlin to collapse "in starvation rage." (She snacked on an emergency stash of malted milk tablets that night.) But the suffragist knew the intimidated wife was on her side when she whispered, "God bless you for trying to help us women." Another benefactor challenged her houseguest to interact more with the host families, no matter how tired she was. "Why, you're just like a circus come to town, you know, and we all want to know all about you." Tell us more about your family, she pressured, and where you came from: "'Tell 'em this kind of thing and you'll never need to say a word about suffrage. The women'll get interested in you and'll make the men vote for it." Catlin admitted this was sound advice.[18]

Danger could be much more sinister for a young, attractive woman traveling in strange areas by herself, and often out at night after her evening meetings. Only once did she find herself in a dicey situation. When a Mr. Buffer picked her up in a horse-drawn carriage to look at a replacement horse, she found him moderately offensive and possibly inebriated, but "still it, like all the other trials of this trip must be endured—with humor. So I fixed my mind on other things and tried to forget him." But when he took an unexplained detour from the main road and "with a swinish runt, he flopped one jellyfish arm around my shoulder," she knew she had to act. They locked eyes and "for a moment he met them insolently;

then he wavered, his arm sagged, and he moved uneasily away from me." Having faced him down, she got safely back to town, where she later learned he had tricked her into checking out the horse in the first place. Her two-word comment: "The cur!"[19]

By August, the physical and emotional strain was beginning to get to her. In Woods Hole, she confided to her diary, "I'm so tired I wish I had never been born." All she wanted was a little peace and quiet. "Must I be questioned, interviewed, for the rest of my life? Was I to hear nothing but suffrage, talk nothing but suffrage, dream, sleep, live nothing but suffrage? Was I becoming a creature with a 'fixed idea'?" On more than one occasion, she had to stay put for several days while she regained her emotional equilibrium.[20]

Once September turned and the Cape emptied of tourists, Catlin focused on getting back for the major suffrage rally on September nineteenth on the Boston Common. She had planned to swap out Diana for Trixie when she went through Woods Hole, but her antisuffrage angel encouraged her to keep Diana for a bit longer. The night before the Boston rally, she stayed in Susan Fitzgerald's attic in Jamaica Plain, where she had started her journey, buoyed by "the General's" praise that the effort so far had been "splendid" and that she had been "an inspiration to us all." The Boston rally was a big success, and Catlin was once again a star attraction, riding on a borrowed horse while Diana nursed a sore foot.[21]

At this point, Catlin had organized fifty-nine meetings in seventy-nine days, averaging daily attendance at her events of around two hundred. She had covered 530 miles and visited thirty-seven cities and towns. Then she hit a snag: Diana was still hobbled, and she had trouble finding a replacement. She could have halted her trip, but instead, she pushed on: "I said I would ride four months—and I will." Once again, her "anti" fairy godmother came to her rescue, providing her with a magnificent new stead named David. "A regular show piece he is," she bragged, "and doesn't he know it." She headed to the western part of the state, adopting Worcester as her home base.[22]

After canvassing and speaking for a week, she was down to her last eight days, planning to ride from Worcester towards Boston for a final election-day rally on Boston Common on November 4. She admitted to conflicted feelings as her journey neared its end. She had grown so close to her final horse companion that she confessed, "That is the one bit of bitter in my cup of joy—joy that this trip is almost over. But I so hate to give up David."[23]

Then, just four days before her final goal, tragedy struck. David was used to cars in town, but he had always been skittish when he met them singly on country roads. Spooked by an electric car speeding towards them, he jumped upward and back, then folded to the ground as Catlin was thrown free. He somehow managed to get up on three legs, but his fourth was "hanging like the broken limb of a tree." A local vet summoned to the scene said the horse must be shot at once. Catlin held his head and fed him sugar cubes, and then left before the sad end, unable to bear it. "Mrs. Catlin Weeps as if Heart Would Break when Bullet Ends Life of David, Her Companion on Suffrage Crusade," read the headline in the *Worcester Daily Telegram*.[24]

Only later did she realize how much worse it could have been. She could have been severely hurt, or the accident might have happened in a remote area without quick access to help. And if it had happened earlier, it would have ended the trip. Even so, the blow cast a pall over her heroic journey. "I loved my horses almost as much as I loved the cause for which I was riding, and it took a long time to recover from David's loss." The Boston suffrage headquarters arranged another horse for her to finish the trip, but although

Catlin had gamely soldiered on for almost four months, she simply could not continue.[25]

Claiborne Catlin dropped out of public view after her daring suffrage ride. She worked as a social worker and school administrator in the Boston area, and she married (and lost) a second husband. She did take the time to write up her notes from her adventure as a memoir titled "Stirrup Cups," in honor of the cup of wine or other drink offered a person on horseback about to depart on a journey. She then made sure her manuscript and newspaper clippings were safely deposited at the Schlesinger Library, along with her saddle bags and the gold, green, and white suffrage sash she wore.

Claiborne Catlin's "Stirrup Cups" saga shows how ordinary women were moved to do extraordinary things for the cause of suffrage. Like many of her peers, she was willing to "risk [her] livelihood for the thing called woman's suffrage." As she observed just past the midpoint of her journey, "It has been worth every speck of tiredness, every minute of loneliness, every throb of fright."[26]

In a postscript titled "A Long Time Afterward," she looked back on the experience, assessing not only the political and social impact of suffrage but also its larger context: "At long last I am clear, and I have had plenty of opportunity in the meantime to see what the Suffrage has meant. Only too well do I realize now that it will never do what I had so fondly and childishly dreamed possible. But what I do recognize is, that what I was really struggling for all along that lonely road, was the removal of one more barrier from the upward journey of half the human race. And so I trust that this diary may serve as a bit of encouragement to any who may be standing alone for something they believe will be of service to all of us."[27] Through dedicated foot soldiers like Claiborne Catlin, on horseback or with their feet firmly on the ground, suffrage cut a wide swath, both before and after the vote was won.

CHAPTER TEN

"How It Feels to Be the Husband of a Suffragette"

IN THE FALL OF 1911, the issue of woman suffrage roiled Harvard University. The year before, John Reed, later a staff writer for *The Masses* and a participant-observer in the Russian Revolution, helped organize the Harvard League for Woman Suffrage. Now the group proposed to bring the militant British suffragist Emmeline Pankhurst to campus. The Harvard administration refused permission for Pankhurst to speak at the university's thousand-seat Sanders Theater, inspiring the memorable *Detroit Free Press* headline "Is Harvard Afraid of Mrs. Pankhurst?" This forced the event off campus to a dancehall nearby on Brattle Street. More than 1,500 students showed up, far more than the hall could hold, but the lecture proceeded without a hitch. Harvard survived this close brush with suffrage militance, and so did the Harvard League's fifty-two by thirty-eight inch banner. Redder than the traditional Harvard crimson, it proudly proclaimed its suffrage allegiance, fringe and all.[1]

The Harvard League for Woman Suffrage was one of men's many public declarations of support in the last decade of the movement. The most influential was the Men's League for Woman Suffrage, founded in 1909 by a group of prominent New

137

Yorkers. George Foster Peabody served as president, with Max Eastman as secretary / treasurer. Its charter members represented a *Who's Who* of the New York intellectual establishment, including Oswald Garrison Villard, William Dean Howells, Rabbi Stephen S. Wise, and the Columbia professors John Dewey and Vladimir Simkhovitch. Frederick Nathan, Maud's husband, was also a founding member.

According to James Lees Laidlaw, himself married to the prominent suffragist Harriet Burton Laidlaw, Men's League activities were intended "to give moral support to men and to give political support to women." Members marched in suffrage parades, attended NAWSA conventions, lobbied in Albany, and spoke at public forums. Never expecting to take over leadership roles, men's groups functioned as adjuncts to the women's suffrage machine, a true role reversal from centuries of women serving as auxiliaries to men. As the historian Brooke Kroeger put it, "they brought up the rear," but they did so by choice.[2]

How it feels to Be the Husband of a Suffragette was published anonymously in 1914 in *Everybody's Magazine* and in pamphlet form the following year to benefit the New York State suffrage campaign. The tract adopted a lighthearted tone to make its case for suffrage. "You are the party aimed at," it opened, meaning the hecklers who taunted marchers at the suffrage parade in New York City. "You who stood on the sidewalk and urged passionately that we who marched go home and wash the dishes or mind the baby." Here is the twist: those hecklers weren't challenging the women suffragists. Instead they targeted the delegation from the Men's League for Woman Suf-

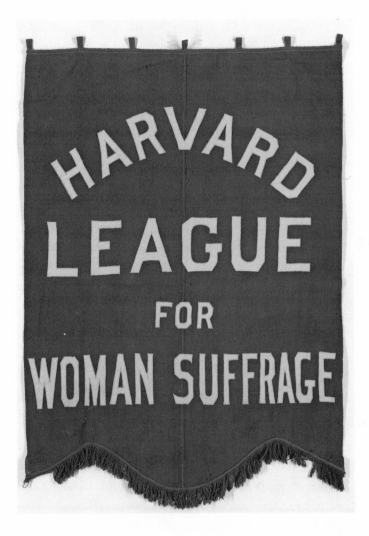

Banner of the Harvard League for Woman Suffrage. *Courtesy of Schlesinger Library, Radcliffe Institute, Harvard University.*

frage who joined the parade. Jeers like "sis" and "henpeck" hurt. "Out in the middle of Fifth Avenue's width we felt a heap isolated; it even went farther than that—we felt ostracized. Tagging along after the girls—that's what we were doing; and nobody would let us forget it."[3]

We now know the author of *How It Feels to Be the Husband of a Suffragette* was Ray Brown, an advertising executive and illustrator married to Gertrude Foster Brown, the president of the New York State Woman Suffrage Association. Himself an avid suffragist, Ray Brown put his creative talents to good use to support the cause monopolizing his wife's time. The pamphlet, and the story of the marriage behind it, offer a window on what happens when suffrage hits close to home. In the case of Ray and Gertrude Foster Brown's marriage, the personal truly was political, and vice versa.[4]

Arthur Raymond Brown was born in Groton, Connecticut in 1865, to a family that traced its roots to the Revolutionary War general Artemas Ward of Shrewsbury, Massachusetts. His father was a Congregational minister who died before Arthur was born, the victim of a freak accident when a tree he was cutting fell on him. His widowed mother kept the family together by opening a girls' school in Connecticut. When Ray was in his teens, he was sent away to the Worcester Polytechnic Institute. Expelled over a prank which involved enticing the deacon's white horse inside the school chapel (newspapers had a field day when administrators couldn't get the horse out), he taught for a while at an Indian missionary school in South Dakota. His main aptitude was for drawing and illustration, and he found his first jobs in the journalism field. Before the technology existed to easily reproduce photographs, newspapers relied on artists to illustrate their stories, so this was a secure niche. By the early 1890s, he was working in Chicago, where his path crossed with his future wife's.[5]

Compared to Ray Brown, Gertrude Foster had already had a very adventuresome life by the time they met. Born in 1868 in the small western Illinois town of Morrison, she was musical from an early age, specializing in the piano. Striking out from conventional expectations for women, she was also ambitious and determined to make something of herself. Despite the strain on her family's finances, she convinced her father to send her to the Boston Conservatory of Music for professional training, where she finished the four-year course in half that time. After a year's teaching gig in Dayton, and once again with full familial support, she left for Berlin in 1886, where she studied with several noted pianists and lived an exciting—and often unchaperoned—life filled with concerts and suitors. By the time Gertrude returned to the United States in 1889, at the age of twenty-one, she had received no fewer than four marriage proposals. Three she dismissed out of hand—"Gentlemen don't appreciate platonic friendship, I'm afraid, as much as ladies do," she said of one—but the fourth was serious enough that she planned to introduce the suitor to her family. For reasons lost to the historical record, that relationship did not work out.[6]

According to her teachers, Gertrude Foster was a "brilliant" pianist with good stage presence, but she worried that she did not have what it took for a full-scale performing career: "a kind of ruthlessness in pushing oneself forward, and an ambition so imperative that one is impelled to sacrifice everything and everybody including oneself." In addition, she was hampered by "faulty memory," a very real problem for a performer. So she decided that she would support herself by teaching at the new Chicago Conservatory of Music and by playing small recitals in private homes, a form of parlor entertainment which was popular among socially prominent as well as upwardly mobile families. Chicago proved a congenial place for her to launch her career—and, as it turned out, her marriage.[7]

Ray and Gertrude "met cute"—they were living in the same boarding house when a fire broke out in Gertrude's rooms, destroying all her possessions. Soon they were spending most of their free time together. With his "mop of unruly hair and heavy shaggy eyebrows" and his total lack of affinity for music, Ray was a stark contrast to Gertrude's earlier cosmopolitan European suitors. Frankly, her family was not very keen on him, and his lack of prospects and social graces concerned them. But confirming Gertrude's strong strand of feminism, her father said, "My daughter usually knows what she wants. If she wants to marry you she will do it." They married in the summer of 1893 in her hometown of Morrison, with the expectation that Gertrude would continue her teaching and recitals in Chicago and Ray would work as an illustrator and specialty writer. In 1896 the couple moved to New York City when Ray received an offer from the Hearst newspaper chain to work as an illustrator. It was a demanding job, and after several years, he had some kind of a physical or mental breakdown. He later became the art director of *Everybody's Magazine*, but poor health and nerves shadowed him for the rest of his life.[8]

The move to New York cut Gertrude off from her musical networks and left her at sea about what to do next. The couple did not have children, and Gertrude always knew she was unsuited for a purely domestic life. "Shall I stay at home and mope?" she rhetorically asked her husband. "There is only one kind of a woman who can live doing nothing and that is a woman utterly without brains." Around 1901, she had an idea that "came like a spark set to tinder." The dramatic operas of Richard Wagner were gaining a following in the United States, and she decided to offer lectures explaining their complicated plots and musical themes to American audiences, accompanied by snippets on the piano. For the next seven years, Gertrude Foster Brown spent most of her time on the road, lecturing to women's clubs and schools across the country.[9]

The success of her career strained their marriage. Although "we were quite frank with each other about it," Ray resented her absences. He probably also resented that she was earning more money—and doing it so easily—than he was. "Don't you see why I cling to my profession and why I like my trips?" she chided her husband. "Who would exchange the experiences I have, the knowledge of the country, the acquaintances, and especially the frequent friendships I make with worth-while people all over the U.S. for the narrow rut of keeping house in N.Y. and doing nothing else?" Ray replied as good as he got, as in this 1905 letter: "Your theory that separation is a good thing is all wrong—that is from the standpoint of the separated *from*. . . . I think when you *do* come you'll probably find me standing on the Western edge of New York State with a telescope looking for my wife."[10]

Their frequent letters are affectionate and loving, but it is not clear how long they could have tolerated these enforced separations. Unfortunately for her—but perhaps fortunately for him—a bout of typhoid sometime around 1908 caused her to put her musical career on hold. At this point, Ray and Gertrude Foster Brown's story becomes a suffrage story.

It happened just after a dinner party in a smart suburban town. The guest of honor had refused to do anything but "grunt and grump," and in desperation, the evening's hostess, inspired by the exploits of militant British suffragettes garnering newspaper headlines that day, asked her guest whether he thought women should vote. "Of course I do, and they would have voted years ago if they hadn't been such damn fools." On the way back to the train station, Gertrude asked her husband whether he believed women should vote. He was somewhat taken aback, never having given it any thought, but answered in the affirmative. "We've been trying to run the world for 2000 years with only one half our available power and nobody likes the result," he reasoned. "Yes, I think women ought to vote, and I believe they ought to vote whether they want to or not, whether the vote will do them any good or not, and whether they will do any good with it or not."[11]

That conversation was Gertrude Foster Brown's introduction to woman suffrage, or as she put it in her memoir, "*our* introduction to the movement which ... practically took possession of our joint lives for the next ten years." Ray also remembered it as a joint plunge: "Personally, we—I and mine—fell into suffrage together and practically made only one splash." And yet when she asked her friends, who were mostly professional women or artists, whether they believed in suffrage, most of them had never given it any thought either. "Their groping and indecision was so universal that I felt something should be done."[12]

Her first visit to the headquarters of New York's local suffrage association was not auspicious. "An elderly lady in dowdy clothes and with gray frizzed hair" gave her and a friend some literature and tried to answer their questions, but failed to impress the "young and bright" women. Brown quickly concluded, somewhat patronizingly, that "if suffrage was to come, it would be we who would bring it, not the little ancient." She organized a woman suffrage study club in New York City with a friend in 1909, and in 1910, she attended her first convention. Soon after, she was giving open-air speeches from the back of her car at the corner of 125th Street and Lenox Avenue in New York City. She marched with the New York delegation in the 1913 suffrage parade in Washington, DC, and in 1914, she was elected president of the New York State Woman Suffrage Association.[13]

Already at ease with public speaking from her performing career, Gertrude Foster Brown now redirected her considerable energy and talent to the suffrage cause. "My musical profession, my social life, even my family duties took second place. . . . The change was as complete as though I had experienced religious conversion." Even as her suffrage work increasingly upended the settled patterns of their life together, Ray generously supported her newfound endeavor. In fact, she noted, "most of the husbands, fathers and sons of active suffrage workers, at whatever personal sacrifice, gave their constant help and support to our cause."[14]

One story captures how suffrage work was woven into their marriage. When Gertrude headed off to the 1914 state convention, Ray made what she called "his usual protest": "Gertrude, I'm really worried. Please don't let them make you president. I want to tell you that if you do I shall feel as badly as you would feel if I should go abroad and leave you at home." Not to worry, dear, she replied. But when she got to the convention, both Carrie Chapman Catt and Anna Howard Shaw took her aside to make personal pitches—"I had no children, they said, I was able financially to give up my time, why should I refuse when so many others were sacrificing more than I was being asked to give?"—and she soon found herself duly standing for election. She wired Ray, "Don't judge me until you see me," but he greeted her warmly at the train station and took her out to dinner. "Now you're in for it, I'll do all I can to help you," he told her, and promptly ordered a bottle of vintage champagne to toast her election.[15]

One imagines similar discussions, with or without the champagne, happening in suffrage households across the country. When a wife signed on to the cause, it was often the equivalent of a full-time job. Not only was it usually unpaid—it could also entail significant outlays of cash for hotel bills, travel, and subscriptions, to say nothing of the disruptions of well-established domestic routines. Many husbands literally and figuratively underwrote their wives' contributions to the cause.

Especially in New York State, the role of socially prominent married women in the final stages of the suffrage struggle was striking. These women's marital status brought respectability and credibility to a cause that still struggled for both. Just as striking was how they were almost always listed by their husband's names: Mrs. Stanley McCormick, Mrs. Clarence Mackay, Mrs. Ogden Reid, Mrs. O. H. P. Belmont, Mrs. Frank A. Vanderlip, Mrs. James Lees Laidlaw, Mrs. Thomas Lamont, Mrs. F. Louis Slade, and so forth.[16] The one exception was the widowed Carrie Chapman Catt, who was simply identified as "Mrs." When Gertrude Foster Brown published *Your Vote and How to Use It* in 1918, she was listed on the title page as Mrs. Raymond Brown.[17]

The National American Woman Suffrage Association cultivated the support of socially prominent men as well, relying heavily on the publicity that groups like the Men's League for Woman Suffrage received in the national press to build support for the cause. Ray Brown was not listed as a charter member of the Men's League—its formation in 1909 was fairly soon after the Browns' joint suffrage epiphany, and he was not quite in the same league as the founders when it came to professional and social status. Nonetheless, it was likely that marching with the Men's League for Woman Suffrage inspired his pamphlet.[18]

How It Feels to Be the Husband of a Suffragette was written on a dare. Gertrude didn't even know about it until it appeared in print. Ray called it not "a defense, an apology, or confession" but rather a "frank statement." There is no question that it was written by a man with strong feminist leanings. He supports women's economic independence and believes in shared finances in marriage. When it comes to who does the dishes, neither does—they leave it to the maid. He summed up his feminist philosophy this way: "Personally, I believe that a lady with a well-worn latch-key, who has healthy interests outside her home, is better company than one whose view of life is circumscribed by the four walls that the landlord refused to paper last spring." Gertrude liked that quote so much she used it as the opening epigram for her memoirs.[19]

The pamphlet is not a closely reasoned pro-suffrage tract. Instead, it uses humor and wit to make points gently, appealing more to emotion and caricature than to logic and facts. Ray Brown was in fact an aspiring short-story writer, with a few publications to his credit, and he knew that if his piece took itself too seriously, it would not reach a broad popular audience. Even so, it is telling that instead of claiming authorship in his own right, the title page only says "by Him."

Ray Brown was likely trying to strike a humorous note when he included the fraught word *suffragette* in the title. That term most accurately described the militant British suffragists from about 1908 on, but it was never embraced by American suffragists, who emphatically wanted to distance themselves from the violence against property their British sisters sometimes displayed. Whenever the term was used in this country, it was almost always a term of derision or disrespect or, at the very least, skepticism. Gertrude Foster Brown would never have referred to herself by that term,

This photo from a 1915 suffrage parade in New York captures a telling mistake: the banner says "Men's League for Women Suffrage," but the correct name of the group was "Men's League for Woman Suffrage." Clearly the person who stitched up the banner wasn't paying attention to the finer points of suffrage terminology. *Courtesy of Bryn Mawr College Special Collections.*

so why did her husband? Perhaps he saw it as a term of playful endearment—he had once addressed a letter to her as "Dear Little Suffragette"—but probably it was simply another satirical ploy to catch the public's attention.[20]

For all Ray Brown's cheery banter about "living in the house with a woman who takes a kind, warm, vital interest in everything that is going on in the world," it wasn't always easy to be married to a suffragist, especially "his" suffragist. What put the most strain on their suffrage marriage was precisely what had challenged the couple earlier: the time she spent away from home. As he wrote to her in March 1913, probably when she was headed down to Washington, DC for the counter-inauguration march, "WOMAN—Your place is *the home* (294 West 92nd Street)." The next year he put it even more forcefully: "I wish after a while, pretty soon, when you get tired of staying away, you would come home. It is all right being married to a famous lady, but there are times when it is a little like having contracted honorary matrimony with Minerva or Diana or some other one of those Olympian ladies who spend most of their time on the top of a high and inaccessible peak and when you do meet them it is a miracle." In a handwritten postscript, he added, "If you live through it." These somewhat plaintive private thoughts contrasted sharply with the cheerful public face he adopted as "Mr." Gertrude Foster Brown. But despite any private misgivings, he never wavered in his support for the larger cause.[21]

Ray and Gertrude Foster Brown's suffrage story reminds us that behind every suffragist was a domestic support system enabling that political activism. Suffragists often spoke of the difficulty of converting male voters, but one place they enjoyed definite success was in their own homes and families. The men who stood behind their suffragist wives, girlfriends, sisters, and mothers are also part of the suffrage story, and it's time to acknowledge them. As for the men who still refused to get on board, Ray Brown, "the husband of a suffragette," had these parting words: "All you can do, my brother, is to pray—pray fervently—that suffrage may never come; but with all due regard to Napoleon's remark about God being on the side that has the heaviest artillery, I'm afraid you lose."[22]

Suffrage bluebird. *Courtesy of Schlesinger Library, Radcliffe Institute, Harvard University.*

CHAPTER ELEVEN

The Farmer-Suffragettes

"THE BLUEBIRD CARRIES the sky on his back," observed Henry David Thoreau. Unique to North America, the eastern bluebird (*Sialia sialis*) is distinctive for its intense blue color and its pleasing musical song. Bluebirds have long been linked with happiness, hope, love, and resilience. To those associations add woman suffrage.[1]

In the summer and fall of 1915, tin bluebirds popped up all over Massachusetts. These die-cut tin birds, with intense blue and yellow coloring, had "Votes for Women" emblazoned down their chests. The prominent placement of "Nov. 2" on their tail feathers confirmed their purpose: to remind voters to support the referendum on woman suffrage scheduled for that date. Massachusetts suffragists did not stint in their promotion of this unique brand of outdoor advertising. On July 17, 1915, "Suffrage Blue Bird Day," they distributed upward of a hundred thousand suffrage bluebirds around the state. A hole in the middle of the tin sign made it attachable to fences, barns, or telephone poles; they were also stuck in lawns, propped up on porches, and displayed in windows. At twelve inches by four inches—much larger than an actual bluebird—they would have been hard to miss.

Like their cheerful tin bluebirds, Massachusetts suffragists had high hopes for the upcoming referendum. Two weeks before the election, more than fifteen thousand suffragists marched and rallied in downtown Boston, in a massive outpouring of public support. But when male electors in this generally conservative state went to the polls on November second, they soundly defeated the referendum. A significant factor was the strength of the Massachusetts Association Opposed to the Further Extension of Suffrage to Women, which counted many prominent women and men among its supporters.

The eastern bluebird's chief competitor is the English house sparrow, which aggressively attacks bluebird nests and destroys their eggs. In many ways, the well-heeled and well-organized Massachusetts antisuffragists played the sparrows against the bluebirds of the Massachusetts Woman Suffrage Association. They prevailed that November, but just four years later, Massachusetts became the eighth state to ratify the Nineteenth Amendment. And bluebirds, suffrage and otherwise, have been making a comeback ever since.

IN THE SPRING OF 1913, two unmarried women bought a farm in the small central Massachusetts town of South Berlin. The women seemed serious about farming, but everyone knew that Molly Dewson and Polly Porter were not typical farmers. Then as now, there was something decidedly "queer" about this whole situation.[2] Where were their husbands? Where were their families? That women could so publicly flaunt their ability to live independently of men raised troubling questions for the residents of this conservative farming community. To make matters worse, the two women had not been in Berlin that long before they became active suffragists, touring the Worcester County countryside to promote votes for women. The neighbors quickly dubbed them "the farmer-suffragettes."[3]

Molly Dewson, born in Quincy, Massachusetts in 1874, was the older of the two by ten years. After graduating from Wellesley College in 1897, she was immediately caught up in the Progressive fervor sweeping the country. In a class book published in 1910, she wrote exuberantly to her fellow Wellesley classmates, "We used to play at choosing the period in which we would rather have lived. But what time could be more thrilling than our own, when in every city and town are springing up hundreds of sane, alert people to fight under scientific leadership the problems of their community with sympathy and sense?" Not the least bit interested in marriage, and in need of paid employment to earn a living, she held three positions in the fifteen years after her graduation: research assistant at the Women's Educational and Industrial Union in Boston, superintendent of probation for the Lancaster State Industrial School for Girls, and executive secretary of the Massachusetts Commission on the Minimum Wage. Many of the causes she worked on during her apprenticeship, especially the minimum wage and protective legislation for working women, remained primary focuses for the rest of her career.[4]

Molly Dewson and Polly Porter met in 1909 at the Lancaster School. Born in Chicago in 1884, Polly was clearly not someone who needed to work for a living. Attractive, impulsive, and conspicuously rich—her family wealth derived from the International Harvester fortune—she was the product of an affluent upbringing that included a stately home in suburban Evanston and a shingled, seven-bedroom "cottage" in Castine, Maine. Orphaned in her late teens, she showed no interest in marriage or settling down. When her guardians insisted she find something to do, she enrolled at the Boston School for Social Work. Her field work assignment took her to Lancaster, where her supervisor was Molly Dewson. Almost immediately, the two became "fast friends." Polly was a frequent visitor to the Dewson family home in Quincy, where Molly still lived with her widowed mother well into her thirties. Mrs. Dewson's death in 1912 meant Molly was finally free to leave the family claim behind.

Taking a break from social work, the Porter-Dewsons—as they called themselves as early as Christmas 1912—decided to try their hand at cow farming. While Molly and Polly thought of themselves as farmers, they were not exactly roughing it. They employed a hired man to tend the cows, extra hands to help with the haying and harvesting in the fall, and local farm girls to run the household. (Neither Molly nor Polly knew how to cook.) The farm turned a small profit, but farm income would never have sustained their privileged lifestyle. Polly's trust fund bridged the gap.

Casting about for things to do, Molly and Polly turned their attention to the issue sweeping Massachusetts: woman suffrage. In 1915, they volunteered their services to the Massachusetts Woman Suffrage Association (MWSA) as suffrage workers in Worcester County. Dewson took over the tenth district, with responsibility for the towns of Berlin, Hudson, Clinton, and Westborough. Polly did not hold an official position; rather, she was Molly's constant sidekick.

With a state referendum scheduled for November, there was much to do. They opened a "Votes for Women" shop in Hudson, which featured a window display of suffrage mottos and banners they created themselves. They wrote numerous letters to the editors of local Worcester county newspapers and distributed brightly colored "Suffrage Blue Birds" for supporters to display on their fence posts and front porches. Less successfully, they tried to convert the local Berlin women's club to a suffrage group, but they only mustered a slim majority in support of giving women the vote.

Truth be told, the farmer-suffragettes were willing to do almost anything for suffrage that involved driving their beloved automobiles. They had two: a stylish Buick and a serviceable Ford. Cars were still something of a novelty in rural areas, especially when driven by women, and Molly and Polly relished the sensation they created as they cruised the Worcester countryside in an open vehicle festooned with suffrage slogans. In one case, a twelve-foot-long banner attached to the passenger's side spelled out "Helen Todd of California" to signal the identity of the out-of-state speaker they were squiring around. In another instance, their featured guest was a former Democratic candidate for governor. The Northboro newspaper captured that scene: "After riding through the main streets in an auto, with a bugler making merry, the party of suffragists drew up at the curbing on Church Street and Miss Dewson of Berlin introduced Mr. Vahey." As Claiborne Catlin had found on her horseback ride across Massachusetts the year before, such dramatic arrivals were sure to attract a crowd.[5]

Another method of garnering publicity was the open-air meeting. Polly Porter never spoke from the platform—except for cameo roles in an occasional suffrage play, she kept pretty much in the background—but Molly loved to be the center of attention, foreshadowing her later role as the head of women's Democratic politics in the New Deal. On the suffrage hustings, Molly pitched her talks to the low level of political sophistication found in these random audiences. "Women would be women just the same whether they had the ballot or not," she reassured listeners in Hudson. "Just as long as women live they will be women; they will work for home, husband, and children." Of course that last sentiment didn't apply to her and Polly, but no matter.[6]

Together the two women kept a scrapbook of their 1915 suffrage activities, which was filled with clippings about Worcester County events they had participated in, as well as more general news about the suffrage cause. The sheer amount of activity documented in local newspapers suggests how deeply this political question had penetrated into even relatively rural areas. Even if woman suffrage was impossible to ignore, opinions remained deeply divided. The scrapbook contained both pro- and antisuffrage clippings, with the latter carefully marked in red. The red ink predominated.

Molly and Polly were soon drawn into the organizational network linking local suffrage workers to state and national groups. As the movement gathered momentum, the same recruitment process was happening in localities all around the country. Molly and Polly signed up for a one-day conference on suffrage techniques in Worcester. In May, they attended a three-day MWSA conference in Boston, which culminated in a "monster" rally on Boston Common. They also represented the town of Berlin in October 1915, in Boston's Suffrage Victory Parade; for this, their car had a starring role, and they decked it out with special care. Unfortunately, talk of victory was premature, as the men of Massachusetts decisively voted down the referendum by a two-to-one margin the next month. Undaunted, suffragists forged ahead, increasingly confident that they would prevail.

In December 1915, Molly and Polly, chosen as Massachusetts delegates to the National American Woman Suffrage Association (NAWSA) convention in Washington, witnessed firsthand a significant turning point for the national movement. At this convention, Carrie Chapman Catt took over the leadership of NAWSA from Anna Howard Shaw. Dewson judged Shaw "a super woman," "the best speaker by far for the suffrage cause," but she thought even more highly of Catt, calling her the "keystone" of the suffrage movement and half joking in 1934 that "without her I believe we still would be voteless!" As a lowly district leader from Central Massachusetts, Dewson had little contact with the national leadership at the convention, although she did befriend younger, less well-known suffrage workers, with whom she would collaborate in the postsuffrage era to increase roles for women in politics. Several fellow attendees, including Sue Shelton White, Lucy Somerville Howorth, Emily Newell Blair, and Florence Allen, later joined Dewson in the Roosevelt administration.[7]

After only a year on the suffrage circuit, Molly Dewson stood poised to break into a substantial leadership position on the statewide level, which was testimony to the professional and organizational skills she had been honing since college. At this point, the suffrage careers of the partners diverged even further. At first, they had been very much in it together: "Molly and Polly, the farmer-suffragettes," always up for an excursion to a neighboring town or putting on an impromptu suffrage play. But Dewson had far stronger organizational talents than Porter, and she felt much more at ease in public than her shy partner did. Polly continued to be active, but she participated more as Molly's companion than as a co-worker.

In the fall of 1916, Dewson agreed to assume the unsalaried position of chair of MWSA's Legislative Committee. She continued to live on the Berlin farm and happily drove the thirty-five miles into Boston for the weekly executive board meetings, chaired by President Alice Stone Blackwell, who by that point had spent almost forty years in the suffrage trenches. While primarily focused on lobbying for suffrage, Dewson tried to push the group to expand its vision to include social welfare measures, such as a bill limiting working hours for women and children to eight hours a day. Many suffragists in fact supported the eight-hour bill, but feared that endorsing that measure in order to build alliances with unions and industrial workers would open suffragists to requests from other organizations on which there might not be such unanimity—such as prohibition or birth control. Those doubts carried the day.

By 1917, a new issue challenged the suffrage movement when the United States formally entered World War I in April. Many women felt torn between their suffrage advocacy and supporting the war effort. While some radical suffragists bravely opposed the war for pacifist reasons, most mainstream suffragists, including Molly and Polly, lined up behind the Wilson administration, vowing to continue their agitation for the vote. The Massachusetts Woman Suffrage Association complied with this dual policy, but Dewson's enthusiasm for the suffrage cause waned in direct proportion to the amount of war-related work she was called on to perform.

Even though the suffrage victory was still three long years away, by 1917, Molly Dewson's active involvement was drawing to a close. So too were her days as a farmer. "Farming in war time is not for us two," she confided to a friend in September 1917. "In 1916 it was no expense. This year the scarcity and poorness of labor and its expense have discouraged Wynott [their tenant farmer] so he is going. We can get no one else. . . . Since we perforce have no farm and our maids have just left and more are hard to get we might as well seize the moment and close up for the winter and take a change." Despite a catchy handbill stating "Attractive Sale by Auction of the Well-Known Herd . . . belonging to Porter & Dewson, South Berlin, Mass," it turned out to be a poor time to sell a farm. So they planted their fields with winter rye, which would not need to be harvested until the summer of 1918, and they arranged for a Berlin family to take care of the house and the remaining stock.[8]

Freed from suffrage and farming responsibilities, Molly and Polly assessed their options. They thought about a six-month cross-country driving trip to California, but they felt a little guilty about planning an extended vacation while the United States was at war. By mid-October, they had signed on as social workers with the American Red Cross in France. "We just couldn't do it Lucy," Molly wrote to a California friend. "We felt it would be like quitters this year to travel. If you were in N.Y. you'd think all the world was going to France."[9]

Before they sailed from New York, with their trusty car packed like a piano onboard the ship, they partook of one final suffrage moment: a massive suffrage parade which Dewson pronounced "superb" and "a thrill." To the suffragists' delight, they won a narrow but conclusive victory in New York in November 1917, the first breakthrough in a major northern industrial state. Molly and Polly heard the news on the boat train from Le Havre to Paris. "What do you think of the gallant men of New York!" Molly bragged to Polly's brother Bill. "Well it certainly gave me about the best send off I could have asked from my native land."[10]

Molly Dewson and Polly Porter's story shows how seamlessly suffrage work and the war effort blended together for many women, especially those who belonged to mainstream suffrage organizations like NAWSA. (The war had a very different meaning for Alice Paul and the militants of the National Woman's Party.) But their story also demonstrates something else: how the suffrage movement provided a safe and welcoming space for a variety of unconventional lifestyles, all hiding in plain sight.[11]

The personal relationships of Carrie Chapman Catt, whose Juniper Ledge suffrage forest opened this book, reveal similar affinities. In 1885, after having graduated from Iowa State University, Carrie Lane married the newspaper editor Leo Chapman, but he died of typhoid the next year. In 1890, she married George Catt, a wealthy engineer. Neither marriage produced children. The Catts had quite an unusual marriage for the time: they often did not live together, while she, with his blessing, continued the suffrage work that kept her constantly on the road. Around 1890, Catt met Mary (Mollie) Garrett Hay, a fellow Midwesterner who was also deeply involved in suffrage organizing. The two women often traveled together, and in 1895, they shared temporary living arrangements. After George Catt's death in 1905, the two women lived together permanently until Hay's death in 1928. When Carrie Chapman Catt died in 1947, she chose to be buried not next to either of her husbands but beside Mary Garrett Hay at Woodlawn Cemetery, where she erected this monument: "Here lie two, united in friendship for thirty-eight years through constant service to a great cause."[12] A queer—as in, strange, odd, and definitely nonnormative—choice indeed.

Susan B. Anthony also led a decidedly queer life. "Man-marriage" held no appeal, so she sustained her emotional life with deep friendships with other women, both married and single. First and foremost was her five-decade relationship with Elizabeth

Cady Stanton—the "thought" to Anthony's "action," according to Stanton's daughter Harriot Stanton Blatch—a partnership with huge implications for suffrage history. In fact, all of Anthony's relationships were suffrage-linked. Her most passionate was with the twenty-four-year-old Anna Dickinson, whom Anthony met in 1866 when she was forty-six. But that cooled after a few years, and the peripatetic Anthony never settled into a long-term relationship with any one woman. Instead, "Aunt Susan" surrounded herself with a range of fictive suffrage nieces, most notably Rachel Foster (later Avery) but also Carrie Chapman Catt and Anna Howard Shaw. She also had deep ties to her blood nieces, and from 1890 on, she shared a home in Rochester with her sister Mary. Labeling Susan B. Anthony queer acknowledges the range and depth of the emotional attachments with which she constructed her non-normative personal life.[13]

The suffrage movement supported a variety of living and working arrangements that fell outside the bounds of heteronormativity. Anna Howard Shaw's longtime companion was Lucy Anthony, Susan's niece. Alice Stone Blackwell considered herself "betrothed" to Kitty Barry, the adopted child of her aunt Elizabeth. Alice Paul never entered into a committed long-term relationship with another woman—it's not clear whether she even had a personal life, so to speak—but instead surrounded herself with like-minded feminists at Belmont House, the headquarters of the National Woman's Party in Washington, DC.[14]

Of course the suffrage movement boasted plenty of married women, starting with Lucretia Mott, Elizabeth Cady Stanton, and Lucy Stone in the founding generation and Alva Belmont, Harriet Burton Laidlaw, Maud Nathan, and Harriot Stanton Blatch in the second. But often, suffrage marriages pushed boundaries. Maud

Wood Park, for instance, married twice but kept both marriages secret, and younger women like Doris Stevens, Alice Paul's sidekick at the National Woman's Party and a self-proclaimed "modern woman," aggressively claimed the right to sexual freedom alongside men— although she also instructed her male paramours not to send her love letters at headquarters, lest her boss spot them. Stevens carried on not one but two affairs with married men while on the suffrage campaign trail between 1915 and 1919.[15]

It isn't simply a case of who's gay and who's not. To speak of "queering the suffrage movement" is to identify it as a space where women felt free to express a wide range of gender non-conforming behaviors, including but not limited to sexual expression, in both public and private settings. This tolerance had its limits, however. From the beginning, the suffrage movement struggled with an undercurrent of accusations that it was engaged in a "sex war" against men. Nor did this openness last. As the work of sexologists like Freud, Krafft-Ebbing, and Havelock Ellis became more widely known in the 1920s and 1930s, being "normal" increasingly came to mean being actively heterosexual. This in turn encouraged a tendency to reinterpret women's feelings for other women in a decidedly more negative light than had been true earlier.

On sabbatical from the professional work that had brought them together, Molly Dewson and Polly Porter were probably not thinking about safe spaces and gender nonconformity when they signed on as suffrage workers. Instead, they were just keen to spend exhilarating days bouncing around the Massachusetts countryside in their open car or attending "monster" rallies on Boston Common, then come home to quiet evenings in front of the fireplace, with Polly reading aloud while Molly listened contently. They didn't aspire to the leadership roles that Carrie Chapman Catt, Anna Howard Shaw, or Alice Paul held; rather, they were happy to do good work in their small bailiwick of central Massachusetts, and they were determined to have fun doing it. "No work I have ever done was more entertaining," Dewson later recalled, "for woman suffrage has nothing to do with economics."[16]

Poster for the International Woman Suffrage Alliance conference in Budapest, 1913.
Courtesy of Schlesinger Library, Radcliffe Institute, Harvard University.

CHAPTER TWELVE

Suffragists Abroad

STARTING IN THE 1830S AND 1840S, American and British abolitionists forged connections that influenced the early history of the suffrage movement. In the decades following the 1840 antislavery conference in London, where Elizabeth Cady Stanton and Lucretia Mott first met, women activists exhibited a remarkable propensity for traveling around the globe to attend conventions. Susan B. Anthony, Frances Willard, Carrie Chapman Catt, and Anna Howard Shaw were all intrepid world travelers.

Women's international networks were especially vibrant in the late nineteenth and early twentieth centuries. In the 1880s, the World Woman's Christian Temperance Union took the lead, promoting political equality for women in places such as New Zealand, Australia, and South Africa. In 1888, the International Council of Women was founded to bring together existing women's groups, primarily from North America and western Europe, with Elizabeth Cady Stanton and Susan B. Anthony as its prime instigators. Its offshoot, the International Woman Suffrage Alliance (IWSA), founded in 1904 in Berlin "to secure the enfranchisement of the women of all nations," fed the growth of the woman suffrage movement worldwide.[1]

Anna So'os Koranyi's block print poster of Atlas and an equally strong woman holding the world was created for the IWSA's seventh annual conference (Internationaler Frauenstimmrechts-Kongress), held in Budapest, Hungary June 15–20, 1913. Undeterred by the distance, Charlotte Perkins Gilman and Jane Addams both made the trip. So did the IWSA president, Carrie Chapman Catt, who traveled by way of meetings in London, Berlin, Dresden, Prague, and Vienna, doing her final leg by boat on the Danube River.

With local arrangements in the highly capable hands of Rosika Schwimmer, the IWSA welcomed its largest gathering to date, attended by representatives from twenty-five countries, including China. "For the first time in the woman movement," Catt boasted, "it is expected that Hindu, Buddhist, Confucian, Mohammedan, Jewish and Christian women will sit together in a Congress uniting their voices in a common plea for the liberation of their sex from those artificial discriminations which every political and religious system has directed against them." Despite this inclusive statement, behind Catt's sentiments lay not an expansive commitment to multiculturalism but a deeply engrained belief in the superiority of Western civilization. The world's women might come together, but the expectation was that women from western Europe and North America would lead.[2]

Flush with success in 1913, the IWSA confidently looked forward to its next biennial meeting in Berlin, but the outbreak of World War I meant it never took place. As a result, many suffragists later looked back on the Budapest congress with special fondness, a halcyon time before the world they knew was forever altered. When women won the vote in a range of countries after the war, many suffragists seamlessly transferred their energies to the promotion of peace and the elimination of war.

In April 1904, Mary Church Terrell, a respected leader in Washington, DC's vibrant African American community, received an invitation to deliver an address to the International Council of Women in Berlin. Deeply honored, she nevertheless struggled to see how she could attend a conference so far away in less than two months. Where would the money come from to pay her way? How could she leave her young daughter? How would she book passage on such short notice? She had moments of self-doubt even after she surmounted those obstacles, but her larger purpose carried the day: "Whenever my courage seemed to be oozing away and the horror of leaving my family seemed greater than I could endure, I would think of the opportunity which had been miraculously afforded me of presenting the facts creditable to colored women of the United States, and my spirit would immediately revive." At this world congress, Mary Church Terrell proudly represented not just the American suffrage movement but the experiences of African American women as well.[3]

When she arrived in Berlin, there was much speculation about *die Negerin* (the Negress) from the United States. Terrell was one of the few American delegates who spoke fluent German, and delegates and the press repeatedly asked her about this unusual honored guest, not realizing that she, who was very light-skinned and often mistaken for white, was the very same person. Finally she revealed her identity to one persistent reporter, whose reaction was a combination of joy at scoring the first interview with the mystery guest and disbelief at the distance between her expectation of what an American Negro might look like—which Terrell parodied as "rings in her nose" and "cake-walking" in the streets—and the well-dressed woman standing in front of her. As she had been doing all her life, Mary Church Terrell confronted racial stereotypes head-on by presenting an eminently respectable public persona.[4]

Once the preconference activities started, Terrell began to hear complaints from the German hosts that the American and British delegates planned to address the congress only in English. (The "poor monolingual Americans" was a frequent complaint at international conferences in those days.) Terrell had painstakingly prepared her address in English, but she decided on the spot to give it in German. Even though she feared she wouldn't have time to adequately adapt the speech to conversational spoken language, she received encouragement from several Americans, including the newspaperwoman Ida Husted Harper, who was covering the conference for the *Washington Post*. "Well, Mary Church Terrell," another delegate weighed in, "if you can deliver an address before this Congress in German and don't do it, I think you are a fool in 57 varieties of languages."[5]

Terrell's main motivation was not showing off her fluency in languages (she also spoke French and Italian), although she was well aware of the symbolism of someone just one generation removed from slavery addressing a major international conference in a foreign language. In the days before simultaneous translation, she wanted German women to hear firsthand what she had to say about the position of African American women in the United States. Then, she hoped, delegates would continue that conversation over the rest of the conference. The stakes were high, she realized: "I represented, not only the colored women of my own country but, since I was the only woman taking part in the International Congress who had a drop of African blood in her veins, I represented the whole continent of Africa as well."[6]

Two days and several sleepless nights later, she stood before the assembled gathering with her new speech. Since many delegates still did not realize that she was "*die Negerin*," she decided to open her talk with a frank admission: "In all this great world gathering of women, I believe I am unique in two respects. In the first place, I am the only woman participating in these exercises who represents a race which has been free so short a time as forty years. In the second place, I am the only woman speaking from this platform whose parents were actually held as chattels and who but for the kindly intervention of a beneficent Providence would have been a slave herself. As you fasten your eyes upon me, you are truly beholding a rare bird." This last phrase brought amused chuckles from the audience, because "rare bird" translates into German as *ein weisser Rabe*: literally, "a white robin." "And so," she continued, "as I stand here tonight, my happiness is two-fold, rejoicing as I do, not only in the emancipation of my race, but in the almost universal elevation of my sex."[7]

Having set the stage so well, Terrell proceeded to give the audience a short tutorial in African American women's history. Hardly glancing down at her prepared text, she contrasted the days of "oppression and despair" under slavery with the "true miracle" of the progress since then, singling out accomplishments in the fields of education, literature, business, and civic improvement. While most of the initiatives came from within the African American community, she noted that black women had also been encouraged "by their more fortunate sisters of the dominant race," singling out Susan B. Anthony, "the veritable Abraham Lincoln of women's emancipation," who was seated in the audience. Her thirty-minute talk was greeted with "tumultuous" applause. Later at the conference, Terrell delivered another well-received speech in French.[8]

Mary Church Terrell was not the only American suffragist who made the long journey to Berlin. Anna Howard Shaw, May Wright Sewall, Hanna G. Solomon, and Mary Wood Swift also attended, as did the eighty-four-year-old Anthony who, when delegates presented her with a bouquet of roses, charmed them by saying, "When I was young men threw stones at me in the street—now that I am old they shower roses upon me." Anthony personally conducted the proceedings at the Berlin congress that led to the formation of the International Woman Suffrage Alliance, a separate transnational organization specifically devoted to suffrage, although she declined to assume its presidency. Carrie Chapman Catt, who was also in attendance, agreed to serve; she held the post for the next twenty years.[9]

The presence of such an impressive American contingent is symptomatic of the strong international ties which linked activists across national borders and promoted a rich circulation of ideas and strategies. As with American suffragism, the international suffrage movement was dominated by a relatively homogeneous group of white, Christian, bourgeois women that mainly operated with often unacknowledged assumptions about western European / North American superiority—"offering a hand to their more oppressed sisters" summed up their stance towards women in the non-Western world. In addition, their mindset contained deep strains of racism, also unacknowledged. That is the world Mary Church Terrell was trying to navigate with her speech in Berlin in 1904, but it is also an apt summary of her experience throughout her long career within the wider suffrage and civil rights movements.[10]

Mary Church was born in 1863 in Memphis, Tennessee, the child of former slaves. Her parents divorced when she was young. Her mother later operated a successful beauty salon, and her father, whose own father was a white slaveholder, invested in Memphis real estate and is often referred to as the South's first black millionaire. Sent north for schooling, Mary graduated from Oberlin College in 1884, where she was one of only a few black women in her class. Unwilling to take up the leisured life that her privileged class background could have afforded, she taught for a year at Wilberforce University in Ohio and then at the esteemed (but segregated) M Street "Colored" High School in Washington, DC.[11]

Still not quite sure of her future direction, she gratefully accepted an offer from her father to send her to Europe. The experience, which spanned the years 1888 and 1889, was eye-opening. As the "cake-walking" quote from 1904 would later confirm, Europe was not free from prejudice, but it was much more fluid than the United States in its racial hierarchies. She found its social freedoms especially exhilarating: "I could take advantage of any opportunity I desired without wondering whether a colored girl would be allowed to enjoy it or not." This relative absence of prejudice was so appealing that she briefly considered settling in Europe permanently. Ultimately, she decided that returning to her country to promote the welfare of her race was her duty.[12]

Traveling in Europe was also attractive because it meant she could temporarily put off the insistent courtship of Robert H. Terrell, an 1884 Harvard graduate who served as the principal of the M Street High School. Although they had tried to be circumspect about their budding relationship, their students had quickly spotted the romantic attraction, quipping, "Mr. Terrell is certainly getting good. He used to go to dances and now he goes to Church," a play on her surname. When she returned from abroad to resume her old job, she finally accepted his proposal, and the couple married in 1891.[13]

The early years of their marriage were challenging: she suffered a serious illness and, in five years, lost three babies shortly after birth. Their daughter Phyllis was born in 1898, and in 1905, the couple adopted her brother's daughter. Making their home in the deeply segregated (and voteless) capital of the nation, the Terrells were, thanks to her leadership roles in civic and educational activities and his position as a municipal court judge, what would now be called a power couple in Washington's African American community.[14]

Mary Church Terrell proudly asserted that she had always been a suffragist. Having seen the vote taken away from black men because of their race, how could she not support such an important citizenship right for women? "Even if I believed that women should be denied the right of suffrage," she wrote in *The Crisis* in 1915, "wild horses could not drag such an admission from my pen or lips, for this reason: precisely the same arguments used to prove the ballot be withheld from women are advanced to prove that colored men should not be allowed to vote."[15]

Terrell came to the attention of the white suffrage movement in part because of her leadership in the black club movement, especially her role as a founder and first president of the National Association of Colored Women (NACW) in 1896. Under the motto "Lifting as We Climb," the NACW pursued a broad agenda that foregrounded women's role in confronting the "race problem." It quickly became the pre-eminent national organization offering black women leadership roles and public prominence. Even though the group did not officially endorse woman suffrage until 1916, it had an active suffrage department from the beginning.[16]

During the 1890s, Terrell attended meetings of the National American Woman Suffrage Association, giving her first address to the group in 1898 on the topic of "The Problems and Progress of Colored Women." She also spoke on "The Justice of Woman Suffrage" at the 1900 NAWSA convention, pleased that she had been tapped to talk about suffrage in general, not just the perspectives of African American women. She counted Susan B. Anthony as a friend—she had been entertained by Anthony and her sister in Rochester—and had warm relations with many prominent white suffragists; in 1908 she was one of the few African Americans invited to Seneca Falls, New York, for the celebration of the sixtieth anniversary of the women's rights convention. Even so, those close associations had not keep her from admonishing "my sisters of the dominant race" at a NAWSA convention four years earlier to "stand up not only for the oppressed sex, but also for the oppressed race." Unfortunately, that call was rarely heeded.[17]

Mary Church Terrell's suffrage philosophy was built around an intersectional vision that embraced race as well as gender, an implicit challenge to white suffragists who tended to focus only on the subordination created by their sex. "A white woman has only one handicap to overcome—that of sex," she argued. "I have two—both sex and race. I belong to the only group in the country which has two such huge obstacles to surmount. Colored men have only one—that of race." Echoing both Sojourner Truth and Ida Wells-Barnett, she always said forthrightly, "However much the white women of the country need suffrage . . . colored women need it more." Yet the white woman suffrage movement consistently refused to make the enfranchisement of black women a priority.[18]

Much of Terrell's vision was shaped by her daily lived experience as a black woman—or as she pointedly titled her 1940 autobiography, "A Colored Woman in a White World." "I assure you that nowhere in the United States have my feelings been so lacerated, my spirit so crushed, my heart so wounded, nowhere have I been so humiliated and handicapped on account of my sex as I have been on account of my race." She always wondered how her life might have been different if she had lived in a country that had not handicapped her by race but instead "had allowed me to reach any height I was able to attain," but she never allowed herself to become bitter.[19]

The challenges of travel, especially in the Jim Crow South, brought this point home. While she never attempted to pass as white, a stance that would have been anathema to her race consciousness and self-respect, her light skin often allowed her to evade the dreaded customs that relegated blacks to separate and distinctly inferior accommodations. This was especially an issue when Terrell began to receive lecture invitations that involved an overnight train ride, where sleeping berths were only available for whites. Rather than sitting up all night in the "colored" car, Terrell purchased first-class accommodations that allowed her to arrive fresh and rested at her destination. But like any person in the South with "one-drop of black blood," she knew an unpleasant confrontation awaited her if a single white person chose to challenge her carefully planned subterfuge.

Terrell's activism and interests cast a wide net. In addition to her key leadership role with the National Association of Colored Women, she was the first black woman appointed to the Board of Education in the District of Columbia and a charter member of the National Association for the Advancement of Colored People

(NAACP), founded in 1909. And despite the suffrage movement's unwillingness to incorporate race into its agenda, she remained loyal to the cause. When Alice Paul staged the 1913 parade down Pennsylvania Avenue the day before President Wilson's inauguration, Terrell marched with the Delta Sigma Theta contingent from Howard University, relegated with the other black marchers to a separate section so as not to offend the sensibilities of white southerners. In contrast, Ida Wells-Barnett had defied suffrage leaders' instructions to march at the back and jumped into the Illinois delegation after the procession began. Each woman made her point in her own way, because both knew how important it was to demonstrate that African American women wanted—and deserved—the vote just as much as white women.

In 1917, Mary Church Terrell and her daughter Phyllis took a turn on the National Woman's Party picket lines outside the White House, possibly the only two African Americans to participate in these demonstrations. Maintaining respectability was a mantra for middle-class African American women—a way to counter whites' negative stereotypes—and such militant action posed a grave risk to their carefully guarded public reputations. (Young African American women who joined the civil rights sit-ins of the 1960s faced similar constraints.) Even though the Terrells avoided arrest, they were later awarded the special prison pin created for those who had been jailed as a result of these public protests. Still, Terrell confided a nagging suspicion to Walter White of the NAACP that if Alice Paul could have gotten the Nineteenth Amendment passed without enfranchising African American women, that would have been fine with her.[20]

As her eagerness to journey to Berlin in 1904 demonstrated, much of Mary Church Terrell's vision for suffrage and race relations

Mary Church Terrell often was the only woman of color at major international conferences. In this group portrait of the Second Annual Conference of the Women's International League for Peace and Freedom in Zurich, in 1919, Terrell stands in the middle of the back row to the left of the woman with the large black hat. *Courtesy of Schlesinger Library, Radcliffe Institute, Harvard University.*

was grounded in an international framework that placed the domestic situation in the United States in dialogue with customs in the rest of the world. When she spoke abroad, she used that platform to educate foreign audiences about conditions for African Americans, about which they were often totally ignorant. When she returned home, she deployed the relative freedom from prejudice found in many European countries as a foil to challenge the rigidity of American racial mores. Thirty years before Hitler's rise to power, she developed an especially acute comparison of the anti-Semitic treatment of Jews in German society with how African Americans were treated in the United States.

As the suffrage movement closed in on victory, Terrell maintained her international connections by joining the Women's International League for Peace and Freedom (WILPF), which was founded at the

1915 International Congress of Women held at The Hague. In 1919, she journeyed to Zurich as a member of the American delegation to WILPF's second annual convention, timed to coincide with the Paris Peace Conference. Once again she was the only woman of color, belying the organizers' statements that women from all over the world were present. "On sober, second thought it is more truthful to say that women from all over the white world were present," she gently chided the organizers. Remembering her experience at the 1904 conference, she explicitly made the link: "For the second time in my life it was a privilege to represent, not only the colored women of the United States, but the whole continent of Africa as well. . . . In fact, since I was the only delegate who gave any color to the occasion at all, it finally dawned on me that I was representing the women of all the non-white countries in the world." On the fourth day of the congress, Jane Addams, the lead American delegate, asked Terrell to represent the United States in an address to the delegates. Just as she had in 1904, she delivered her speech in German.[21]

Mary Church Terrell's international experiences underscore the rewards and challenges of suffrage activism that crossed national borders. Like many of her white allies, she journeyed to Europe for conferences and reveled in the friendships and connections she made abroad. But she always had an additional item on her agenda—an urgent plea that the concerns of African Americans, especially African American women, not be forgotten. "You may talk about permanent peace until doomsday," she told the delegates assembled in Zurich in 1919, "but the world will never have it until the dark races are given a square deal."[22] And that had to include women, a point too often lost on the white suffrage movement, no matter in what language Mary Church Terrell was speaking.

PART THREE

Winning Strategies

According to Willa Cather, "The world broke in two in 1922 or thereabouts," but for the woman suffrage campaign, that moment happened about fifteen years earlier.[1] In the years on either side of 1910, there was a palpable, almost electric change in practically every aspect of the suffrage movement. New tactics, new recruits, new strategies—all came together to energize the cause. Suddenly, the prospect of victory was tantalizingly in sight, even if the actual steps necessary to reach that goal remained unclear.

Part of the shift was generational. By then, the original founding mothers had all passed from the scene, and the second generation—women like Carrie Chapman Catt, Harriot Stanton Blatch, and Anna Howard Shaw—weren't getting any younger. A rising generation, represented by Alice Paul and Lucy Burns at the National Woman's Party, challenged the status quo, and younger recruits swelled the membership of the National American Woman Suffrage Association as well. For the first time, it was possible to speak of suffrage as a mass movement.

A huge factor in the new suffrage dynamism was its more aggressive deployment of public spectacle. Suffragists literally took to the streets—in parades and pageants, in open-air meetings, in strikes, and on picket lines—often decked out in the suffrage colors of white, purple, and gold. More and more women, and a few intrepid men, were willing to stand up and be counted in very public ways, and even to risk arrest and possible jail sentences for their actions. This brash "in your face" mentality made suffragists very hard to ignore.

Often the new vibrancy of the American suffrage movement is ascribed to the influence of militant British suffragettes, who burst into American consciousness around 1908–1909. While the British impact is undeniable, there were plenty of precedents on American soil for this new militancy, including a productive link with working-class women in the labor movement and the breakthroughs in western states. The actions of Ida Wells-Barnett and Mary Church Terrell demonstrate that African American suffragists experienced a quickening of their own. Taking risks and pushing boundaries, the suffrage movement entered its final decade in a militant mood.

CHAPTER THIRTEEN

Mountaineering for Suffrage

IN 1909, the Washington Equal Suffrage Association (WESA) published a cookbook with this credo on the frontispiece: "Give us a vote and we will cook the better for a wide outlook." The cookbook was the brainchild of WESA president Emma Smith Devoe, who had three thousand copies printed and made sure it was advertised widely in the *Woman's Journal*. When critics suggested the cookbook was just a political ploy for the upcoming 1910 Washington state referendum, Devoe demurred, although she did add playfully, "Not that I say that the book hasn't made us friends among the men." How could it not, when its preface presented this appealing picture: "Home, a smiling woman, and a good dinner—does not the heart of man yearn toward this trio at evening time? In the best interests of all concerned, we offer you this little book."[1]

The *Washington Women's Cook Book* was one of a number of cookbooks produced over the course of the suffrage campaign, all designed to promote some combination of "good cooking and sure voting." Modeled on the popular genre of charity cookbooks, their format followed familiar forms: recipes and menus for ordinary meals and special occasions, as well as a range of practical advice on matters such as housekeeping and beauty, with quotes and anecdotes designed to advance the cause of votes for women interspersed throughout. The cookbooks were designed primarily as fundraisers, but they also proved quite helpful in building good will for the cause. Cookbooks reinforced the key suffrage argument that voting would not strip women of their domestic skills—or, as the cover of the *Washington Women's Cook Book* put it: "Votes for Women / Good Things to Eat."[2] But alongside that paean to women's traditional roles was intriguing evidence that suffragists no longer confined themselves to hearth and home: a recipe "To Cook Trout in the Forest," which begins, "First catch your trout."

The recipe was part of a chapter contributed by a group of women climbers affiliated with the Mountaineers, a Seattle-based outdoor recreation club. Dr. Cora Smith Eaton, a well-respected physician and officer of the Washington Equal Suffrage Association, was one of its members. In addition to a list of recipes suitable for cooking while camping, the chapter included a three-page list of the supplies and equipment a woman would need for mountaineering, including a sleeping bag, a tramping suit featuring bloomers or knickerbockers, a mosquito head net, three pairs of cotton hose, light and heavy undersuits, toilet articles, a jackknife and a needle and thread. Just months later, to prove the point that mountaineering and woman suffrage went hand in hand, Cora Smith Eaton planted a "Votes for Women" banner on the summit of Columbia Crest on Mount Rainier.

Cover of the *Washington Women's Cook Book* (1909). *Courtesy of Schlesinger Library, Radcliffe Institute, Harvard University.*

AMERICA'S LOVE AFFAIR with world's fairs was on full display in the decades on either side of 1900, the very years the suffrage movement was picking up momentum. In 1893, the World's Columbian Exposition in Chicago brought twenty-seven million visitors to the so-called "White City" for the four hundredth anniversary of Columbus's voyage. One of the most popular exhibits there, the Woman's Building, highlighted women's contributions to literature, art, and civic life. The wildly successful Chicago World's Fair was followed by Buffalo's Pan-American Exposition in 1901—notable, unfortunately, as the site of the assassination of President William McKinley—and the St. Louis World's Fair in 1904, which marked the centennial of the Louisiana Purchase. Next up was Seattle.

In the five months after June 1, 1909, when the Alaska-Yukon-Pacific Exposition opened on the campus of the University of Washington, over 3.7 million people visited the fair. But the A-Y-P Exposition was not Seattle's only big event that summer: the National American Woman Suffrage Association held its forty-first annual convention there in July—a deliberate choice to take advantage of the expected crowds. To garner publicity, suffragists planned a dramatic entrance into the city. A special Northern Pacific train set out from Chicago and picked up supporters on the way to Spokane, where they were treated to a tour of the city and a banquet. Their ranks swollen by Spokane supporters, the suffragists continued westward, delivering whistle-stop speeches to crowds in Pasco, Yakima, and Tacoma. By the time the train pulled into Seattle's King Street Station, it boasted more than 250 suffragists.

Once in Seattle, NAWSA conventioneers made good use of the connection to the Alaska-Yukon-Pacific Exposition, and vice versa. Fair managers offered free passes to speakers, officers, and delegates for Sunday, July 4, when Reverend Anna Howard Shaw was scheduled to address the crowd, and July 7, which was designated "Woman Suffrage Day." NAWSA staffed a suffrage booth on the fair grounds, handed out "Votes for Women" buttons and balloons, and even sponsored a dirigible towing a "Votes for Women" banner, all the while capitalizing on the crowds and free publicity. The strong suffrage presence at the fair built goodwill for the upcoming 1910 Washington state referendum.[3]

The convention was also conveniently scheduled to coincide with various other activities likely to draw suffragists to Seattle that summer, as the NAWSA monthly newsletter *Progress* suggested: "Among the many attractive side trips which may be taken, one of the most alluring is the ascent of Mount Rainier. The Mountaineers' Club will take its annual outing on this peak July 17 to August 7. The dunnage will go by pack train of horses, the Mountaineers on foot, through the flowery meadows, and in and out of the rugged canyons, the trip reaching its climax in an ascent to the summit by way of the White Glacier," all for the bargain price of forty dollars. Even though suffrage luminaries such as Alice Stone Blackwell, Charlotte Perkins Gilman, and Harriet Taylor Upton journeyed to Seattle to attend the annual convention, none of them signed up for the side trip, which was a shame, because they missed the chance to join Cora Smith Eaton planting her banner on the summit.[4]

The ascent was a first for the suffrage movement, but it was also part of a long, proud tradition of women climbing. Inspired by pioneers such as Lucy Walker and Meta Brevoort, who first climbed the Matterhorn in 1871, women took to the mountains, both in Europe and the United States. The Appalachian Mountain Club was founded in Boston in 1876, and soon afterward, it admitted women to membership. "In these days of advocacy of female suffrage and woman's rights," said an early member with just a whiff of condescension, "it needs hardly to be stated that American ladies can accomplish nearly everything which is possible to their sturdier brethren." On the West Coast, groups such as the Mazamas, based in Portland, and the Mountaineers, founded in Seattle in 1906, welcomed women from the start; over half of the founding members of the Mountaineers were female, including four physicians. (By contrast, the Explorer's Club in New York did not admit its first female members until 1981.) With challenging mountain ranges in close proximity to major urban areas, the Pacific Northwest quickly became "a cradle of mountaineering activity."[5]

Besides lingering prejudice and outright sexism, women climbers faced the additional challenge of finding suitable gear. A Mountaineers flyer for its first annual outing to Mount Olympus in 1907 stated flatly, "all women of the party who expect to go on side trips or climb any of the peaks, must be prepared to wear bloomers or better still knickerbockers, as on all these trips no skirts will be allowed." The bicycle craze of the 1890s had set a precedent for women to discard heavy Victorian outfits in favor of clothing that actually allowed physical movement, and women climbers showed no qualms about setting off for the mountains sans corsets or skirts. When Cora Eaton hiked in Yellowstone in 1902, she wore corduroy jodhpurs, a gingham shirt, and a jaunty straw hat.[6]

Eaton's 1909 suffrage feat was part of the Mountaineers' annual summer outing, on which sixty-eight climbers (gender breakdown unknown, but probably close to equal) reached the summit of Mount Rainer. In those days, climbers hiked in large parties and expected to spend a significant amount of time on the mountain. The large group left Seattle by train on July seventeenth and planned to be gone for three weeks, with their gear and supplies transported by horse-drawn wagons and pack trains. After hiking eleven miles up the Carbon River to their first camp, "in drizzling rain camp was made, and tents erected to protect everyone, and in spite of the discomforts of wet garments it was a happy party that gathered around the campfire." Over the next few days they established a base camp at Moraine Park, interspersed with "try-out trips . . . to see the surrounding country with the greatest possible dispatch and to drill members of the party and test their mettle." Their final high camp was on Ruth Mountain at 9,500 feet.[7]

On the morning of July 30, a clear but windy day, seven different summit teams set out. The plan was to plant two pennants on the summit—a large one in honor of the Alaska-Yukon-Pacific Exposition and the smaller "Votes for Women" that Eaton carried. Unfortunately, the wind was too strong, and the climbers were forced to leave the pennants in a nearby crater. If Cora Eaton had planted the pennant, taken a picture, and then brought back either the pennant or a photograph documenting its proud deployment, that image would certainly have been included in this book. In this case, the key artifact was literally lost to history, a reminder of the serendipity that allows some objects to survive and others to disappear forever.

Women climbers were often quite independent characters, accustomed to breaking down barriers and not being held back by prejudice or custom, and that description applied to Cora Smith Eaton. Born in 1867, she attended the newly established University of North Dakota, where she became interested in suffrage, from 1884 to 1889. After graduating from the Boston University School of Medicine in 1892 and marrying Dr. Robert A. Eaton, she returned to Grand Forks, North Dakota, where she was the first woman licensed to practice medicine in the state. She also served as president of the Grand Forks Equal Suffrage Association.[8]

In 1896, Cora Smith Eaton relocated her medical practice to Seattle. Soon she was involved in both the local suffrage movement and local mountaineering. In 1907, she became the first woman to climb the 7,780-foot East Peak of Mount Olympus; eventually she climbed all six of Washington's major peaks. When Eaton climbed Glacier Peak, she wrote "Votes for Women" after her name in the register on top. In July of 1909, when she planted the "Votes for Women" flag on top of Mount Rainier, she was serving as the treasurer of the Washington Equal Suffrage Association.

Given the turmoil roiling the local suffrage scene that summer, Eaton had probably welcomed the chance to escape to the mountains. When national suffrage leaders arrived in Seattle for the NAWSA convention in early July, the local newspapers were full of stories of a nasty battle between two wings of the Washington suffrage movement. Personality conflicts, regional rivalries between Seattle and Spokane, and clashes over strategy fueled the dispute, and Cora Smith Eaton was right in the thick of it.

Emma Smith Devoe, a talented suffrage organizer, had moved to Washington in 1905 and was elected president of the Washington Equal Suffrage Association the next year. Devoe proved an especially gifted fundraiser but a somewhat autocratic leader. Soon, certain suffragists grew tired of Devoe's controlling ways, her lack of executive skills, and her constant need to be the center of attention. (Cora Eaton, her trusted lieutenant, didn't have any problems with that, reassuring Devoe, you "are the State general, or 'boss.' You speak and I obey.") There were also grumblings about Devoe's conflicted loyalties as a "professional suffragist" (she collected a stipend from NAWSA) who followed the money "from state to state." In 1909, a challenge to her leadership came from the eastern part of the state in the person of May Arkwright Hutton, a flamboyant, thrice-married suffragist whose husband had made a fortune in Idaho mining silver.[9]

Mainly, the turmoil came down to a matter of political style. Whereas Devoe carefully cultivated the state's politicians with what she considered ladylike behavior, Hutton had no qualms about aggressively confronting them to present her demands. As the suffrage bill worked its way through the legislature, Devoe was appalled by Hutton's pushy behavior, and she later claimed that her "aggressiveness was such that it nearly lost us our success in the state." Cora Smith Eaton totally agreed with this negative view of Hutton, and even suggested to Carrie Chapman Catt later that Hutton had tried to buy votes at $250 a shot. The bill authorizing a referendum for November 1910 did pass, but Devoe and Eaton were determined to sideline Hutton—and they were prepared to play hard ball to do it.[10]

The matter came to a head at the annual Washington Equal Suffrage Association convention in June. Hutton forwarded membership dues from a large number of new recruits, primarily from the Spokane area, but Eaton, then the treasurer, saw it as a blatant attempt to stack the upcoming election and refused to accept the money. She informed Hutton that she was no longer eligible for membership "because of your habitual use of profane and obscene language and of your record in Idaho as shown by pictures and other evidence placed in my hands by persons who are familiar with your former life and reputation," a reference to Hutton's supposed connections to a brothel and other illegal activities, a version of Western history which respectable suffragists hoped to leave behind. Even though Eaton insisted to Carrie Chapman Catt that "every word of it was true, and capable of proof," an independent investigator was unable to corroborate the charges.[11]

Nevertheless, Eaton threatened Hutton in language that sounded like a crude blackmail attempt: "The publicity of the evidence I hold against you depends entirely on yourself. These matters will not be made public by me unless you make further claim to membership." Privately, Eaton was even more direct about the need to silence Hutton, deploying vivid medical imagery to make her point: "It was a terribly hard thing to do, but . . . it was a surgical operation—an amputation, following the opening of a very foul abscess."[12]

Hutton refused to back down and defiantly showed up at the state convention with many of her supporters. When they were not seated, "pandemonium broke out." Eventually they walked out, and the remaining delegates re-elected Emma Smith Devoe to a fourth term.[13]

The matter was still far from settled. The insurgents appealed directly to the NAWSA executive board to overturn the election results. NAWSA leaders, looking ahead to the upcoming Washington referendum, were not pleased at the discord in the state organization, and they instructed Devoe to work out a compromise or risk losing her NAWSA salary. Taking the high road, Devoe claimed she had done nothing wrong and refused to apologize. NAWSA promptly fired Devoe, an embarrassing rebuke for the elected head of the local suffrage organization on the eve of hosting the national convention. Eaton was not singled out for censure for her role in the affair.

Despite this nasty internal dispute, just over a year later the voters in Washington approved the state woman suffrage referendum by a hefty two-to-one margin, an unprecedented victory at a time when referenda usually just squeaked by, if they passed at all. But when it came time to write the summary of the Washington State campaign for the final volume of the *History of Woman Suffrage*, all the chapter had to say about the contested events of 1909 was this: "The Political Equality League of Spokane, Mrs. May Arkwright Hutton, president, worked separately for fourteen months prior to the election, having been organized in July, 1909." Maybe that omission shouldn't come as too much of a surprise, since the chapter was written by none other than Cora Smith Eaton. Still, the incident is an important reminder of all the personality conflicts and local bickering that never made it into the *History of Woman Suffrage* and other official narratives of the suffrage struggle. Instead of harmonious unity towards a common goal, the real story on the ground was often much messier.[14]

The Washington state victory in 1910 proved a major turning point for the national woman suffrage campaign. It had been fourteen long years since Utah and Idaho had given women the vote, a period often referred to as "the doldrums." But that pejorative term does a disservice to the amount of suffrage organizing that occurred in individual states throughout that period—activity which laid the groundwork for the emergence of new techniques and leaders who would guide the suffrage movement towards victory in the following decade. In 1911, California voted in favor of woman suffrage; it was followed by Arizona, Kansas and Oregon in 1912, and Nevada and Montana in 1914. Suddenly, an awful lot of women were actually voting and politicians were forced to take notice. Western states played a critical role in these breakthroughs, first by successfully orchestrating state-by-state victories and then by showing the rest of the country what the political landscape looked like when women started to vote.

Cora Smith Eaton's suffrage career was not over yet. Widowed in the midst of the 1909 campaign, she married Judson King in 1912 and moved to Washington, DC, where she established a sanatorium in northwest Washington under her new name of Dr. Cora Smith Eaton King. In March 1913, she marched—or rather, rode horseback—in the Washington, DC suffrage parade, carrying the banner of the National Council of Women Voters (NCWV), an organization founded in 1911 to take advantage of women's combined political clout from the five western states where they were enfranchised. As the NCWV congressional chair, she and a delegation of western women voters met with President Woodrow Wilson in the spring of 1913 to press the suffrage cause. That summer, she welcomed another group of western women voters to her home in Hyattsville, Maryland, and together they drove in a caravan to the nation's capitol to present petitions to their elected representatives. Allying herself with the Congressional Union and later the National Woman's Party, she also served as Alice Paul's personal physician, and even smuggled notes in and out of the Occoquan Workhouse on several supervised visits with her patient, who had been imprisoned for picketing the White House and promptly undertook a hunger strike.[15]

There are no mountains to climb near Washington, DC, but there are certainly parallels between the woman suffrage campaign and mountaineering. Annie Peck Smith, one of the best-known climbers of her day and also an avid suffragist, linked women's conquests of mountains with the larger struggle for women's emancipation: "We should be free to do whatever we think we are qualified for." When the president of the Joan of Arc Suffrage League of New York asked Smith to represent the club on future climbing expeditions, she readily agreed. In 1911, two years after Cora Smith Eaton's triumphant ascent of Mount Rainier, Annie Peck Smith planted a "Votes for Women" banner on the summit of the second highest mountain in Peru, the twenty-one-thousand-foot Nevado Corpuna. She was then sixty-five years old and still going strong.[16]

Annie Peck Smith later reflected on the satisfaction she derived from her mountaineering feats: "The chief joy is the varied and perfect exercise, in the midst of noble scenery and exhilarating atmosphere, for the attainment of an object, the conquest of the mountain. The peak utters a challenge. The climber responds by saying to himself, I can and I will conquer it."[17] Change "himself" to "herself," and that's not a bad description of what it took to win the vote. When Cora Smith Eaton King celebrated cresting the peak of the battle for woman suffrage in August 1920, she likely remembered the proud moment eleven years earlier when she planted her "Votes for Women" pennant on top of Mount Rainier.

Official program of the Woman Suffrage Procession, Washington, DC, March 3, 1913. *Courtesy of Library of Congress, LC-USZ62-20185.*

CHAPTER FOURTEEN

Hazel MacKaye and the "Allegory" of Woman Suffrage

WHAT'S A PARADE without a souvenir program? When Alice Paul took the lead in organizing what she called "a procession of our own" to coincide with President Woodrow Wilson's March 1913 inauguration, she underscored her grand aspirations by commissioning an elaborate twenty-page program clearly meant to be saved if not treasured by participants and spectators alike. Paul planned the entire event in just nine weeks, which might explain why she didn't have time to find a female artist to do the cover art. Instead, she turned to a twenty-four-year old Washington, DC illustrator named Benjamin Moran Dale.

The full-color cover image was striking. Whether or not Paul gave the artist specific suggestions, he gravitated towards themes that were often featured in suffrage propaganda. The palette, for example, featured purple and gold, colors already associated with the suffrage cause. The central figure was an elaborately attired woman suggestive of a medieval knight—or perhaps Joan of Arc—astride a horse also decked out with medieval cloth barding. As in numerous pieces of suffrage literature, the figure was portrayed as a herald with a bugle, spreading the word with a "Votes for Women" banner. And she was broadcasting this message in a decidedly public space—the streets of the nation's seat of government, as shown by the visual prominence of the US Capitol.

The rest of the official program was black and white, a mixture of paid advertisements (Terminal Taxicabs was an especially loyal backer), photographs of suffrage leaders with short biographies, and narrative text on subjects such as "Why Women Want to Vote." But the program's main purpose was to describe the intricately plotted order of the "Progression," as the organizers referred to the marching procession, starting with the "Great Demand" float ("WE DEMAND AN AMENDMENT TO THE CONSTITUTION OF THE UNITED STATES ENFRANCHISING THE WOMEN OF THIS COUNTRY"), followed by seven carefully curated sections of marchers, ranging from representatives of countries where women already voted to wage-earning and professional women grouped by occupation (and dressed accordingly), state delegations, and a separate section for male suffragists. There was no mention of the segregated section for African American marchers—presumably this was put into effect as the parade assembled. The suffrage parade also featured twenty floats, four mounted cavalry brigades and three bands. The event culminated with Hazel MacKaye's suffrage pageant *Allegory*, which was staged on the steps of the Treasury Building.

The official program anticipated a dignified and orderly procession. In contrast, the actual parade was marred by an unruly crowd and a totally inadequate police presence. Yet the marchers persisted, bravely claiming the streets of the nation's capital to press Congress and the new president for the vote.

Hedwig Reicher cut an imposing figure as Columbia on the steps of the Treasury Building. Visible behind her are members of *Allegory*'s supporting cast. While Hazel MacKaye's production featured approximately one hundred participants, some pageants had casts that numbered in the thousands. *Courtesy of Bain Collection, Prints and Photographs Division, Library of Congress, LC-B2-2501-14.*

HAZEL MACKAYE worked out the logistics carefully in advance, setting up a telephone relay to coordinate her suffrage tableau with the progress of the larger parade. At 3:00 p.m. on March 3, 1913, almost ten thousand marchers would leave their gathering spot at the Peace Monument near Capitol Hill and begin the fifteen-block procession down Pennsylvania Avenue. At precisely that same moment, her suffrage pageant *Allegory* would begin to unfold on the marble steps of the Treasury Building—the first time, thanks to Alice Paul's persistent lobbying, that women had secured permission to use a federal building for such a purpose. Both events were part of the suffragists' attempt to create in effect a counter-inauguration to Woodrow Wilson's official investiture the next day—to claim public space in the nation's capital in support of women's demand for the vote at a time of presidential transition.

At first things unfolded as planned. To the musical accompaniment of the "Star-Spangled Banner," the figure of Columbia—decked out in breast-plate and helmet and cloaked in a blue velvet cape with a red and white lining to symbolize the American nation—majestically emerged from between the classical columns framing the entrance to the Treasury Building and proceeded slowly to a flat, plaza-like area where the action was to take place. In pantomime, she used her eagle-topped scepter to salute the grandstand audience, who had paid five dollars per seat for admission to the spectacle, as well as the crowd of curious bystanders. MacKaye remembered that both groups greeted the start of the pageant "with a veritable Niagara of applause."[1]

Then, to musical accompaniment ranging from Verdi to Wagner to Mendelsohn, Columbia began to summon her court, who were gathered out of sight inside the main entrance to the building at the top of the stairs. First came Justice with her entourage, then Charity, accompanied by a girl and boy (the only male in the cast) scattering rose petals. Liberty, portrayed by the event's choreographer, Florence Fleming Noyes, leapt and skipped down the Treasury stairs "with great, free limbed steps" in a low-necked crimson gown. Next came Peace, who released a white dove in the direction of the White House, followed by Plenty, who descended to the plaza with attendants decked out with olive branches and cornucopias of fruit. The final character was Hope, accompanied by fifty young girls dressed in bright colors and clutching balloons. Led by the commanding figure of Columbia—the event's "visual crux . . . allegory-turned-suffragist"—the group of approximately one hundred actors, now assembled together in a tableau on the

Treasury steps, stood silently as they awaited the procession of marchers, whose impending arrival was to be announced by heralds of trumpets.[2]

No trumpets sang out, MacKaye remembered, only "a most deadly pause." The spectators craned their necks up Pennsylvania Avenue, but there was no sign of the procession. The pageant director grabbed the nearest telephone and learned that unruly crowds had disrupted the suffrage parade and the police had been unable—or unwilling—to intercede. The cavalry was on its way, but it was unclear how long it would take to re-establish order. In the meantime, the tableau of characters stood frozen on the Treasury steps.[3]

MacKaye acted quickly, sending out a messenger (presumably in costume) to convey to Columbia what had happened. Calmly assessing the situation, Hedwig Reicher, the experienced German-born actress who played the lead role, signaled the bandmaster to play "America" while she explained to the cast what had transpired. "Whereupon, as though they were veteran players, the entire cast wheeled about and, group by group, mounted the steps again as though the whole thing had been rehearsed." Once safely inside the Treasury Building, they warmed up (many were dressed in loose-flowing gowns and sandals on a cool March day) and waited.[4]

When word came that the march was finally on the move again, MacKaye sent the groups of actors out a second time. Columbia, Justice, Charity, Liberty, Peace, Plenty, Hope and their colorful entourages re-enacted the pageant, and then, this time with perfect timing, the allegorical figures finished their final tableau just as Inez Milholland, widely credited as "the most beautiful suffragette," rode by on her white horse at the front of the procession. "With a friendly lilt of her head, she acknowledged the acclaim and then turned to raise her hand in solemn greeting to Columbia and her assembled court who stood in silent review. Then she passed on and the radiant young crusader was swallowed up in the surging crowds beyond."[5]

After the masses of suffragists had marched past the tableau on the Treasury steps, the actors fell in line at the end of the procession and proceeded to the planned meeting, featuring Anna Howard Shaw, Carrie Chapman Catt, and Helen Keller, at Continental Hall. But Hazel MacKaye rushed off to catch a train to Chicago, where she was directing another pageant. As she later observed, "Thus ended one of the most eventful days in my career as well as a day fraught with significance in the history of woman suffrage."[6]

Hazel MacKaye was absolutely right about the importance of this event. In part because of the rowdiness of the crowd and the inability of the Washington police to maintain control, the suffrage parade received an enormous amount of press coverage, especially when President Woodrow Wilson's inaugural parade went off without a hitch the following day. The sheer visual impact of thousands of suffragists marching down Pennsylvania Avenue won new converts to the cause, and MacKaye's *Allegory* was singled out for special praise. The *Washington Herald* called it "one of the most beautiful spectacles ever seen on the stage or in the open in Washington," while the *New York Times* deemed it "one of the most impressively beautiful spectacles ever staged in the country." The *Woman's Journal* offered an especially positive endorsement: "To those who feared that equal suffrage would make women less womanly, to those who feared that in becoming politically free woman will become coarse and mannish looking, to those who fear the loss of beauty and grace, art and poetry, with the advent of universal suffrage, the pageant offered the final word, the most convincing argument that human ingenuity can devise."[7]

The coordination of *Allegory*'s climax with the suffrage parade's passing in review confirms that the pageant was conceived as an integral part of the Progression. The official program described the link in this way: "The story told in the Progression shows what woman is striving to achieve, as well as what she has so far attained. The Allegory, on the other hand, illustrates those ideas towards which both men and women have been struggling through the ages and toward which, in cooperation and equality, they will continue to strive."[8]

Open-air suffrage parades and pageants were both still quite unusual in 1913. The pageant movement in the United States dates to 1905, when an outdoor masque in honor of the sculptor Augustus St. Gaudens was held in Cornish, New Hampshire. Relying exclusively on amateur performers and often featuring huge casts, pageants prized participation and inclusion. The format, which usually offered six episodes with musical or dance interludes designed to "deliver wholesome and uplifting entertainment to the general public," proved especially adaptable to town histories and other historical commemorations. While most pageants consciously steered away from controversial topics, Hazel MacKaye took a different tack. If pageants were such a popular form of entertainment, she reasoned, why not use them as a vehicle for social change? Specifically, why not stage pageants as a creative way to build support for a movement like woman suffrage? As MacKaye wrote to a supporter, "A pageant is the most potent means of welding the women themselves together as well as poignantly to set the question of suffrage before the voters."[9]

Hazel MacKaye came from a family with deep roots in theatrical production. Her mother, Mary Medbery, was a writer and actress; her father, Steele MacKaye, was a playwright best known for *Hazel*

Kirke (1880), reputed to be the most widely performed play of its time after *Uncle Tom's Cabin*. The play provided a name for their daughter, who was also born in 1880. Her older brother Percy, who wrote the prologue to the 1905 St. Gaudens production, became a leading pageant director; he was especially well known for staging a pageant featuring 7,500 actors in honor of St. Louis's 150th anniversary in 1914 and for his series *Caliban, by the Yellow Sands*, staged in 1916 for the tercentenary of Shakespeare's death.

Hazel started her career as an actor. After working on several of her brother's productions, she switched to directing pageants on her own. When she masterminded *Allegory*, she was thirty-two years old and "not averse to the wonder I caused among the people to see a woman in the position of stage manager." Showing the male professional stagehands that "I knew my business," she confessed, caused her "pleasurable pride." Looking back, she felt that this experience helped to strengthen her already well-established feminist tendencies and proved "that a stage manager's job had nothing to do with sex—it was whether or not an individual was fitted for the task."[10]

MacKaye had quite a capacious approach to pageantry, which she laid out in a 1914 article for *The Suffragist*: "I can only state my firm belief that a pageant has more power to convince people of the truth of our cause than any other means. A pageant is a forceful and vivid form of drama. It combines the medium of the spoken word, the dance, pantomime, stirring music, masses of people in striking costumes, strong contrasts in situation, in its appeal." That very fluidity of form made it especially appealing for theatrical professionals, but MacKaye realized pageants were also very effective at reaching audiences: "When our emotions are swayed, our very innermost being is touched. The light comes to us in a single flash, instead of by dim and cautious flickerings."[11]

MacKaye made special note of what the pageant experience meant for participants. Pageants subsumed the individual to the larger whole, encouraging a "remarkable esprit de corps," which according to MacKaye "welds a heterogeneous mass of participants from every class and creed into an army disciplined to withstand the onslaughts of any disaster." Taking part in a performance—in effect fulfilling the dream of generations of would-be thespians—was truly thrilling: "To enter to a blaze of trumpets in a sweeping costume with a banner or a wand, or a star upon one's brow, whether it be down lofty steps or through winding paths of greensward, makes the commonplace days of one's ordinary life seem drear and dry, indeed." Performers were just as touched as audiences, according to MacKaye. "Not one of those women or girls who participated in the pageant could ever again feel indifference towards the cause of Equal Rights."[12]

Like many others involved in the pageant movement, MacKaye emphasized the underlying aesthetics. "I stress the beauty of the ceremony because I have an intense belief in the importance of beauty to the health of the world," she wrote. But she didn't want to merely present a vision that imitated neo-classical forms without linking them to modern themes: "If pageantry is to endure and live we shall have to use pageantry—not alone as a review of the past—but also to interpret the problems of the present and our hopes for the future." Her brother Percy captured this sense of inhabiting parallel worlds when he described the experience of seeing his sister's *Allegory* performed: "gazing up at the double background of mysterious pillars—before them the sun-blazed plaza and steps, a-flutter with rose and iris and pale gold—one sank, under the spell of music, into a day dream of old Athens, only to thrillingly awake at the thought: 'No. This is to-day, 1913,

America—our own living age and festival! This is Washington—the Athens of tomorrow.'"[13]

Unfortunately, this "Athens of tomorrow" was totally white. Whether intentionally or not, *Allegory*'s depiction of female beauty served to reinforce prevailing standards of race and class—what scholars call "performing whiteness"—in its presentation of elite white women as the caretakers and upholders of culture. There was no room on the Treasury steps for women of color, and if suffrage leaders had had their way, there would have been no room for them in the suffrage procession either, unless they marched segregated at the back. The black suffragist Ida Wells-Barnett of Chicago's Alpha Suffrage Club had made it clear what she thought of that capitulation to southern suffragists when she joined the Illinois delegation midway through the parade. Maybe she should have walked on to the "Allegory" set as well.[14]

After *Allegory*, Hazel MacKaye mounted three more suffrage-themed pageants. The first, *Six Periods of American Life: Past—Present—Future*, sometimes referred to as *The American Woman*, was staged in New York City for the Men's League for Woman Suffrage in collaboration with the Equal Franchise Society. Presented at a ball held April 17, 1914 at the Seventy-first Regiment Armory in front of several thousand guests, the pageant drew on the talents of more than five hundred participants, male and female—more than five times the scale of *Allegory*. Alas, the *New York Times* review only had eyes for the women, headlining its article about the event "Real Beauty Show in League Pageant; Handsomest of Their Sex Chosen for Suffrage Allegorical Scene."[15]

MacKaye's narrative in this pageant was much more hard-hitting and antagonistic to men than the generalities that floated *Allegory*. Perhaps she thought the supporters of the Men's League would be more open to such an interpretation than the general public. In what was basically a parody of the laudatory tone of most town histories, she reframed the historical narrative to speak out boldly against sexism (although that word had not yet been coined) from colonial times to the present and clearly laid the blame for women being "powerless and ignored" at the feet of men. While her portrayal of recently emancipated male slaves was positive, her staging reinforced reigning racist tropes regarding Native Americans.[16]

The pageant unfolded in six parts, accompanied by music composed by Bertha Remick. The first scene, "The Indians—Before the Coming of the White Man," portrayed Native American men lazing about while their women did all the work. The next episode blamed male Puritan leaders for not listening when a suspected witch's female friends vouched for her innocence. A third portrayed a colonial-era scene of men and women working productively together, until only the men were called by the town crier to attend the town meeting. A fourth, set immediately after the Civil War, featured Susan B. Anthony unsuccessfully arguing that women should be enfranchised alongside black men.

Then it was to "The Present—Side by Side." Here MacKaye employed the favorite tactic of featuring a well-known personage—in this case New York City suffrage leader Harriet Burton Laidlaw— as an onstage actor. In another insider's wink, Laidlaw's husband James also had a role in the tableau. This scene argued that despite women's working alongside men in "all occupations, trades, and professions," the law still prevented women from passing through the "portals of state." After a short, dream-like interlude, the pageant concluded in "The Future," with the figures of Man and Woman (as embodied by Spencer Miller and Inez Milholland) now truly equal, celebrated by the Spirit of Triumph in a dance choreographed by

Florence Fleming Noyes from *Allegory*, as well as by the choruses of Future Men and Future Women. Despite tackling patriarchy head on, the pageant seems to have been well received, although it was never performed again.[17]

MacKaye's third suffrage pageant was decidedly more inspirational in tone. In yet another innovative gesture, she focused on a single individual, Susan B. Anthony. The pageant presented her life in ten biographical scenes and five symbolic tableaux, which were based on material drawn from the *History of Woman Suffrage*. The performance, which netted $4,000 for Alice Paul's Congressional Union and was timed to the convening of the sixty-fourth Congress in Washington in 1915, featured four hundred actors, a chorus of sixty, and a twenty-five-piece orchestra. The play's emotional climax was Anthony's disruption of the celebrations surrounding the US Centennial in Philadelphia on July 4, 1876, which MacKaye called "the first militant act ever committed in the cause of Votes for Women." Functioning both as entertainment and suffrage advocacy, this pageant proved MacKaye's most popular and was performed by suffrage groups and amateur theatrical organizations around the country. She proudly considered it her most important contribution to the suffrage cause.[18]

Over the next few years, MacKaye produced pageants for groups such as Vassar College, the Women's Peace Party, the YWCA, and a soap manufacturing company in Buffalo. After the Nineteenth Amendment was ratified, she continued her activism in the fight for equal rights. When the National Woman's Party looked to stage an extravaganza in 1923 to launch its campaign for the Equal Rights Amendment and to celebrate the seventy-fifth anniversary of the Seneca Falls declaration, she eagerly accepted the commission.

MacKaye had a different agenda for this final feminist pageant. Now that suffrage had been won, she could be less didactic and more celebratory. Her *Equal Rights Pageant* recruited more than a thousand women to portray the history of the women's rights movement. Usually pageants ended with a grand finale, but MacKaye inverted the practice and opened with one: a huge procession of women carrying banners in the colors of the National Woman's Party. Another unusual touch was the illuminated barges on nearby Seneca Lake that ferried brightly dressed Banner Bearers to the pageant's outdoor set. The move that best wedded MacKaye's theatrical sense to her commitment to women's history was the giant sign that flashed on, like an oversize roadside advertisement, spelling out "Declaration of Principles"—the 1848 Seneca Falls manifesto—in electric lights, symbolically bringing suffrage history into the modern age.[19]

The performance was such a hit that it was restaged two months later for twenty thousand people in the Garden of the Gods near Colorado Springs, and then, retitled *Forward into Light*, at the annual National Woman's Party conference in Westport-on-Lake Champlain in New York State. This pageant was the last spectacle the women's movement mounted until feminism's revival in the 1960s and 1970s. By 1923, the pageant movement had basically run its course, falling prey to the competition of far more exciting forms of mass entertainment, such as movies, newsreels, Victrola records, and radio, which were readily available nationwide by the 1920s, especially in urban areas. This new popular culture made extravaganzas like pageants seem increasingly quaint and outdated.

Hazel MacKaye considered herself one of the "old guard" of the National Woman's Party, having been present at the very first meeting in Washington in the winter of 1911–1912, which led to the formation of the Congressional Union under Alice Paul's char-ismatic leadership. Like so many others, she had not set out to become a suffragist, let alone a suffrage pageant-maker, but when suffragists took to the streets in 1913 to stage their response to Woodrow Wilson's inauguration, she found herself standing up to male authority in a very public way. According to MacKaye, "that procession and allegory in their novelty marked a new era in the political campaigning of women," confirming her insight about the importance of spectacle to the suffrage cause.[20]

CHAPTER FIFTEEN

"Bread and Roses" and Votes for Women Too

ACCORDING to the Massachusetts suffragist Florence Luscomb, "no state was ever carried for suffrage until it was sown ankle deep in leaflets." These fliers—"brief, snappy arguments in handbill form on the cheapest, gay newsprint"—were distributed by the hundreds of thousands to the so-called "man on the street," who held the fate of woman suffrage in his hands. The fact that so many male voters were immigrants—in 1910, approximately 15 percent of the American population was foreign-born—called for some creative campaign material to drive the point home.[1]

Around 1915, NAWSA began to circulate suffrage fliers in a variety of foreign languages, including German, Polish, Italian, Yiddish, and French. Since suffrage speakers fluent in foreign languages were in short supply, these fliers were a novel and efficient way to reach this untapped constituency. The foreign-language fliers usually employed the same typeface and layout as their English language counterparts; in fact, they were such literal facsimiles that it was possible to move back and forth between the two using the English version as a crib sheet and vice versa.

209

No matter what language they were in, the fliers explained the reasons women should be enfranchised in simple, direct, and compelling terms. Why do women want to vote? "*Frauen sind Bürger und wollen ihre Bürgerpflicht erfüllen*" (Women are citizens and wish to do their civic duty). This sentiment was widely shared among "*arbeitende frauen*" (working women), "*hausfrauen*" (housewives), "*mütter*" (mothers), and "*lehrer*" (teachers). "*Gerechtigkeit*" (justice) and "*Gleichheit*" (equality) support their demands.

It turns out there are lots of ways to say votes for women: "*Das Stimmrecht für Frauen!*" "*Voti per le Donne!*" "*Le Suffrage Pour Les Femmes!*" "*Votos par alas Mujeres!*" "*Glos Dla Kobiet!*" Learning how to reach out to these constituencies—both male voters and female family members who could use these arguments to convert them—broadened the suffrage movement and contributed to its ultimate success.

ON MARCH 25, 1911, a fire broke out at the Triangle Shirtwaist Company factory off Washington Square in Greenwich Village. The employers had locked the doors and blocked the emergency exits, supposedly to keep the workforce from leaving early, but now they were trapped. Because of that callous decision, 146 workers (primarily young women, but also including twenty-three men) lost their lives, many having jumped from the upper floors to escape the flames. Two years earlier, the labor organizer Rose Schneiderman had led many of those same workers on strike as part of the Uprising of the Twenty Thousand that swept through the sweatshops on the Lower East Side. The strikers won many of their demands, but

Gerechtigkeit   **Gleichheit**

Warum die Frauen stimmen wollen:

Frauen sind Bürger

und wollen ihre Bürgerpflicht erfüllen

Arbeitende Frauen brauchen den Stimmzettel, um die Arbeitsverhältnisse, unter denen sie beschäftigt sind, zu reguliren.

Die **Männer** wissen ganz gut, daß sie selbst ohne den Stimmzettel schutzlos wären.

Hausfrauen brauchen den Stimmzettel, um die sanitären Zustände zu reguliren, unter welchen sie und ihre Familien zu leben gezwungen sind.

Glauben die **Männer,** daß sie in ihren resp. Distrikten Verbesserungen erlangen können, wenn sie nicht die richtigen Vertreter erwählen?

Mütter brauchen das Stimmrecht, um die moralische Umgebung, unter welcher ihre Kinder aufwachsen, zu reguliren.

Glauben die **Männer,** daß sie verdammenswerthe Zustände, welche ihre Kinder bedrohen, ändern können, ohne daß sie Gelegenheit haben, die Beamten der Gemeinde zu wählen.

Lehrer brauchen den Stimmzettel zur Erlangung gerechter Saläre, und um die Leitung der Schulen zu beeinflussen.

Glauben die **Männer,** daß sie bessere Schulverhältnisse schaffen können, ohne für den Mayor zu stimmen, welcher die Schul-Behörde ernennt.

Geschäftsfrauen brauchen den Stimmzettel, um sich Bewegungsfreiheit in geschäftlichen Unternehmungen zu sichern.

Glauben denn **Geschäftsmänner,** daß sie sich gegen schädliche Gesetzgebung ohne den Stimmzettel schützen können?

Steuern zahlende Frauen brauchen den Stimmzettel, um ihr Grundeigenthum zu schützen.

Wissen die **Männer** nicht, daß „Besteuerung ohne Volksvertretung" Tyrannei ist.

Alle Frauen brauchen den Stimmzettel, weil sie in gleichem Maaße wie die Männer ein Interesse daran haben, ob die Regierung gut oder schlecht ist, und weil sie in gleichem Maaße für bürgerliche Tugend verantwortlich sind.

Alle Männer brauchen die Hilfe der Frauen am Stimmkasten, um eine bessere und gerechtere Regierung aufzubauen und

Frauen brauchen **Männer,** welche ihnen helfen, das Recht zu erlangen, ihre Bürgerpflichten zu erfüllen.

National American Woman Suffrage Association
Headquarters: 505 FIFTH AVENUE, NEW YORK

Foreign language flier, National American Woman Suffrage Association. *Courtesy of Schlesinger Library, Radcliffe Institute, Harvard University.*

the Triangle Shirtwaist Company was one of the shops that held out. If its owners had agreed to the strikers' demands for a half-day on Saturday, there would have been no workers inside when the fire broke out that fateful afternoon.

Rose Schneiderman lost several friends in the conflagration, but she hardly needed a personal connection to fuel her outrage. At a mass meeting the wealthy socialite Anne Morgan organized to demand stronger laws protecting the health and safety of New York garment workers, Schneiderman's response was impassioned. Only ninety pounds and four and a half feet tall, with fiery red hair and the rhetoric to match, Scheiderman quickly shushed the restive audience at the Metropolitan Opera House. "I would be a traitor to these poor burned bodies if I came here to talk good fellowship," she told the huge crowd. "This is not the first time girls have been burned alive in the city. Every week I must learn of the untimely death of one of my sister workers. Every year thousands of us are maimed. The life of men and women is so cheap and property is so sacred. There are so many of us for one job it matters little if 143 of us burned to death." Then she drew this powerful conclusion: "I can't talk fellowship to you who are gathered here. Too much blood has been spilled. I know from my own experience it is up to the working people to save themselves. The only way they can save themselves is by a strong working-class movement."[2]

Too often the images of the suffrage movement are of elite, white, native-born women, but that is an incomplete view. Working-class women played active and vibrant roles in the movement, especially in its last decade. These suffragists, coming out of the trade union movement and committed to organizing women into unions alongside men, were street-smart and politically savvy. They helped to revitalize the suffrage movement in its final years, and they contributed a broader theoretical perspective by arguing that class solidarity must always be prominent alongside gender. As experts on their own lives, they sought the vote as a critical tool to increase their power vis-à-vis employers, the state, and, not incidentally, middle-class female allies. Working women insisted they should have a say in what happened to them. It was literally that simple.

Rose Schneiderman had traveled a long way to get to the stage of the Metropolitan Opera House. She was born to an Orthodox Jewish family in the small village of Saven, in Russian Poland, in 1882. Her father was a tailor and her mother was a skilled seamstress, who made sure that her oldest daughter had access both to public education and traditional Hebrew schooling. In 1890, the family migrated to New York City, settling on the Lower East Side. Although it was only a few miles from the Schneiderman's tenement to the uptown enclave of successfully assimilated Jews like Maud Nathan and Annie Nathan Meyer, they lived in separate worlds. Two years after the family immigrated, her father died, leaving her mother pregnant with their fourth child. She tried to support the family by taking in boarders and doing piecework sewing, but for a time, the three older children lived at a Jewish orphanage. When the family reunited, Mrs. Schneiderman went back to work, and young Rose took over running the household.[3]

Rose Schneiderman first entered the paid labor force at the age of thirteen, working as much as seventy hours as a department store cash girl for the paltry wage of just two dollars a week. When she turned sixteen, she switched to industrial work, which was lower status but paid somewhat higher wages. Settling into the cap-making industry, she discovered not only the camaraderie of the shop floor but also the exploitation that workers, especially working women, faced at the hands of their male employers. In 1903, she and two other women organized the first female local of the Hat and Cap Maker's Union. Two years later, she emerged as a leader during a successful thirteen-week strike in which the workers resisted employers' attempts to introduce an open shop (that is, a non-union factory). For the rest of her life, she was involved in broader questions of trade unionism and working women, primarily through the International Ladies' Garment Workers Union (ILGWU) and the Women's Trade Union League (WTUL).

The Women's Trade Union League, founded in 1903, brought together working-class activists and middle- and upper-class reformers in a single organization devoted to unionizing working women and securing labor legislation to improve their lives both on and off the job. Margaret Dreier Robins, the president of the New York branch, recruited Schneiderman to the organization in 1905. She was dubious at first, fearing she would just be a token, but Robins convinced her that this was a unique opportunity to participate in a true cross-class coalition. By then, Schneiderman had grown weary of male union leaders' total lack of interest in organizing women in the trades. Hoping that this new organization offered a different way to work for social change, she threw her lot in with the women reformers, an association she maintained for the rest of her professional life.

Being a young, working-class woman in an organization where she was expected to interact with older, middle- and upper-class allies was challenging. For one thing, unlike elite women who could volunteer their time, Schneiderman needed a salary to live on. The NYWTUL put her on the payroll, her salary made possible by contributions from wealthy women; no doubt there were times she had to tone down her outspoken socialism in order not to offend her wealthy benefactors. Other working-class activists got caught in this trap as well. The Irish shirtmaker Leonora O'Reilly, also a dedicated socialist, was a paid organizer for the WTUL until she had a falling out with Margaret Dreier Robins and quit; she later returned, but she never totally overcame her suspicions. This divide between the majority of reformers, who could contribute their time and energy to the cause, and the minority that needed to earn a living often complicated the union's internal organizational dynamics. As a general rule, the leadership of the woman suffrage movement was almost exclusively in the hands of those who could afford to forego a salary.[4]

Schneiderman's suffrage activism began in 1907, when she joined the newly established Equality League of Self-Supporting Women, which Harriot Stanton Blatch had conceived as an independent organization to attract working-class women to the suffrage movement. In part because of her time in England (her husband was British), Blatch was probably the most class-conscious elite American suffragist. Like Alice Stone Blackwell, she boasted a proud suffrage patrimony but, in response to changing political and economic conditions, took her activism in new directions. Charlotte Perkins Gilman was another influence on the Equality League—and an early member. Building on Gilman's emphasis on the importance of work and economic independence for women's emancipation, the group welcomed "any woman who earns her own living, from a cook to a mining engineer." More than two hundred showed up for the first meeting.[5]

Schneiderman made her first public speech for suffrage at an April 1907 meeting at Cooper Union and quickly became the Equality League's most popular speaker. She was especially at home as an impromptu street speaker, drawing directly on her years of union organizing to spontaneously attract a crowd when a factory let out for the day or wherever strollers congregated in public parks and squares. Besides being a good way to reach working people, these impromptu meetings were basically free, and certainly much cheaper than hiring a hall and distributing fliers.[6]

In May 1908, the Equality League of Self-Supporting Women sponsored a trolley tour campaign between Syracuse and Albany to commemorate the sixtieth anniversary of the Seneca Falls Convention. The plan was to bring suffrage speakers to small towns in upstate New York using the inexpensive and convenient intercity trolley system. Harriot Stanton Blatch had already developed a close working relationship with Rose Schneiderman through the League, and she recruited her to join the tour.

In Poughkeepsie, one of the tour's last stops, Blatch and Schneiderman crossed paths with Inez Milholland, later known as the beautiful suffragist on a white horse, but in 1908 still a student at Vassar College. Milholland wanted to hold a suffrage rally on campus, but Vassar's conservative male president flatly forbade any such political gatherings. Undeterred, Milholland decided that if she couldn't hold the meeting on campus property, then she would hold it off campus in a public space. And what could be more convenient—and newsworthy—than holding it in the local cemetery?[7]

That was how, on a May afternoon, around two dozen brave Vassar students and a smattering of alumnae and spectators gathered under a banner beseeching, "Come, let us reason together," for one of the most stellar impromptu suffrage protests ever held. Blatch, herself a Vassar graduate (class of 1878), addressed the small crowd, as did the successful lawyer Helen Hoy (class of 1899). Next up was none other than Charlotte Perkins Gilman, whose *Women and Economics* was practically a Bible to that generation of college students. But the speaker who made the strongest impression on the students was Rose Schneiderman, "a very youthful, popular industrial worker, graduate of that University of Life down on the East Side of New York," as Blatch later described her. Only twenty-six years old, Schneiderman more than held her own with seasoned suffrage speakers twice her age.[8]

Schneiderman began to make a name for herself during the 1909–1910 garment workers' strike in New York. As the historian Annelise Orleck has argued, the Uprising of the Twenty Thousand represented "a moment of crystallization, the sign of a new integrated class and gender consciousness among US working women." By 1919, half of all women garment workers in the country belonged to labor unions. The strike was notable for the cross-class alliances it supported, with wealthy women—the so-called "Mink Brigade" of Alva Belmont, Anne Morgan, and others—marching on picket lines and raising money for bail and strike support, a harbinger of the roles wealthy women would play in the final stages of suffrage. During the strike, Schneiderman was all over the place—giving speeches, raising money, bailing out strikers, and forging strategy, all under the auspices of the NYWTUL.[9]

Schneiderman's strong sense of class solidarity undergirded much of her suffrage advocacy. As a self-supporting working woman, she was able to point out how far women's lives had already strayed from the domestic sphere. For example, she often poked fun at the idea that voting would somehow "unsex" women, especially in comparison to the rigors of industrial work. "Surely . . . women won't lose any more of their beauty and charm by putting a ballot in a ballot box once a year than they are likely to lose standing in foundries or laundries all year round." Or as she said on another occasion, "What does all this talk about becoming mannish signify? I wonder if it will add to my height when I get the vote. I might work for it harder if it did."[10]

So far, Rose Schneiderman's story—and by extension, those of other working-class suffrage activists such as Leonora O'Reilly, Clara Lemlich, and Pauline Newman—has mainly been a New York story, for good reason: between 1868 and 1908, over 70 percent of all Jewish immigrants stayed in New York, mainly settling and working on the Lower East Side. But in 1912, Rose took a leave of absence from the NYWTUL to campaign in Ohio for NAWSA, which had hired her to reach out to voters in urban and industrial regions who were crucial to the campaign's prospects. As usual, Schneiderman did not disappoint. An Ohio suffrage leader reported to national headquarters, "'we have had splendid speakers here before, but not one who impressed the people as she did. Strong men sat with tears rolling down their faces. Her pathos and earnestness held audiences spellbound." Still, Ohio voters decisively defeated the suffrage referendum.[11]

Soon Schneiderman was back in New York, which was gearing up for a massive referendum of its own in October 1915. This referendum was initially Harriot Stanton Blatch's idea, and she had spent several years in Albany laying the groundwork for the legislature to agree to put the question before the voters. Her argument was brilliantly simple—I'm not asking you to endorse suffrage, she told legislators, just throw your support behind a referendum to allow male voters to register their opinions. By now, Schneiderman was channeling her suffrage work through the Industrial Section of the New York Woman Suffrage Party, which she oversaw along with Leonora O'Reilly and Pauline Newman. (The earlier Wage Earners' League for Woman Suffrage, announced just three days before the Triangle Shirtwaist Fire, had come to naught.) Vast resources of money and energy poured into this 1915 campaign, and hopes were high. But once again, the referendum went down to defeat, a discouraging turn of events for New York suffragists.

At this point, a consensus was emerging that passing a national constitutional amendment to enfranchise women in one fell swoop was likely to be quicker than the state-by-state approach. Alice Paul had been single-mindedly pursuing this course since she took over the Congressional Committee in 1913, and Carrie Chapman Catt in effect endorsed this strategy with her "Winning Plan" of 1916, but with a significant asterisk. Mindful of the political clout that newly enfranchised women could wield, Catt realized that a victory in a state like New York, with its large congressional delegation and forty-five electoral votes, could play a significant role in the amendment's chances of passage in Congress. So New York suffragists decided to try again with a second referendum in 1917. Rose Schneiderman had spent most of the prior two years organizing for the International Ladies' Garment Workers Union, but in 1917, she was back in the suffrage fold for this one last battle. This time, the New York suffragists prevailed.[12]

Rose Schneiderman's suffrage story differs from other suffrage stories, and not simply because of class, although that is a major factor. Rather than a single thread or story line, her suffrage activism was part of a broad palette of social justice issues, mainly driven by her concern for empowering working-class women. She never had any illusions that suffrage would be a solution or panacea to their problems, but she was convinced that the vote would be an important tool to confront the class and gender discrimination that belied the American dream of freedom and equality for all. Since so much organizational energy and momentum was gravitating toward woman suffrage, Schneiderman deliberately allied herself with this progressive movement, but because of her class consciousness, her vision was always broader than just the vote—something that was not true for all suffragists, many of whom saw the vote solely through the lens of gender.

Like African American suffragists, Rose Schneiderman anticipated the modern intersectional approach which posits that oppressions cannot be singled out or ranked, because they operate in tandem with each other. She knew from her own experience that class could not be separated from gender, and that awareness informed her entire political career. The "race" leg of the intersectional triangle was less well-developed, even though she proved quite forward-looking in trying to organize African American laundry workers in the 1920s, a time when the labor movement totally ignored them. In the early twentieth century, however, especially on the Lower East Side of New York, where most of the working-class suffragists lived and worked, their world was predominantly white. The factories were white, the neighborhoods were white, and the suffrage organizations were white. That was the world that Rose Schneiderman inhabited, for better or worse.

Yet that world opened amazing opportunities to this young Russian immigrant. In 1919, she and Mary Anderson, later director of the US Women's Bureau, represented the Women's Trade Union League at the Paris Peace Conference. In the 1920s, Schneiderman and her partner Maud Schwarz played a key role in educating Franklin and Eleanor Roosevelt about the conditions of the female working class. When the Roosevelts went to Washington in 1933, Rose Schneiderman joined the advisory board of the National Recovery Administration, where she spent two of the most exciting and professionally satisfying years of her life. She remained a close friend of Eleanor Roosevelt's until the first lady's death in 1962.[13]

Rose Schneiderman once said, "The woman worker needs bread, but she needs roses, too." Bread stood for basic human rights, such as decent wages and hours, safe working conditions, and respect for labor. Roses meant friendship, education, leisure, and recreation— what she called "the spiritual side of a great cause that created fellowship." In Schneiderman's view, working women deserved both. In 1916, twenty-six years after her family arrived on Ellis Island, she took out citizenship papers in anticipation of women's enfranchisement. There could be no more fitting image of how American democracy and woman suffrage were fundamentally intertwined than Rose Schneiderman's becoming a new citizen and a new voter almost simultaneously.[14]

Nina Allender, "Come to Mother," cover of *The Suffragist*, March 31, 1917. *Courtesy of Schlesinger Library, Radcliffe Institute, Harvard University.*

CHAPTER SIXTEEN

Cartooning with a Feminist Twist

IN ITS FINAL DECADES, the suffrage movement was an intriguing mix of old and new. It drew on the energy of New Women, who took advantage of expanding opportunities for higher education, entry into the professions, and more egalitarian relationships with men to move confidently into many aspects of modern life. At the same time, it deliberately allied itself with notions of women's traditional roles as wives and mothers—conservative ideals that helped offset the often unsettling connotations of its political activism. Cora Smith Eaton's mountaineering exploits featured in a suffrage cookbook or Hazel MacKaye's suffrage spectacle drawing on classical tropes of virtuous (white) womanhood exemplify this dual thrust.

Another example is Nina Allender's "Come to Mother," an illustration created for the cover of the March 31, 1917 issue of *The Suffragist*, the official publication of the National Woman's Party. The cartoon spotlighted Jeannette Rankin, the first woman elected to Congress, who is clearly identified by a purse stamped "J. R." and "Montana," her home state. Even though Rankin never married or had children, she is portrayed as a kind and friendly mother reaching out to a young girl, who has "Susan B. Anthony

Amendment" embroidered on her skirt. Two well-dressed and attractive suffragists stand in the background, saying *sotto voce*, "That child needs a woman to look after her." Effectively coopting traditional female values of motherhood and maternal concern while hitching them to women's new political roles, the cartoon reinforces the ideology that women are different from men and thus will bring a fresh perspective to public life. As suffragists pitched their arguments to politicians and the general public, they were careful never to stray too far from prevailing gender norms.

"Political cartooning gives you a sense of power that nothing else does," Nina Allender told a *Christian Science Monitor* reporter the year the Nineteenth Amendment was ratified. For so long, women's rights activists and suffragists had been the butts of jokes and cartoons, with satirists lampooning their supposedly unnatural aspirations, mannish appearances, and frivolous mannerisms. Now the tables were turned. As female political cartoonists took up the pen for woman suffrage, they created positive images in service of the larger feminist cause. Nina Evans Allender, the official cartoonist of the National Woman's Party, was one of the most prolific.[1]

Political cartooning is by definition a pointed and aggressive act. A form of propaganda, it challenges or destabilizes the status quo in a single image, the message of which must be instantly grasped by its viewer. Humor, allegory, satire, metaphor, and irony are its stock in trade. Until the 1910s the field had been entirely dominated by men. Thomas Nast, the creator of the Republican elephant, the Democratic donkey, and the Tammany tiger, as well as the popularizer of Uncle Sam and Columbia as symbols of the American nation, was the nineteenth century's preeminent American political cartoonist. His work and that of other cartoonists and illustrators found an audience in the proliferating newspaper print culture and a range of humor magazines founded in the 1870s and 1880s, such as *Puck*, *Judge*, and *Life*. Politicians quickly realized the power of such images to sway voters and influence public opinion. As William Tweed, the boss of New York's Democratic Tammany machine, said in reaction to a Thomas Nast cartoon exposing the corruption of the so-called "Tweed Ring," "I don't care so much what the papers write about me—my constituents can't read; but d—n it, they can see pictures."[2]

By the early twentieth century, conditions were ripe for women artists to enter this realm. Foremost was the expansion of higher education for women, which opened possibilities for careers beyond just marriage and motherhood. Just as important was the opening of formal artistic training to women, both in Europe and the United States, which laid the groundwork for women's professional (as opposed to amateur) careers as artists or in art-related fields. Finally, the woman suffrage movement was gaining momentum, and victory was now a distinct possibility rather than a distant dream. Since professionally trained women artists were already pathbreakers in their field, they often harbored feminist sensibilities that made them stick up for their sex, both in their professional lives and in the art they produced. The woman suffrage movement, with its network of publications and outreach, offered a perfect place to combine these dual thrusts. As a result, at least three dozen female cartoonists, mainly born in the 1870s and therefore in their thirties and forties at the height of suffrage activism, plied their trade and their feminism in the movement's final decade.[3]

Annie Lucasta "Lou" Rogers, who published several hundred suffrage cartoons in newspapers and magazines such as *Judge*, the *Woman's Journal*, *The New York Call*, and *Woman Voter*, was one of the most successful members of this pioneering cohort of cartoonists. Born in rural Maine in 1879 and possessed of both artistic and independent bents, she gravitated first to Boston, where she enrolled at the Massachusetts Normal Art School, then decamped to New York, "certain of only one thing: I would be a cartoonist."[4] Submitting her work under the name Lou Rogers to sidestep the sexism she faced as a female artist, by 1911 she had turned her attention primarily to suffrage. The *Woman's Journal* proudly noted that she was the "only woman artist to devote all her time to feminism." Her cartoon "Breaking into the Human Race" inspired the title of the lecture series on feminism in Greenwich Village in 1914 where Charlotte Perkins Gilman and others spoke. One of her best known images, "Tearing off the Bonds," featured a suffragist bound in rope which spelled out "politics is no place for women." This image clearly influenced William Marston, the creator of *Wonder Woman* in the 1940s, whose cartoon panels often featured women in chains or bondage—until, that is, they break free. Like Lou Rogers, Marston was a staunch feminist.[5]

Blanche Ames embodied the vibrancy of the cartooning tradition in Boston. Born in 1878 in Lowell to a prominent Massachusetts family—her grandfather was the Civil War general Benjamin Butler, who later served in Congress—she was an early graduate of Smith College, class of 1899, where her professors strongly encouraged her to pursue her interest in art and illustration. In 1900, she married the Harvard botanist Oakes Ames (no relation), with whom

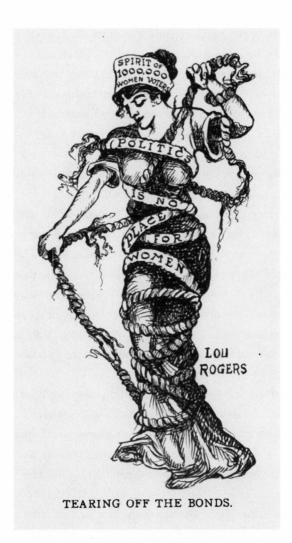

TEARING OFF THE BONDS.

Lou Rogers's "Tearing off the Bonds," which appeared in the
October 19, 1912 issue of *Judge*, shows a woman doing just that,
aided by the "spirit of 1,000,000 women voters." Soon there would
be many more. *Courtesy of Schlesinger Library, Radcliffe Institute,
Harvard University.*

she had four children. Determined to pursue interests beyond the home, she served as an illustrator on many of her husband's botanical expeditions and became his trusted partner and collaborator. When not off searching for orchids, both husband and wife were avid suffragists. Blanche Ames frequently contributed cartoons to the Boston-based *Woman's Journal*, and from 1915–1917, she served as its art editor.

Ames preferred pen-and-ink sketches, whose sharp contrasts were well-suited to the *Woman's Journal*'s text-heavy format. Her 1915 cartoon captioned "Meanwhile They Drown" is particularly notable. It depicts a woman ("We don't need it") sitting on a dock alongside a man who holds a life preserver inscribed "votes for women" ("When ALL women want it, I will throw it to them"). The man steadfastly refuses to extend the life preserver to the struggling women and children in the water who are being swamped by waves identified as "white slavery," "sweatshop," "filth," and "disease." Meanwhile his female companion, seated on a box labeled "antisuffrage," passively watches.[6]

New York and Boston were important beachheads for suffrage activism, and so was Washington, DC, especially after Alice Paul came to town in 1912 and took over the Congressional Committee of NAWSA before breaking away to found what became the National Woman's Party. Based in the nation's capital, Nina Allender emerged as one of the most influential members of this cohort of pioneering suffrage artists. "Mrs. Allender is the first woman artist who has ever won a name in the magazines of the country as a cartoonist," noted an article in *The Suffragist* in 1918. "Mrs. Allender not only brings to politics quick insight, but also the eye of a feminist. No man could have projected such a series of cartoons on the suffrage situation. . . ." The suffragist Inez Haynes Irwin made a similar point:

Blanche Ames knew her cartoon "Meanwhile They Drown" had hit its mark when it drew a public rebuttal from William Howard Taft. The former president was quite a large man, and his hefty girth is prominently featured in her cartoon reply, "Our Answer to Mr. Taft," which appeared in the *Woman's Journal and Suffrage News* on September 18, 1915. *Courtesy of Schlesinger Library, Radcliffe Institute, Harvard University.*

"It would be impossible for any man to have done Mrs. Allender's work. A woman speaking to women, about women, in the language of women."[7]

The future suffrage cartoonist was born Nina Evans in Auburn, Kansas, on Christmas day 1872—just a few years after the decisive and divisive Kansas referendum of 1867 dealt both woman suffrage and African American male suffrage resounding defeats. After moving from Philadelphia to Kansas in its early days of frontier settlement, her mother, Eva Moore, began teaching school at the age of sixteen. In 1871, the young schoolteacher married David J. Evans, a somewhat older superintendent of schools who had been a teacher in Oneida County, New York before migrating west. The couple had two daughters, but Mrs. Evans grew dissatisfied with the relationship and took the highly unusual step of leaving the marriage and moving with her daughters to Washington, DC, where she found a clerical position with the Department of the Interior in 1881. As far back as the Civil War, the federal government had become the employment option of first choice for genteel if often impoverished women who needed or wanted to work. Clearly an independent-minded woman, Eva Evans passed that trait on to her elder daughter.

From an early age, Nina showed an interest in drawing and art, primarily painting. Her mother encouraged her aspirations, arranging for lessons at the newly opened Corcoran School of Art in Washington, DC. While training to become an art teacher in the 1890s, Nina met and married an Englishman named Charles Allender. Like her parents' marriage, this one did not last. After stealing money from the bank where he was employed, Allender skipped town with another woman. The couple, who did not have children, quickly divorced, and Nina Allender set out to support herself. She shared a home with her mother and, following her mother's lead, found good employment opportunities in the federal government, landing a position in the Treasury Department. She continued to be active in the local arts scene, and she also joined the woman suffrage movement, taking time off from her job to campaign in Ohio in 1912.

In early 1913, she had a fateful meeting with Alice Paul, who was new in town and eager to revitalize NAWSA's Congressional Committee to lobby for a federal suffrage amendment. Paul arranged to call on Nina and her mother, whom she had never met. After a brief conversation, they agreed to donate both time and money to the cause, specifically to help pay the office rent for the headquarters Paul needed to coordinate plans for the upcoming suffrage parade in March. As Inez Haynes Irwin later recounted, "their amazement arose partly from the fact that they had not been begged, urged, or argued with—they had simply been asked; and partly from the fact that, before this arrival of this slim little stranger, they had no more idea of contributing so much money or work than of flying." That story perfectly captures Alice Paul's legendary ability to get people to do things they hadn't planned to do. And she wasn't done yet with Nina Allender.[8]

The next year, Paul asked Allender to contribute political cartoons to *The Suffragist*, the publication of the recently formed Congressional Union. No matter that Allender was by training a painter and had never drawn a cartoon in her life—once again she couldn't say no to Alice Paul. Her first drawing appeared on the cover of the June 6, 1914 issue. Somewhat busier and denser than her later drawings, "The Summer Campaign" depicts an attractive, slim suffragist addressing a mixed crowd from the back of an open automobile. One week later, she contributed her first cartoon: a crowded slum street scene featuring a young mother and two children, a babe in arms and a young girl playing with a cat in the gutter, under the caption "The Inspiration of the Suffrage Worker." In late July, she linked suffrage to protective labor legislation under the banner "Child Saving is Woman's Work—Votes for Women." In general, working women did not often figure in her cartoons, although when they did, they were treated sympathetically. For example, under the intentionally ironic header "Woman's Place is the Home," a shawl-clad immigrant mother glances back sadly at her six children as she trudges off to her factory job.[9]

Herself an independent, modern professional woman, Allender drew respectful portraits of women that were sympathetic to their new roles. As the suffrage historian Alice Sheppard noted, "Allender created an image of suffragists in sharp contrast to the typical caricature of the bespectacled old maid seen in the national press. Her suffragist appeared infused with a new spirit, the spirit of pride and daring, and possessed the vigor of youth." Drawing mainly in charcoal, her cartoons presented their central points in an uncluttered and straightforward fashion. As *The Suffragist* noted, "she gave to the American public in cartoons that have been widely copied and commented on, a new type of suffragist—the young and zealous women of a new generation determined to wait no longer for a just right. It was Mrs. Allender's cartoons more than any other one thing that in the newspapers of this country began to change the cartoonist's idea of a suffragist." This type of suffragist was so identifiable that it was often referred to as "The Allender Girl."[10]

In 1916, Nina Allender was part of an innovative National Woman's Party campaign that combined Valentine's Day on February 14 and Susan B. Anthony's birthday on February 15 to flood Congress with valentines making the case for suffrage. "We have tried reasoning, eloquence of the soapbox, cart tail, and back of an automobile variety," explained a suffrage spokesperson, "and we hope rhymes may influence the politicians where the other forces did not." Over a thousand "Dripping Hearts and Rhymes" valentines were sent, many of them hand-drawn and tailored to the recipient. Nina Allender's valentine to Woodrow Wilson, which was one of several reproduced in *The Suffragist*, featured a group of attractive suffragists from the various states where women already voted carrying baskets of hearts with "vote" on them, accompanied by this caption: "Will you be our Valentine if We will be Your Valentines."[11]

President Woodrow Wilson, who in the eyes of the National Woman's Party never did enough as the leader of his party or the nation to support woman suffrage, was one of Allender's frequent targets. Even though Allender never picketed the White House and never was arrested, she was in total sympathy with the radical turn NWP activism took after 1917. One cartoon titled "President Wilson says, 'Godspeed to the Cause,'" shows three comely suffragists behind prison bars, unlikely criminals whom readers would know were in jail for the minor charge of obstructing traffic while picketing the White House. Gazing out from their cells, they entreat Wilson: "Mr. President what will you DO for woman suffrage?" In the past, political cartoons of transgressive women like the pickets would have painted them as harridans or ugly, mean spirited women. Instead, Allender portrays them with sympathy and understanding.[12]

Allender was not afraid to take on the division between the two wings of the suffrage movement after the Congressional Union split away from the National American Woman Suffrage Association and formed the National Woman's Party. In 1915, Senator John Shafroth and Representative A. Mitchell Palmer introduced a rival constitutional amendment that would require a state to hold a suffrage referendum if 8 percent of the voters petitioned for the move. NAWSA signed on to this approach, but the NWP strongly opposed it because the strategy undercut their push for a clean and simple amendment with national reach. In a drawing entitled "The Anthony and Shafroth Suffrage Amendments," Allender makes it clear where her sympathies lie. She represents the Democratic-controlled sixty-fourth Congress as a donkey which a suffragist leads to a crossroad, clearly demarcated as "Anthony Road," which leads straight to the franchise shining on the horizon, and "Shafroth Road," which takes a far more circuitous route. The caption reads, "But I can't get the old dear to take both roads at once." Precisely. Soon after, NAWSA dropped its support for the rival constitutional amendment.[13]

Nina Allender's wartime cartoons were especially provocative in linking the justice of the suffrage cause to the larger ideals of a democracy at war. In a cartoon that mimicked Wilson's 1916 campaign pledge, a suffragist carrying a purse labeled "Suffrage Amendment" asks a man labeled "Congress," who is spreading ashes on the slippery pavement, "Will you Make 1918 Safe for Democracy?" When the Congress finally passed the Anthony amendment in 1919 and sent it to the states for ratification, she penned a powerful image of a huge "V" for Victory ("One Vote for Victory Women") with a suffragist proudly in the middle. And in a cartoon that truly says it all, "Any Good Suffragist the Morning After," she paints an exhausted suffragist fast asleep under the covers with newspapers proclaiming "victory" littering the floor around the bed.[14]

Nina Allender's suffrage imagery leaves a proud but muted legacy. There is no question that she portrayed women positively, but she did so in ways that gently tweaked existing gender roles rather than tackling them head on. In other words, she never distanced suffragists too far from prevailing notions of femininity as they stepped into their new roles in public life. One case in point is a

Drawn by Nina E. Allender

Any good Suffragist the morning after.

Contrary to popular perceptions, "any good suffragist" did not simply roll over and go back to sleep after the ratification of the Nineteenth Amendment. Suffragists enthusiastically embraced their status as women citizens and prepared to take on new roles in the postsuffrage era. Nina Allender's cartoon appeared in *The Suffragist* in September 1920. *Courtesy of Schlesinger Library, Radcliffe Institute, Harvard University.*

cartoon depicting a small girl throwing a snowball labeled "vote" at a figure representing the Democratic Party, which causes a police officer (labeled "Judiciary Committee") to challenge "Wha' jer goin' to do next?" But the girl is adorably dressed in a cute outfit and hat, which downplays the threatening aspects of the challenge to authority. And yet the snowball still hits its target.[15]

And, as is true of so much of suffrage history, Allender's cartoons often reinforced class and race prejudices. The "Allender girl" was an affluent, educated, middle-class white woman. Working women appeared only occasionally in her portfolio, and African American women were totally absent, not just in Allender's NWP cartoons but in all the surviving suffrage images. (There was no equivalent of Nina Allender in the African American press.) In the end, Nina Allender's cartoons were very much a mirror not just of the racism of the suffrage movement but of the racial and class hierarchies of Progressive-era American society.

Despite these limitations, Nina Allender's cartoons demonstrate a willingness and ability to harness women's expanding professional opportunities with new media technologies to get the word out about suffrage. More broadly, her corpus of work, especially when linked with the images produced by her sister cartoonists, is an important addition to our understanding of what female creative artists contributed both to artistic endeavor and politics in early-twentieth-century America. As Lou Rogers said in 1913, "It is not art as art that I am interested in; it's art as a chance to help women see their own problems, help bring out the things that are true in the traditions that have bound them; help show up the things that are false."[16]

Ironically, since the cartoons of these pioneering and politically engaged artists were published mainly in suffrage organs rather than mass-market newspapers or magazines, their impact was limited. In other words, they primarily reached the already converted, which helps to explain why the cartoons are so little known today. This is unfortunate, because most of these sketches are just as fresh and compelling a century later as they were in the 1910s.

CHAPTER SEVENTEEN

Jailed for Freedom

ON A SUNDAY AFTERNOON in December 1917, several thousand women filled the Belasco Theater in Washington, DC for a mass meeting organized by the National Woman's Party. The event was planned to honor the "self-respecting and patriotic American women" who had picketed the White House and served time in jail that summer and fall, including Alice Paul, who had recently been released after five weeks in prison. Alva Belmont, the NWP chair, set the charged tone of the gathering with these opening words: "A flame of rebellion is abroad among women, and the stupidity and brutality of the government in this revolt have only served to increase its heat."[1]

At the climax of the meeting, the eighty-nine women to be honored, all dressed in suffrage white, marched to the stage where they were presented with a specially designed brooch in the shape of the locked door of a prison cell. Said Elizabeth Thatcher Kent, herself a veteran of the picket line, as she gifted each former prisoner with a small (1-by-1½-inch) metal pin: "In honoring these women who were willing to go to jail for liberty we are showing our love of country and devotion to democracy." The audience was so moved by the spectacle that it quickly pledged almost $100,000 to continue the campaign.[2]

Alice Paul drew inspiration for the NWP prison pin from several sources. The main one was Sylvia Pankhurst's "Holloway Brooch," which was distributed to members of the British Women's Social and Political Union who had been jailed for the cause, including Alice Paul, who had been incarcerated three times in 1909 during her stay in England. Paul may also have remembered the Daughters of the American Revolution pin worn by the NWP activist Helen Hill Weed, which had bars representing her fourteen ancestors who died in the revolutionary conflict. No matter what the inspiration, these metal brooches became treasured mementoes of membership in an incredibly select society. Many of the former pickets wore them for the rest of their lives.[3]

In the 1940s, the long-time National Woman's Party member Betsy Graves Reyneau showed her pin to the Howard Law School student Pauli Murray, a civil rights activist and feminist who later developed the "Jane Crow" legal strategy linking race and sex discrimination. Murray was profoundly moved both by the artifact and by the story behind it. When Reyneau died in 1964, her daughter gave the pin to Murray, for whom it became "one of my most cherished possessions" as well as a literal link to the generations of feminist activists who preceded her.[4]

ALMOST FIVE HUNDRED women were arrested on the suffrage picket lines between 1917 and 1919, and close to 170 served time in prison. These militant suffragists were so committed to the cause

Prison pin, National Woman's Party. *Courtesy of Schlesinger Library, Radcliffe Institute, Harvard University.*

that they voluntarily risked their reputations and possibly their lives to secure women's right to vote. Some, like Alice Paul and Lucy Burns, were legendary in suffrage circles and have dominated suffrage histories ever since, but most, like Hazel Hunkins (later Hunkins-Hallinan), remain footnotes to history. Hunkins-Hallinan is not included in standard biographical dictionaries such as *Notable American Women* or *American National Biography* and has only a stub for a Wikipedia entry, but her life demonstrates the courage and commitment suffragists brought to what, in their eyes, was the most burning issue of their day.

Hazel Hunkins was born on June 6, 1890 in Aspen, Colorado and was brought up in Billings, Montana. The only child of Anna Whittingham and Lewis Hunkins, a jeweler and watchmaker, she later joked that the Revolutionary War lived on in her family because her father was "a die-hard Puritan from New England and my mother was English." Despite not having a brother, she was aware from an early age that boys and girls were raised with different expectations based on gender. When she announced that she planned to become a doctor, her father replied that only men could be doctors. Instead, he told her, she could become a nurse.[5]

After she graduated from high school in Billings in 1908, her family sent her east for a year of college preparatory classes at the Mount Ida School in Newton, Massachusetts. She then enrolled at Vassar College, where she spent four glorious years taking every course offered in chemistry and graduated with that major in 1913. She began working towards a Master's degree at the University of Missouri, focusing on agricultural economics, but found her career aspirations increasingly stymied because of her gender. Then suddenly, she was summoned home to nurse her sick mother. What Jane Addams called "the family claim"—the propensity to regard daughters as dependent possessions rather than as autonomous individuals in their own right—still held sway in 1916.

After her exciting time at Vassar and the University of Missouri, coming home to Billings was a huge letdown. When the principal of her high school asked if she was interested in joining the science department, she leapt at the chance of teaching chemistry again, only to be told that she would be expected to teach geography and botany, subjects she knew nothing about, because only men taught chemistry. Bored by her familial domestic duties as her mother's health mended, she experienced "a summer of despair and unhappiness." She claimed that she wrote to every chemistry laboratory from Portland, Oregon to Portland, Maine, but the replies were all the same: we don't hire women.[6]

At that low point, she was introduced to Anna Louise Rowe, whom Alice Paul had sent to Billings to establish a Montana branch of the National Woman's Party. "For the first time in my life I heard the full philosophy of feminism described and explained to me. And I bought it—hook, line and sinker." Not all suffrage epiphanies were so complete or quick, but for twenty-six-year-old Hazel Hunkins, her conversion literally changed her life. She threw herself into NWP activities, organizing a Billings branch and then becoming Montana state chair. From there she became a paid organizer, traveling to California, Colorado, Utah, and New York to work in various NWP campaigns. At the 1915 Panama-Pacific International Exposition in San Francisco, when flying was still a dangerous novelty, Hunkins dropped suffrage leaflets on the crowd from an airplane.[7]

Described as "young, beautiful and brilliant," Hunkins proved to be a very persuasive organizer and soon was ensconced in Washington, DC overseeing the fieldwork of organizers sent out to the states. At NWP headquarters, Hazel quickly fell under the sway of the organization's brilliant young leader. "After a talk with Alice Paul about what had to be done, one left her presence twice one's size and ready to do anything for a cause she made you feel so deeply." Like so many others, Hunkins recognized Paul as nothing less than a great leader. "Within her spirit was a flame forcing her to make right what she thought to be wrong to her sex and she communicated this in full strength to others."[8]

Hunkins arrived in Washington, DC just as Alice Paul escalated her battle to force President Woodrow Wilson to endorse woman suffrage by posting "Silent Sentinels" at the White House gates. Picketing the White House is now such a staple of political life that it is often forgotten that the suffragists were the first ever to use this tactic at that symbolic location. With banners like "Mr. President! How Long Will Women Have to Wait for Their Freedom?" and "Democracy Should Begin at Home" the first pickets took their places on January 10, 1917, with Hazel Hunkins proving one of the most loyal and dedicated.

Taking a shift as a sentinel was much harder work than it might appear. The pickets stood outside no matter what the weather, feet frozen and hands numb from holding the heavy banners, subject to taunts from young boys and bemused stares from passersby. Luckily those reactions were balanced by heartening encouragement from supporters: "I just couldn't go by without shaking hands with you splendid women!" gushed a woman with a small baby. When the "militant suffs" were pointed out to one man, he said with surprise, "Why, they don't look so bad." As Hunkins summed it up for a reporter for the *Washington Post*, "In a day's work we meet them all, rich and poor, men and women of all classes and from every rank of life. . . . After all is said and done, we enjoy the experience, and being firm in our convictions of the justice of our cause, we are

National Woman's Party members representing colleges as diverse as Vassar and the University of Missouri picket the White House in February 1917. Their banners starkly call out President Woodrow Wilson for his failure to rally the country behind woman suffrage—a decidedly unladylike attack on the country's highest elected official. *Courtesy of Library of Congress, LC-USZ62-31799.*

happy in whatever sacrifices we make in standing the cold or the fatigue of long vigils."[9]

For the first six months of 1917, NWP pickets literally "stood up" to President Woodrow Wilson as he came and went through the gates of the White House, making their case rhetorically with an ever-changing array of banners. "If we had given out a long, scholastic dissertation on the political status of women in this country," Paul realized, "nobody would have paid any attention to it" but with the banners "the people were knocked into thinking." ("I think we made millionaires out of those banner makers," Hunkins later joked.) To maintain interest and break the monotony, Alice Paul organized days that featured picketers from specific states, alumnae of colleges and universities (only women were allowed to picket), and all-nurses or all-teachers days. The protestors' task grew more fraught after April, when the United States entered World War I and the NWP refused to give up its suffrage advocacy. Even so, the picketers incited mainly curiosity, never violence, and the police did not interfere with their right to assemble. That changed in June with the so-called "Russian banners," which provocatively, some said treasonously, linked Wilson's war aims with the Russian Revolution.[10]

Things got ugly very fast. An angry passerby tore a banner from the hands of a Silent Sentinel—the first violent confrontation after six months of peaceful protest. Then a second banner was destroyed. When Hazel Hunkins came back on line the next day, with a fairly innocuous banner that read "We demand democracy and self government in our own land," she was suddenly rushed by a woman who took hold of the banner and spit on it. "One minute I was standing there in perfect peace and quiet holding a banner that has had its duplicate in every fight that has ever been made for political rights; three minutes later I was holding a broken staff with no banner and the center of a surging crowd." Because the sentinels were pledged to nonviolent resistance, Hunkins could not fight back, even when the crowd pressed toward her. "I never felt so alone and so helpless in my life," she said. She then admitted tellingly, "I never felt so superior before and I never expect to again."[11]

A corner had been turned. After the Russian banner incident, the local police, apparently with the tacit support of the Wilson administration, started arresting and jailing picketers for disorderly conduct and obstructing sidewalk traffic, even though they were doing nothing differently than they had for the past six months. These pickets became the first American women to be jailed for the "crime" of advocating women's rights. They were also among the first victims of wartime repression of dissent.

Undaunted, Alice Paul raised the stakes, planning large demonstrations for the Fourth of July and Bastille Day. Hazel Hunkins was arrested for the first time at the Fourth of July demonstration. She was selling copies of *The Suffragist* outside the Belasco Theater when a man stole her banner, which she demanded he return because it was NWP property. This altercation led to her arrest for disturbing the peace. She was not officially charged and did not go to jail, but other suffragists did.

As brave as Hazel Hunkins was on the picket line, she cowered at the thought of telling her mother back home in Billings what was going on, especially once the newspapers picked up the story of her arrest. Like countless other cross-generational dialogues between bold daughters and their cautious mothers—Alice Paul exchanged strikingly similar messages with her mother when she was imprisoned and force-fed in England in 1909—Hazel Hunkins tried to make the case for her actions to a doubting mother. "How can I ever make you see these things as I do. . . . Every minute has been darkened by the thought of what you were suffering. . . . I can imagine you walking up town and feeling that every eye is on you as the mother of a notorious character." The telegrams she received from her mother left her in tears and wanting to catch the next train home. And yet she wrote her mother, "I am in some what the same position as a soldier in the trenches who has the choice of going back or of going on—and he chooses to go on." Not at all sure she had made her case, all she could say was "try to be with me in spirit even when it is easiest to condemn."[12]

Hazel Hunkins continued to serve on the picket lines over the coming months, risking arrest but never going to jail. Other suffragists were not so lucky. By October 1917, seventy women were imprisoned, six of them for terms as long as six months. Sent to serve their sentences at the Occoquan Work House, they were subjected to inedible food, humiliating treatment, lack of communication with the outside world, and—especially on the infamous "Night of Terror" on November 15, 1917—physical intimidation and violence from prison authorities. Doris Stevens pointedly labeled these reprisals "Administration Terrorism."[13]

Alice Paul was then serving a seven-month sentence for obstructing traffic. When her demand for political prisoner status was refused, she and other suffragists began a hunger strike. Removed to the psychiatric ward, she was then forcibly fed three times a day for more than three weeks. Among her few visitors was Cora Smith Eaton King, her personal physician.

The administration had hoped to cripple suffrage activism with long prison sentences and mandatory forced feeding, but that strategy backfired. With so many suffragists serving time and close to thirty on hunger strikes, the authorities faced the real possibility that a suffragist would die on their watch. From that point on, sentences were kept deliberately short. Reflecting this change in policy, Alice Paul, now a genuine martyr to the cause, was abruptly released in late November after serving only five weeks of her sentence.

Throughout these months of picketing, Hazel Hunkins managed to stay out of jail. By then, she had taken a position as a researcher with the National War Labor Board, a temporary agency tasked with investigating labor issues in wartime. She loved her job, but she still remained deeply involved with the National Woman's Party. "It is huge fun working for them when it is volunteer work," she told her mother. "I don't feel the slave to them that I did when I worked for them for a salary."[14]

In the summer of 1918, with the Senate about to adjourn without considering the suffrage amendment, the NWP called a protest.

It would be held on August sixth, the birthday of Inez Milholland, the movement's first true martyr, who had collapsed and died of acute nephritis while on the campaign trail in November 1916 at age thirty. Of course Hazel Hunkins would be there, even though it was a Tuesday and she must have taken time off from work.

The demonstration was set for Lafayette Square, a public space directly across from the White House dominated by a large statue of the Marquis de Lafayette, the French hero of the American Revolution. Doris Stevens recreated the scene: Women "dressed in white, hatless and coatless in the midsummer heat of Washington, marched to the monument carrying banners of purple, white and gold, led by a standard bearer carrying the American flag." That standard bearer was Hazel Hunkins. "They made a beautiful mass of color as they grouped themselves around the statue" in an entirely peaceful protest. But when Dora Lewis of Philadelphia stepped forward to speak, she was "roughly seized by a policeman and placed under arrest." Hazel was the next speaker, but she got no further than, "Here at the statue of Lafayette, who fought for the liberty of this country, and under the American flag, I am asking for—" before she was arrested. As speaker after speaker came forward, each met the same fate. According to one newspaper account, Woodrow Wilson exited the White House at the height of the arrests, glanced across the street, and smiled.[15]

The protestors were transported in police wagons to the booking station and ordered to appear in court the next week. Free on bail, Hazel Hunkins and others defiantly returned to Lafayette Square, where they were arrested several times over the next few days. The outcome of the trial was never in doubt. For the crimes of "holding a meeting in public grounds" and "climbing on a statue," they were given sentences of between ten and fifteen days. Elsie

Hill injected a rare moment of levity into the otherwise grim proceedings when she observed, "During my years of suffrage work I've been told and re-told that woman's place is on a pedestal; and the first time I get on one, I'm arrested." Hazel Hunkins put her best face forward when she cabled home, "TWENTY SIX OF AMERICAS FINEST WOMEN ARE ACCOMPANYING ME TO JAIL ITS SPLENDID DONT WORRY LOVE HAZEL."[16]

The prisoners were sent not to the Occoquan Workhouse, the site of all previous incarcerations, but to an abandoned jail building in the swampy District prison grounds. Hazel Hunkins's account for *The Suffragist* described the ordeal in sparse, straightforward prose: "In a moment we were on the other side of the iron gate and the clang of the great lock meant we were prisoners held by our government for daring to proclaim it cannot yet hold high the torch of liberty while millions of its adult citizens are still denied a voice in the power that rules them." Conditions were so bad that, save for two elderly women, all the protestors immediately began a hunger strike to protest their treatment. Prisoners dragged the straw pallets from their cells to the cement floor of the yard, where they huddled together to fight off the cold and tried to keep up their spirits by singing songs, including an energetic "Happy Birthday" to Helen Hill Weed who turned forty-three on the second day.[17]

By then the most acute pangs of hunger passed, but the women soon became violently ill with something more ominous than the usual symptoms of a hunger strike: "The horrible smells coming from the antiquated sanitary arrangements and from the open drains, the absolute lack of sunlight, the cold and dampness were all contributing causes but the real cause was the water. We had saturated ourselves with water from the source which was one of the causes the jail had been declared unsanitary and abandoned years before." Soon Hunkins too had succumbed to the poisonous gases and water, "absolutely limp" in her cell.[18]

As word got out about these terrible conditions, pressure built on the Wilson administration to intercede, and at the end of the fifth day, all the prisoners were released. Hunkins came home in an ambulance. According to fellow prisoner Julia Emory, "it was hard to realize that the same girl who carried the American flag so steadily and bravely at the head of our processions was now being brought home wrapped in a blanket and violently ill." Hazel Hunkins had more than earned her treasured prison pin.[19]

After her release, Hunkins once again had to do damage control at home. "An endless chain of exciting events has made life kaleidoscopic for the last month and I have no idea when you last heard of me," she began, somewhat disingenuously. Despite "that awful piece" her mother had seen in the paper, she reassured her jauntily, "Well—I'm fully recovered from the hunger strike and am getting altogether too fat to please myself." Somehow it seems unlikely that those cheery words reassured her mother, although the following sentence probably helped: "There is to be another demonstration in Wash. to-morrow and I am just dying to take part but another jail sentence so soon would not be fair to the N.W.R.B. so I'm not going to join in."[20]

Hazel Hunkins's final arrest came in January 1919, when she took part in the NWP strategy of lighting perpetual "watchfires for freedom" outside the White House gates and burning Wilson's speeches. While the NWP continued to pressure Congress until the suffrage amendment finally passed the Senate in June 1919, their militant actions and the resulting arrests basically ended in February and March.

By then, Hazel Hunkins was moving on as well. A free spirit when it came to feminist politics, she also embraced emancipated ideas about sex and marriage. Some time after her release from jail, she met journalist Charles Hallinan at a pacifist meeting where he was speaking, and they began an affair. He was married at the time, with a daughter, and his wife resisted a divorce. In July 1920, Hazel headed to England to conduct research for the American Railway Brotherhood, and Hallinan soon followed, becoming the London financial editor of United Press International. Their daughter was born in 1921, and they had three other children together but did not marry until 1930.[21]

Hazel Hunkins-Hallinan spent the rest of her life in England. In 1922, she joined the Six Point Group, Britain's leading feminist organization, which worked towards improving the status of women in the economic, social, and political realms. She served as the group's chair in the 1950s and 1960s, boasting to American feminists, "My very modest distinction is that I am the only American woman who has achieved the chairmanship of a national organisation (British) without having climbed to that office through marriage to an English title!"[22] She never lost her admiration for Alice Paul, and she journeyed back to the United States in 1977 to speak at her memorial service. And while she was there, she marched in a demonstration organized by the National Organization for Women for the Equal Rights Amendment. Once a feminist, always a feminist.

CHAPTER EIGHTEEN

Maud Wood Park
and the Front Door Lobby

THERE ARE several ways to read the handbill "Seeing is Believing! Finish the Fight" distributed by the National American Woman Suffrage Association in 1919. A pessimist might focus on how slow the progress had been: in the forty years after territorial Wyoming gave women the vote in 1869, only three states followed suit. An optimist could see it another way, marveling at the dramatic breakthroughs that occurred in the decade between 1909 and 1919. Even so, that optimist might have cause for concern in those black areas on the map to follow that covered large chunks of the South and most of the industrial Northeast. The woman suffrage movement had definitely gained strength, but it was still far from a truly national phenomenon.

NAWSA's map encapsulated the challenge that suffragists faced in their final years. Where would they get the necessary votes to push it over the top? State suffrage referendums were still possible, but the New York State victory in 1917 notwithstanding, it wasn't clear what more could be done in states like Massachusetts, Ohio, or New Jersey, which had recently voted down similar initiatives, or in southern states where there was scant prospect of success. That left a constitutional amendment,   251 but to win approval in Congress meant dealing with the same political map, with large swaths of the country unsympathetic if not downright hostile to women's cause. And after approval in Congress, the amendment would need to be ratified by thirty-six states, far more than currently allowed women to vote.

Yet the map held clues about the path to victory in the number of states where women enjoyed full suffrage, primary suffrage, or presidential suffrage. We don't need to be reminded that close elections are often decided in the Electoral College, and by 1919, the states where women voted counted for 339 electoral votes. Elected officials in those states were beholden to women's support, and politicians in states that hadn't yet enfranchised women could see it coming. Mobilizing the actual and potential power of the women's vote was critical to breaking the stalemate.

Don't nag

Don't boast

Don't threaten

Don't lose your temper

Don't stay too long

Don't talk about your work where you can be overheard

Don't give the member interviewed an opportunity to declare himself against the amendment

Don't do anything to close the door to the next advocate of suffrage

The last "don't" was the one that Maud Wood Park dwelt on most in her pep talks with her loyal corps of suffrage workers. "If we can't do any good, at least we must be sure that we don't do any harm."[1]

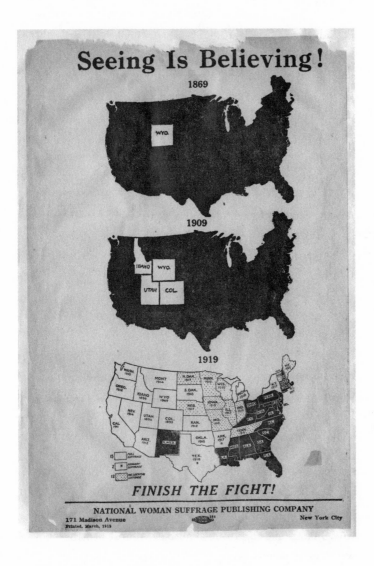

"Seeing is Believing! Finish the Fight!" handbill, 1919. *Courtesy of Schlesinger Library, Radcliffe Institute, Harvard University.*

Suffrage lobbyists quickly absorbed other lessons as well. They always went in twos, because their presence was harder to ignore and because it was useful to have one designated as the talker and the other as backup. They learned never to go into the congressional office buildings after six o'clock because "we had heard rumors that in the evening offices were not always devoted to public business." They became adept at cultivating elevator men, doorkeepers, and friendly secretaries who could help them track down members of Congress who were trying to make themselves scarce. One cardinal rule was to do everything possible to keep a man from taking a stand against the amendment, even if he was clearly not in favor of it. And if he later came on board? Never ask him why he changed his mind.[2]

The "front door lobby" was the "half-humorous, half-kindly" name one of the press-gallery journalists gave to NAWSA's Congressional Committee in Washington because, he explained, they "never used backstairs methods." At the height of the campaign, as many as twenty-five regular lobbyists lived at Suffrage House, the Congressional Committee's combined office and living quarters on Rhode Island Avenue. They were backed up by the state congressional chairmen in the association's forty-four state branches, as well as by ninety-five congressional aides who were available to light "backfires" to stir up constituent or press support in the cases of wavering members of Congress. Compared with the large staffs and bloated budgets at the disposal of more entrenched male lobbyists, NAWSA's size and costs were minuscule. Almost all of the lobbying was done by volunteers.[3]

Keeping track of portfolios on 435 members of the House of Representatives and ninety-six senators was difficult and often tedious work. It lacked the glamour of marching in a suffrage parade, addressing an open-air meeting, or picketing the White

House, but it was absolutely crucial to the long suffrage campaign's success. "The lobbying route," according to the historian Nancy Cott, "should be seen as pioneering in the modern mode of exerting political force—that is, interest group politics." The methods the highly disciplined suffrage lobby employed therefore put the drive to win the vote at the forefront of twentieth-century political history—and the person who made it happen was a Boston-born, 1898 Radcliffe graduate named Maud Wood Park.[4]

Park's Radcliffe classmate (and fellow suffragist) Inez Haynes Irwin once said of her, "I was always admiring the length, breadth and height of her mind. It had great floor space." By the time Park took over the Congressional Committee in late 1916, she had spent almost twenty years in the suffrage trenches. Her first suffrage encounter came during her student days, when a Radcliffe professor assigned an English paper on suffrage. Out of seventy students, Park was one of only two who supported it, composing this succinct affirmation: "I see no more reason for the men of my family to decide my political opinions and express them for me at the polls than to choose my hats and wear them, or my religious faith and occupy my seat at church." Over the course of her career, Park gave hundreds of suffrage speeches, but she always felt that this brief undergraduate statement expressed her sentiments most clearly.[5]

Wishing to do something to promote the cause on campus, Park reached out to Alice Stone Blackwell, a local suffrage legend, who came to Radcliffe to speak. At first Park was concerned that the students "would think her a little queer" because of how she was dressed, but "that fear vanished completely during the first few minutes of her speech, which was so lucid and temperate that I knew at once the fastidious Harvard standards were being met." In turn, Blackwell recruited the two Radcliffe students to join the suffrage movement. For the rest of her life, Park considered Alice Stone

Blackwell her personal link to the suffrage cause. Repaying that debt was a prime reason Maud Wood Park took the lead in setting up the annuity for Blackwell when she faced impoverishment in the 1930s after a bad investment robbed her of her savings.[6]

In 1900, the twenty-nine-year-old Park became chair of the executive board of the Massachusetts Woman Suffrage Association, a position which Lucy Stone had held for many years and which was currently held by her daughter, who graciously stepped aside in favor of her new recruit. "With you as chairman, dear Mrs. Park," wrote Alice Stone Blackwell, "I shall feel as if a strong young horse had come to help us drag the suffrage chariot out of the mudhole in which it seems to be stuck at present." Soon after, Park joined with the Boston suffragists Mary Hutcheson Page and Pauline Agassiz Shaw to found the Boston Equal Suffrage Association for Good Government (BESAGG), a progressive group dedicated to both suffrage and civic reform. She also convened the first College Equal Suffrage League in Boston, with twenty-five charter members; in 1908, representatives from twelve of the fifteen states with college leagues came together to form the National College Equal Suffrage League under the leadership of Bryn Mawr president M. Carey Thomas. The following year Park and Mabel Caldwell Willard set off on an eighteen-month round-the-world tour with a special focus on the political and social situation of women. The trip was underwritten by Mary Hutcheson Page, who was already providing Park with a yearly stipend of $500 for her suffrage work. Park, who was not from an elite background despite her Radcliffe degree (her father was a police officer), could not afford to volunteer her time.[7]

Park's ongoing financial struggles were closely linked to her marital situation, which was rather unusual. While she still was at

Radcliffe—she was an older student who didn't start college until she was twenty-three—she married a Boston architect named Charles Edward Park, but she kept the marriage secret until after her graduation. He died in 1904, and for the rest of her life, she was known as Mrs. Park. Four years later, she entered into a second marriage, this time to the theatrical agent Robert Freeman Palmer, which she also kept secret. Her reasoning this time was that she didn't want to complicate plans for her upcoming round-the-world trip, plus she didn't want to be known as his wife until his debts were paid. That didn't happen for many years, and by then, they were used to the subterfuge. Even more to the point, "I realized that my kind of work could be better done by a supposed widow than by a woman known to be married and therefore suspected of neglecting her husband." Only a few close friends knew of her second marriage, which lasted until Palmer's death in 1928.[8]

When Carrie Chapman Catt was considering asking Park to come to Washington, DC to head up the Congressional Committee, she reached out to Alice Stone Blackwell for an assessment of Park's work at the Massachusetts Woman Suffrage Association and BESAGG. As Park told the story, Blackwell replied that she had "two drawbacks as a worker; I *wouldn't* write letters and I *couldn't* attend to the necessary publicity, but otherwise I was efficient." She was efficient indeed, especially at tasks like "arranging meetings, increasing membership and directing continuous work," all of which would be vital to her new position. Catt chose well. Without Maud Wood Park and her team of lobbyists stalking the "marble halls" in the nation's capitol, the Nineteenth Amendment might never have cleared Congress.[9]

Park arrived in Washington ready to implement the "Winning Plan" that Carrie Chapman Catt had laid out at NAWSA's annual convention in September 1916 in Atlantic City. Park had been electrified by Catt's presentation: "I felt like Moses on the mountain top after the Promised Land had been shown to him and he knew the long years of wandering in the Wilderness were soon to end. For the first time I saw our goal as possible of attainment in the near future." Catt's plan was twofold: to focus on passage of the national amendment while continuing legislative activity on a state-by-state basis. Why both? Because increasing the number of women voters in individual states put enormous pressure on their representatives in Washington to support the amendment. Unlike the National Woman's Party's concentration solely on passage of a federal amendment, Catt said forcefully, "We must do both and do them together."[10]

When Maud Wood Park took over as head of the Congressional Committee, she had no legislative experience, so she gave herself a crash course in how Congress worked—or didn't. She spent time in the galleries observing the speechifying and parliamentary procedures, trying to put names to the faces of the men (and woman—Jeannette Rankin had just been elected from Montana) she would need to convert. Much of the routine business was quite boring, and she passed the time by bestowing nicknames on the politicians—the Undertaker, Puss-in-Boots, the Floorwalker. Other times she kept herself awake by assembling a cast for a comic opera with players like the Bald Brigade, the Moustache Contingent, and the Young Things. Mainly, though, she was carefully laying the groundwork for a coordinated lobbying effort that would reach every member of Congress, guided by the multi-page "Directions for Lobbyists" which laid out step-by-step instructions on how to get the job done.

Park's job was complicated by the April 1917 entry of the United States into World War I. "Overnight, it seemed, the shadow of the

Great War fell upon Washington," she recalled. Further complicating the suffragists' mission, a so-called Gentlemen's Agreement stipulated that Congress would take up no general legislation while war measures were under consideration; luckily congressional allies helped the suffragists find ways to work around that prohibition. There was never any question of suffragists abandoning their agenda in order to support the war. "Do both," Carrie Chapman Catt said succinctly.[11]

Another complication was the competition from the National Woman's Party, which continued its controversial policy of picketing the White House in spite of the declaration of war. There was no love lost between the two groups. "Nothing about our work was more unpleasant than the need of explaining that we did not agree as to method with other women working for the same end," Park asserted. "Why don't you women get together?" congressmen complained, conveniently forgetting that men hardly agreed on everything. Senator Reed Smoot from Utah, a conservative Mormon Republican who nevertheless was a suffrage supporter—"the only forward-looking movement that he was known to support," Park observed—was especially disdainful of the NWP's tactics: "Do they think United States senators are going to change their opinions and their votes because a parcel of women stand round the doors, holding banners? Who are they, anyway? Little young things, just out of school or old ladies who ought to be at home enjoying their grandchildren." NAWSA lobbyists worked hard to earn their designation as "the sane suffragists."[12]

They plotted their strategy carefully. In January 1918, the front door lobby won a huge victory when the House of Representatives passed the suffrage amendment by a vote of 274–136, with literally one vote to spare. One supporter who had broken his shoulder refused to have it set until after the vote had been taken; another interrupted the preparations for his wife's funeral to cast his ballot. The morning after the vote, Carrie Chapman Catt reached out to NAWSA's state congressional chairmen with a clarion call to mobilize pressure on the Senate, confidently predicting to Maud Wood Park that their task would be over in a month or two. Park was more cautious, realizing how difficult winning a two-thirds majority in the Senate would be. She suspected that she and her corps of lobbyists wouldn't be leaving Washington anytime soon.

So the suffragists went back to work. In May they were still two votes short, but Woodrow Wilson's recent declaration of support encouraged them to bring the measure up for debate on the senate floor. When it was clear that those votes were not forthcoming, the Democratic leadership abruptly cancelled the vote, a humiliating experience for the suffragists. After the fiasco, a furious Carrie Chapman Catt lost her temper with one of the floor managers, leaving Park with the task of making amends for the offense her hot-headed boss had caused. Later, she realized that the floor leader's action had been motivated by his desire to help, not hinder, the amendment, but at the time it was a low blow.[13]

With the 1918 off-year elections looming, the suffragists geared up for another attempt in September. "Mrs. Catt has been here for weeks," the *Woman Citizen* reported. "Mrs. Park is always here." Five days of debate began on September 26, with much pontificating, especially on the antisuffrage side. Catt couldn't bear to sit in the gallery listening to the debate, so she decamped back to Suffrage House. When it became clear that no minds were being changed, Catt appealed to President Woodrow Wilson to address the Senate, with the hope that he could personally change enough votes for it to pass. Wilson gave one of the most impassioned speeches he ever delivered on the subject, calling the suffrage amendment "vital to the winning of the war." If only the vote had been taken then, they might have prevailed, Park later thought. But when the matter came to a vote the next day, Wilson had not changed a single mind, and the amendment went down to defeat, 62–34. Park's response? "We've got to act like merry sunshine no matter what we think for we can't afford to have any one know that we feel beaten." Anna Howard Shaw took revenge by inserting this dig in her speeches: "When I sit in the gallery of the Senate and look down on the senators," she would begin, then pause and add: "and I don't have to sit in the gallery to look down on them."[14]

By this point, there wasn't much more lobbying that could be done to convince recalcitrant opponents, so the suffragists concluded they would need to change the composition of the Senate. With just five weeks until the November 1918 election, they targeted the Republican senator John W. Weeks of Massachusetts and the Democratic senator Willard Saulsbury of Delaware, helping to defeat both of them in the midst of the terrible influenza epidemic gripping the country. With the Republicans poised to take control of both the Senate and the House when the sixty-sixth Congress convened in March 1919, the suffragists pushed for one more vote while the Democratic-controlled sixty-fifth Congress was still in session. Once again, they came up two votes short.

Now that a new Congress was convening, the suffragists had to start all over again. Luckily, the momentum had begun to shift—the successful 1917 New York State referendum proved a huge turning point. The measure galloped through the House, picking up supporters in direct relation to the increasing number of states where women had full or partial suffrage. On May 10, 1919, it passed the House by a vote of 304–90, "the ayes . . . tumbling in so fast and close together that I could hardly set them down," Park remembered.[15]

Prospects in the Senate were still guarded. Suffragists had experienced such bad luck with supporters dying in office that Maud Wood Park "dreaded to look at the morning paper for fear that one of our friends in the Senate had died during the night."[16] During the two agonizing days of debate, "when victory was within our grasp, I completely lost the self-control with which I had sat through the previous debates," Park admitted, emitting "murmurs of angry impatience" during the final antisuffrage speeches. With the support of sixty-six senators, on June 4, 1919, more than two and a half years after Maud Wood Park took over as congressional chair, the suffrage amendment finally passed.[17]

When it came time to parse the reasons for victory, Park repeatedly emphasized the key insight of Carrie Chapman Catt's winning plan: that increasing numbers of enfranchised women would put pressure on Congress. While some commentators linked the victory to women's participation in the war effort, Park did not believe any votes were swayed by that issue. She could not point to a single case where Woodrow Wilson's intervention had made the difference, either, although victory would have been difficult if not impossible without the president's change in heart. Never one to gloat or make grandiose claims, she even downplayed the role of the front door lobby: "Much as I like to think that we had our part in the successful outcome, I am sure that no member of that lobby failed to recognize that without the backing of the women at work in the states, our best efforts would have been futile." And she adamantly deflected attention away from her own role, keeping very much in the background and letting Carrie Chapman Catt bask in the public limelight.[18]

Maud Wood Park was too modest. When a final tally comes down to a few votes, the role of lobbyists takes on heightened importance. Senator Henry Hollis of New Hampshire made that point directly to Park: "The narrow margin of two votes gives you a right to feel that you personally are a tremendous factor in the final result. If the margin had been large, no one could have claimed much credit. But those two votes certainly represent the result of your individual efforts." Especially significant was Park's ability to work with members of both parties. Throughout her years of service to the suffrage campaign, Maud Wood Park had remained scrupulously non-partisan, a stance she would maintain when she became the first president of the National League of Women Voters in 1920. "Perhaps God knew which party Mrs. Park favored," observed one Washington insider, "but if so, He hasn't told anybody in Washington."[19]

Carrie Chapman Catt was not in the gallery when the final senate vote was taken. After witnessing the defeat the previous fall, she vowed never again to listen to a congressional suffrage debate, and she kept her word. Besides, she was too busy preparing the campaign for ratification. The long hard haul was not over yet.

Alice Paul sews a star on the suffrage flag while members of the National Woman's Party look on. *Courtesy of Schlesinger Library, Radcliffe Institute, Harvard University.*

CHAPTER NINETEEN

Tennessee's "Perfect 36"

ALICE PAUL was not included in Carrie Chapman Catt's suf-frage forest, but her fingerprints are all over the struggle. To say that Alice Paul was a polarizing figure is a wild under-statement. To her devoted followers in the National Woman's Party, she was practically a saint—Joan of Arc reincarnated, the most inspirational leader any feminist movement could ever want. The views of her opponents were just as extreme. In the words of a Dutch activist who clashed with Paul in the 1930s, "The opinion that 99% of all the people whom I have met and who have had to deal with Miss Paul" is "A. P. can ONLY lead!" In the suffrage veteran Doris Stevens's telling phrase, "In order to work with Miss Paul, one has to surren-der all."[1]

Some leaders build their followings by spellbinding ora-tory, but Alice Paul was never an especially charismatic public speaker, and she generally shunned the limelight. Paul's greatest skill was her ability as a tactician and strategist. Lucy Burns, her co-conspirator from British suffrage days onward, captured her ability to work on both the macro and micro levels: "Her great assets, I should say, are her power to make plans on a national scale; and a supplemental power to see that it is done down to the postage stamp.["2](...)

If she had been a man, she might have been a business tycoon or a college president, but she always preferred the world of women. As a leader—and she always had to be in charge—Paul crafted flexible, panther-like responses, almost counterinsurgencies, deploying different strategies as different situations demanded. She never repeated her tactics, and she kept upping the ante as needed. She was willing to take risks, and she never took her eyes off the prize. The veteran of repeated hunger strikes, she always seemed on the verge of collapse, but of course she never did, which in turn added to her mystique.

And she could sew. One of the most iconic images of Alice Paul is her unfurling a suffrage flag from the balcony of NWP headquarters. Each time a state approved woman suffrage, she would personally sew a ratification star on the flag. In this picture, it looks as though there are still at least five states to go. New Mexico, Oklahoma, West Virginia, and Washington all ratified in February and March 1920, but then progress came to a halt. With the election of 1920 fast approaching, it all came down to Tennessee in August. One key to that victory was sitting at the table to the right of Alice Paul, holding the fabric steady: Tennessee's own Sue Shelton White.

THE POPULAR APPEAL of Harry Burn's story is easy to understand: a minor Republican legislator in Tennessee dramatically removes the antisuffrage red rose from his lapel and casts the deciding vote that puts the Nineteenth Amendment over the top. And what causes his sudden change of heart? Nothing less than a heart-felt appeal from his mother to follow Carrie Chapman Catt's call to "put the RAT in ratification." This is no urban legend. Harry Burn did indeed cast that vote, and his mother strongly lobbied him to do so. But reducing the final battle to such a simple story flattens out the political intrigues and machinations raging in Nashville those hot August days in 1920. The Tennessee suffragist Sue Shelton White was right in the thick of them and had been for the past eight years.[3]

"I come of good American stock. The blood of Thomas Jefferson and John Marshall flows in my veins. My father fought under Lee."[4] That is how Sue Shelton White, a proud southern Democrat, described her family's background. Her carefully curated facts told only part of the story, however. The White family, like many other formerly well-to-do southern slave owners, had experienced financial difficulties since the Civil War. When Sue was born in Henderson, Tennessee in 1887, her father was serving as the local superintendent of schools and active in the Methodist ministry. After his death in 1893, when Sue was just six, her mother struggled to keep the family together. Southern white women were not supposed to work outside the home, so she cobbled together various ways to get by—selling pianos, giving voice lessons, and writing for the local newspaper. "I never classed my mother as a feminist," her daughter later recalled, "but I suspect she was one. Life would have made her one in the end if she had not been in the beginning." When Mary White died in 1901, fourteen-year-old Sue was looked after by an aunt.[5]

Sue Shelton White remembered a childhood in which both brothers and sisters shared the household chores, and gender distinctions were minimal. It soon became clear to her that unless she married, she would need to support herself. Being of an independent frame of mind and influenced by her mother's feminism, this prospect did not daunt her and may in fact have been quite appealing. The most obvious path was to enter the teaching profession, and in 1904 she graduated from Georgie Robertson Christian College, a teacher training school which also offered courses in stenography. Forgoing teaching, she set her sights on the law. In 1907, she became a court reporter in Jackson, Tennessee and later a private secretary to one of the members of the Tennessee Supreme Court. Clearly loving her immersion in the legal world, she was frustrated by the barriers that she faced, such as being called "impractical" or "visionary" whenever she talked of studying law. (Not until 1923, while working in Washington, DC as a secretary to Senator Kenneth McKellar, would she finally get her law degree.) In the meantime, she was gaining valuable political contacts that she would soon put to good use. As Governor Thomas Clarke Rye later said, "Anyone who is a friend of Miss Sue's, is a friend of ours."[6]

In 1912, Sue Shelton White embraced woman suffrage, a cause that came later to the South than elsewhere in the country. She helped found the Jackson League of the Tennessee Equal Suffrage Association and was soon promoted to recording secretary. Even when the Tennessee Equal Suffrage Association split in two because of regional factionalism, White maintained cordial relations with both groups. Yet because the leadership of the southern suffrage movement was almost uniformly held by older, wealthy, socially elite white women—a status White did not enjoy as a self-supporting stenographer—she found herself shut out of the top positions, no matter how much energy and talent she brought to the cause. White was well aware of the limitations of her respectable but modest status. As she wrote to Carrie Chapman Catt about a fellow suffragist who was lobbying the Tennessee senator John Shields, "Mrs. Warner knows him quite well socially. I know him quite well also, but my acquaintance has been more political than social. There is sometimes a difference."[7]

In these years, Sue Shelton White juggled the need to support herself with her time-consuming commitment to suffrage advocacy. With a wide range of contacts on the Tennessee political scene to draw on, she was a superb organizer. She was also an effective speaker, but one of her early suffrage exploits involved not speaking at all. In December 1916, Tennessee suffragists wanted to present a petition to the Farmer's Institute convention in Nashville. When that request was denied, they stood silently on the main floor of the state capitol, holding suffrage signs and banners that the delegates had to walk by. White later thought this demonstration may have given Alice Paul the idea for the Silent Sentinels that started picketing the White House in January 1917.[8]

The onset of World War I in April 1917 affected Sue Shelton White's suffrage career in ways that she had not anticipated. By that point, the National Woman's Party had long broken from NAWSA, but it had only the faintest footprint in the South. Suffrage itself seemed such a radical idea that the NWP's militance seemed over the top, and their strategy of targeting Democrats in the 1914 and 1916 elections as the party in power did not sit well in the solidly Democratic South. The NWP's reputation got even worse when Alice Paul decided to continue picketing the White House after war was declared. Now, in addition to being militant and unladylike, suffragists were accused of being unpatriotic and un-American.

In 1917, the National Woman's Party sent Maud Younger on a southern tour to build support for the Nineteenth Amendment—a hard sell in the states-rights South—and to recruit talent for the

organization. So strong were the pro-war and antisuffrage sentiments in Tennessee that Younger found herself unable to secure
speaking venues. Sue Shelton White was ashamed of her home state's
affront to free speech, and she offered to use her political capital on
Younger's behalf. As she later explained to Carrie Chapman Catt, "I
was appealed to, to do the only thing and the least thing that I could
do under the circumstances, which was simply to state that while
I did not subscribe to the policy of the Woman's Party and was not
working with it, I did not regard either the party or Miss Younger
as disloyal, pro-German, or un-American."[9]

The NWP organizer Rebecca Hourwich Reyher later provided a
much more vivid description of White's role: "She got on the phone.
She called the Mayor, and the Police Chief. She demanded that we
be given the privilege of speaking, and that we have the protection
we might need, and she guaranteed to stand behind us and anything we said on her word of honor. We were women asking for the
vote, and there was nothing anyone could call *unpatriotic* in that."
Sue White was especially impressive on her home turf of Jackson,
according to Reyher: "She spellbound the hostile audience. The
rumblings stopped, the atmosphere became friendly; we hated to
leave Jackson." White temporarily closed down her stenography
office to accompany them on the rest of their tour of Tennessee,
"and everywhere, thanks to her the hostility vanished." Reyher especially appreciated the gesture of support: "In those days Sue lived
by what she earned, and her shutting up shop to help us was a real
sacrifice."[10]

Carrie Chapman Catt first learned that things might be amiss
in Tennessee when she read an account of White's efforts on behalf
of Maud Younger in *The Suffragist*, the NWP weekly newspaper. (It
is telling, but hardly surprising, that the president of NAWSA kept

tabs on the NWP.) Alarmed, she contacted the president of the Tennessee suffrage association, fearful that White might be sharing NAWSA plans with their rivals. "No one can now carry water on both shoulders," Catt asserted. She admitted the Woman's Party was "doing some good work. But its chief stock in trade is to get our plans and try to frustrate them, and for that we can not stand."[11]

When White learned that aspersions were being cast on her loyalty, she wrote a lengthy reply to Catt. Clearly upset that Catt had shared her unfounded suspicions behind her back, she recounted the Maud Younger saga in great detail—"You now have before you a full confession"—stressing that the issue of free speech was paramount in her intercession. But she also got in a few digs about NAWSA's disinterest in organizing southern states, which stood in stark contrast to the NWP's recognition of "the need of waking up the South." More broadly, White tried very hard to appeal to a sense of larger solidarity for the cause. Even when there were disagreements about tactics and strategies, she felt that much common ground remained. Carrie Chapman Catt would have none of this. "This is the point in which women everywhere must take a big view and try to consider all the data before making up their minds." She asked White to "take your stand fair and square, one side or the other."[12]

Meanwhile, Alice Paul recognized that she had a hot prospect in Tennessee. White had not been ready to jump ship in November— she was "still 'too good a Democrat,' too well grounded in my faith in the President's ultimate purpose, to take my stand at that time with the women who were in the front line trenches of the fight"— but she was finally ready to make the break five months later. She accepted a position as the Tennessee chairman of the National Woman's Party, finding opportunities for influence and power in the upstart NWP that her lack of social status and southern roots denied her in NAWSA. In 1919, after Alice Paul offered her a position as the editor of *The Suffragist*, she moved to Washington, DC.[13]

As 1919 dawned, suffragists in both camps were increasingly discouraged at the stalled amendment in the Senate. Once again, the National Woman's Party stepped up its militance, and this time Sue Shelton White was fully on board. On February 9, she took part in a demonstration where an "effigy" of President Woodrow Wilson was burned in Lafayette Park, an act that risked being labeled as treason when repressive wartime restrictions on free speech remained in force despite the armistice the previous November. White personally read their dramatic manifesto: "We burn not the effigy of the President of a free people, but the leader of an autocratic party organization whose tyrannical power holds millions of women in political slavery." (The protesters actually burned a Lou Rogers cartoon of Woodrow Wilson so it would catch fire quickly. Still, the protest troubled African American suffragists, who found it far too closely resembled the heinous practice of lynching.) Alice Paul looked on, admiring their bravery: "I saw Sue White at the urn— the flames flashed. She gave me a nod; I knew the deed was done." White was quickly arrested and, along with more than two dozen NWP protestors, spent five days in jail, where she promptly went on a hunger strike. When she was released, she was personally awarded her prison pin by Alice Paul, just as Hazel Hunkins had earned hers a few months earlier.[14]

Just days after her release White embarked on a cross-country whistle-stop tour on the "Prison Special." On February 15, 1919, twenty-six women who had been imprisoned since the arrests started in summer 1917 boarded a railroad car they christened "Democracy Limited." They carried a message "from the prison to the people" in a last-ditch effort to change votes before the Senate adjourned. With public attention focused on Woodrow Wilson's peace negotiations in Paris, the National Woman's Party wanted to remind the country of "the lawless and brutal length to which the Administration has gone to suppress the lawful agitation for suffrage." What better way to make both of those points than to appear on platforms in replicas of their prison garb—"all 'jail birds' and proud of it," White recalled. Once again, Alice Paul had upped the ante.[15]

Sue Shelton White remembered the Prison Special tour as an exhilarating but exhausting experience, but she never doubted that it was worth it: "Twenty-five nights on the same sleeper, with the same fellow passengers, going through the same routine at stops, practically the same food (always chicken, at luncheons), snatching a cup of coffee at a lunch counter in the early morning, the everlasting photographers, parades, pilgrimages to mayors' offices for the keys to cities, open air meetings, indoor mass meetings snatching spare moments to get shoes polished, handkerchieves washed, clothes pressed,—all the miserable worry of traveling." When the tour finally ended, they parted "friends with each other, and with the consciousness that each had done what she could and that it all had been worth while."[16]

Ironically, the Prison Special tour coincided with the end of militant action by the National Woman's Party. As did NAWSA's front door lobby, the NWP recognized that nothing could happen until Congress passed the amendment. It finally did so in June, after intense lobbying by both sides. Then all energy turned to the ratification campaign. The enmity between the NWP and NAWSA was as strong as ever—it would continue to play out in postsuffrage politics well into the 1940s—but in this final stage, the similarities between the two groups' approaches were far more salient than their differences. Both focused on traditional lobbying and the mobilization of public opinion to win over state legislators. Of course, neither side would admit to any common ground, so the battle for ratification went forward on separate but parallel tracks.[17]

Sue Shelton White's unswerving loyalty to the cause of suffrage, her keen political instincts, and her ability to rise above factional disputes were put to good use in the successful ratification fight in Tennessee. Finding what NAWSA called "the perfect 36"—a reference to the number of states needed to ratify as well as to the ideal female figure—had proven harder than expected, and Tennessee offered probably the last chance to accomplish this goal in time for women to vote in the 1920 election.

For several weeks in August, practically everyone descended on the state capital. Carrie Chapman Catt was in town, but she mainly holed up at a hotel supervising her legions of NAWSA lobbyists. Alice Paul was in close contact with her NWP lieutenants by telegraph and telephone from Washington, DC. Tennessee contributed its own seasoned suffragists to the cause, as did both political parties. Right in the thick of things was Sue Shelton White, officially on the NWP team but playing a critical role navigating this chaotic scene. Because of her political contacts and her insider's knowledge of how things worked, White was in a unique position to affect the outcome. To keep her spirits up, she wore her prison pin every day, even though she realized its association with militance might be off-putting to some of the local politicians she was trying to sway.

Unlike Maud Wood Park's painstaking "front door" lobbying, which literally stretched over entire congressional sessions, the Tennessee ratification campaign unfolded at breakneck speed, evoking far "more excitement and agitation than the long fight in Congress." First the Tennessee governor had to be convinced that it was constitutional to call a special legislative session. Drawing on her legal expertise, White played a key role in overcoming his objections. That hurdle cleared, the legislators dutifully if reluctantly returned to Nashville to consider the amendment, not at all keen, in those days before air-conditioning, to return to work in the summer heat, but resigned to fulfilling their civic duty. For or against, they literally had a chance to participate in making history.[18]

On August 9, 1920, White opened a temporary National Woman's Party headquarters in Nashville, and it was flat out for the next two weeks. As always, the NWP was strapped for cash, so White could only count on a small team comprised of Anita Pollitzer, Betty Gram, and Charlotte Flanagan. Gram recalled working day and night together "against a formidable opposition—a lobby of wealthy anti-suffragists, ostentatious liquor interests, and clandestine railroad executives." (It wasn't all work, though: she also remembered White treating her to the best watermelon she ever tasted in her life.) Telegrams flew back and forth to Alice Paul at Belmont House in Washington, DC, and lobbyists roamed the corridors of the statehouse. As to Sue Shelton White herself, "she worked at white heat, directing the lobbyists day by day, hour by hour, so that every moment they knew where the legislation stood in the Legislature." With so many outsiders flooding the state capital, pro- and anti-, "her contacts, her good judgment, and her fire accomplished wonders."[19] Activists at the time and historians ever since have singled out White "for her skillful coordination of suffragists of all factions." Betty Gram concluded dramatically, "I think it can be said that the date of victory might have been delayed many years but for her brilliant strategy."[20]

The amendment breezed through the Tennessee Senate on August 13 by a margin of 25–4, but prospects were much dimmer in the House, especially because House Speaker Seth Walker was firmly against ratification. A master parliamentarian, he repeatedly used delaying tactics to try to undermine still shaky support for the amendment. With legislators increasingly restless to go home, however, he was forced to bring the issue to a vote on August 18. At that point, both suffragists and antis knew it was a dead heat. Walker's motion to table the question indefinitely resulted in a 48–48 tie, not enough to cause the motion to pass, but certainly a bad omen for the final vote.

So now the official vote on the amendment began. Moving alphabetically, the results mirrored the earlier voting breakdown on the motion to table—until the roll call got to Harry Burn. It was at this point that he dramatically laid aside his red rose and changed his vote to "aye." Even so, this did not guarantee victory for the suffragists, and the roll call continued through the alphabet. When it got to Banks Turner, a legislator who had been allied with the state's pro-ratification governor but who had earlier voted with the antis, he asked to be counted as not voting, and the tally ended once again in a 48–48 tie. When those results were announced, Turner stepped forward and asked to be counted in favor, making the final tally 49–48.

Even with these two changes of heart, the amendment still might have gone down to defeat, because it lacked a clear constitutional majority of fifty votes in a ninety-nine member lower chamber. Where did the final vote come from? Ironically, it came from House Speaker Seth Walker, who changed his vote to yes so that he could immediately move for a reconsideration. His plan was to delay the proceedings once again, in the hopes of convincing a single legislator to flip his vote and kill the amendment. That scheme failed, as did a last-minute injunction holding up certification of the vote. Not until six days later, on August 24, was the vote officially certified, and not until two days after that did the official documentation arrive in Washington, DC, making August 26 the date usually associated with the passage of the Nineteenth Amendment.

Finally, Alice Paul could sew the last suffrage star on her flag and unfurl it out the window at NWP headquarters. The century-long struggle to win the vote for women was over, but not so the quest for women's equality. One hundred years later, the struggle continues.

"Leaving All to Younger Hands"

History matters. Susan B. Anthony knew that, but she refused to stay stuck in the past. When the fourth volume of the *History of Woman Suffrage* appeared in 1902, the eighty-two-year-old Anthony looked back with pride at what the movement had accomplished, but she also looked forward to what still needed to be done. With a firm hand and a penetrating choice of words, she penned this inscription in her friend Caroline Healey Dall's personal copy: "This closes the records of the 19th century of work done by and for women—what the 20th century will show—no one can foresee—but that it will be vastly more and better—we cannot fail to believe. But you & I have done the best we knew—and so must rest content—leaving all to younger hands. Your sincere friend and coworker, Susan B. Anthony . . . Rochester, N.Y."[1] Anthony had devoted more than fifty years of her life to the woman suffrage movement, and victory was nowhere in sight when she wrote those words. Yet she remained proud of what she and her co-workers had done for the cause, and confident that the future would bring even more progress. I suspect that the suffrage leaders who guided the movement to its successful conclusion on August 26, 1920 felt the same way.

That hard-fought victory, the culmination of three generations of sustained political mobilization and spirited public advocacy, represented a breakthrough for American women as well as a major step forward for American democracy. By the early twentieth century, women's lives had already moved far beyond the domestic sphere. Barriers had fallen, and opportunities had opened up. Yet the fundamental responsibility of citizenship—the right to vote—was arbitrarily denied to half the population. The Nineteenth Amendment changed that increasingly untenable situation, and that is no small achievement.

Participating in the suffrage campaign provided women with the kind of exhilaration and camaraderie often described by men in periods of war or political upheaval. Women were proud to be part of this great crusade, and they cherished the solidarity it engendered for the rest of their lives. Frances Perkins, a veteran of the New York suffrage campaign and the first woman to serve in the cabinet as Franklin D. Roosevelt's secretary of labor, remembered it this way: "The friendships that were formed among women who were in the suffrage movement have been the most lasting and enduring friendships—solid, substantial, loyal—that I have ever seen anywhere. The women learned to like each other in that suffrage movement."[2]

The campaign also honed women's political skills. As Gertrude Foster Brown observed at its conclusion, "We were wiser politically than any group of women had ever been." Because the opposition of politicians had been so fierce and because most of the public remained indifferent if not outright hostile, women were forced to become extremely effective campaigners, lobbyists, and publicists. Once learned, these skills were put to use after the vote was won. "Men are saying perhaps 'Thank God, this everlasting woman's fight is over!'" Crystal Eastman observed. "But women, if I know them, are saying, 'Now at last we can begin.'" That sentiment is just as true today as women approach their second century of full voting rights.[3]

Once the Nineteenth Amendment passed, activists claimed a new moniker—that of women citizens. The sustained activism of suffragists-turned-women-citizens provides the clearest answer to why suffrage mattered. Historians agree that there was no significant difference in the level or intensity of women's activism "across the great divide"—that is, before and after 1920. In many ways, the suffrage movement was an anomaly, the rare time when a broad range of women came together under one banner. Women collectively won the vote, but they exercised that right as individuals. In the postsuffrage era, politically engaged women embraced a wide variety of causes rather than remaining united around a single goal. A similar insight applies to antisuffragists once the Nineteenth Amendment was ratified. Either way, progressive and conservative women remained active in public life. When it came to politics, women were saying forcefully, "We have come to stay."[4]

In this enlarged perspective, the suffrage victory is not a hard stop but part of a continuum of women's political mobilization stretching not just between 1848 and 1920 but across all of American history. It is still appropriate, indeed welcome, to celebrate the centennial of the Nineteenth Amendment as an important marker in American women's history, but rather than positioning 1920 as the end of the story, it is far more fruitful to see it as initiating the next stage in the history of women's political activism, a story that is still unfolding.

When thinking about the larger implications of the suffrage victory, we also need to remember that many women, especially those in western states, were already voting in the years before the passage of the Nineteenth Amendment. In addition, women across the country had recourse to a range of voting opportunities on the local level, such as municipal suffrage or participating in school committee elections, well before the Nineteenth Amendment took effect. Focusing too much on the 1920 milestone downplays the political clout that enfranchised women already exercised. The focus on the 1920 victory also tends to overshadow women's earlier roles as community builders, organization founders, and influence wielders. Throughout American history, women have been political actors, even without the vote. Women's political history is far broader than the ratification of a single constitutional amendment.

Another reason for decentering 1920 concerns the plight of African American voters, for whom the Nineteenth Amendment was at most a hollow victory. To be sure, African American women in the North, such as Ida Wells-Barnett and Mary Church Terrell, could now exercise the right to vote—although Terrell would lack full voting rights even today as a resident of Washington, DC, which is not entitled to voting representation in Congress. In 1920, however, the vast majority of African Americans still lived in the South, where their voting rights were effectively eliminated by devices such as whites-only primaries, poll taxes, and literacy tests. For blacks, it was the Voting Rights Act of 1965, not the Fourteenth, Fifteenth, or Nineteenth Amendments, that finally removed the structural barriers to voting.[5]

In a parallel disfranchisement, few Native American women gained the vote through the Nineteenth Amendment. After the Supreme Court ruled in 1884 that the Fourteenth Amendment did not automatically confer citizenship on Native Americans, it took Congress until 1924 to pass legislation declaring that all Native

Americans born in the United States were citizens, which cleared the way for tribal women to vote. But as with African Americans after the 1920 milestone, Native American women still faced ongoing restrictions and barriers to voting on the state and local levels, especially in the West, well into the twentieth century.[6]

Today, the battle for voting rights is far from over. A Supreme Court decision in 2013 significantly weakened key provisions of the Voting Rights Act. People of color and other minorities face obstacles deliberately designed to keep them from exercising their right to vote, such as photo ID laws, purging of voter rolls, and widespread delays at under-resourced polls which serve to suppress voting, especially in urban areas. And large groups, especially convicted felons, are prevented from voting altogether in many states. When assessing who can exercise the right to vote, it is always essential to ask who cannot.

In addition to the importance of woman suffrage for American political history, women's demand for fair and equitable treatment in the political realm emerges as an integral part of the history of feminism. To protest women's exclusion from voting demanded an assault on attitudes and ideologies that treated women as second-class citizens; to formulate that challenge involved conceptualizing women as a group whose collective situation needed to be addressed. Even though white suffragists were often clueless that they were speaking primarily from their own privileged class and race positions, the growing consciousness of women's common concerns fostered a unique sense of sisterhood in early twentieth-century America. The fact that certain groups of women, especially women of color, were often excluded from this supposedly universal vision demonstrates how racism intersected with feminism throughout the woman suffrage movement and during its aftermath. Contemporary feminists have significantly broadened their commitment to recognizing the diversity of women's experiences and worked hard to include multiple perspectives within the broader feminist framework, but it is still a struggle. The suffrage movement is part of that story, warts and all.

Suffrage mattered to the later careers of suffragists as well. Not all of the women in this book lived to see the suffrage victory, but many enjoyed significant careers in the postsuffrage era. Most of their names are little known within the realm of mainstream history, which says a great deal about how the contributions of politically engaged women are often marginalized or overlooked. Maud Wood Park served as the first president of the National League of Women Voters, and Gertrude Foster Brown oversaw *The Woman Citizen*, the LWV's main publication. Ida Wells-Barnett ran for political office in Illinois. Molly Dewson, Rose Schneiderman, and Sue Shelton White all served with distinction in Franklin Roosevelt's New Deal administration. Nina Allender pursued her career as an artist. Alice Stone Blackwell continued her activism through the American Civil Liberties Union and the League of Women Voters. Hazel Hunkins-Hallinan joined the British feminist movement. In her eighties, Mary Church Terrell marched on a picket line in Washington, DC to protest segregation in the nation's capital.

These examples point to the public continuities of women's activism before and after suffrage, but the suffrage experience also played out in less visible ways. To paraphrase Betty Friedan about her own involvement in second-wave feminism, participating in the movement changed lives. For women such as Maud Nathan, Cora Smith Eaton, Mary Johnston, and Charlotte Perkins Gilman, their suffrage activism came towards the end of long and productive public careers, and thus served as something of a valedictory. For others, such as Claiborne Catlin, who remarried and worked as a school administrator, or Hazel MacKaye, who stepped back from her theatrical career to take care of an ailing mother before succumbing to ill health herself, it was more of a temporary if exciting blip. In ways large and small, suffrage made a difference to all of their subsequent lives.

If there is a clear take-away to these suffrage stories, it is that we need to keep individual lives in focus while also tracking the big picture. Suffragists participated in one of the largest mobilizations of women the United States has ever seen, and being part of that collective effort was immensely rewarding. Even though many of these women were foot soldiers—after all, not everyone aspires to be a leader or a general—their rank-and-file contributions made a difference to the larger movement, to the larger society, and to the participants themselves. "It was a continuous, seemingly endless, chain of activity," Carrie Chapman Catt and Nettie Rogers Shuler realized. "Young suffragists who helped forge the last links of that chain were not born when it began. Old suffragists who forged the first links were dead when it ended." As one character states in Oreola Williams Haskell's *Banner Bearers: Tales of the Suffrage Campaigns*, "It's not hard to tell what I am. Just an ordinary woman trying to do her best—often with a prayer in her heart—for a great cause. . . . I am just a cog in a big machine."[7]

Biography captures the power and passion of those individual "cogs"; material culture helps make the stories even more real. Sojourner Truth's carte de visite shows how commitment to a cause could also sustain a livelihood. Hazel MacKaye's souvenir program from the 1913 Washington, DC suffrage parade demonstrates how the movement marshaled traditional iconography in the service of radical new forms of public spectacle. The treasured prison pins of

Hazel Hunkins and other National Woman's Party members passed down through the generations remind us that women were literally willing to die for the cause. And the lowly ballot box provides a physical reminder of what the movement was all about: the chance for women to cast their ballots alongside men.

That paean to objects and artifacts brings us full circle to Susan B. Anthony's inscription and the Schlesinger Library, whose archives document so many of the stories told in this book. While women's history is extraordinarily broad overall, the history of the woman suffrage movement provides a central strand, especially in terms of extant archival material.[8] Maud Wood Park was one of those who honored suffrage history by donating her extensive Woman's Rights Collection to Radcliffe College in 1943. The Woman's Rights Collection became the Radcliffe Women's Archives, which in 1965 was renamed the Arthur and Elizabeth Schlesinger Library on the History of Women in America.

There is a direct link between Anthony's inscription in the *History of Woman Suffrage* and the emergence of the field of women's history. Anthony foreshadowed not only the significance of women's contributions to public life—what the historian Mary Beard, another early supporter of the Women's Archives, called "woman as force in history"—but also the need for collecting the material that would make studying those contributions possible. Park's decision to give her suffrage collection an institutional home demonstrated suffragists' determination to document their story so their legacy would be available to future generations. Their collective decisions in turn laid the foundations for the exponential growth of the field of women's history since the 1970s, whose scholarship has been central to reclaiming the history of feminism and keeping its legacy alive.[9]

The specific volume that contained Susan B. Anthony's hand-written inscription was not part of the original 1943 donation, and there is a story behind that too. The *History of Woman Suffrage*, especially its first three volumes, was probably found in the library of every prominent suffrage supporter in the country. When suffragists donated their papers to Radcliffe, the Schlesinger Library accumulated multiple copies—sometimes a full set, other times a partial one, some inscribed, some not. No one had paid any special attention to this specific volume included in Caroline Healey Dall's bequest. Only years later, when every last volume in the library's vast book collection was barcoded for retrieval and tracking, did a cataloguer pick up Dall's volume and gasp with astonishment at the inscription it contained. It was almost as if the physical object spoke.

And now, more than a century later, Susan B. Anthony's inscription speaks again, reminding us that feminism and women's rights are an ongoing struggle with no clear endpoint in sight and that the woman suffrage movement is a vital part of that story. The strategies and lessons of the suffrage campaign link past and present to provide a clear blueprint for the mobilization of women in our contemporary political landscape. To wit: Embrace a broad definition of political activism which goes beyond electoral politics but still encourages women to change the political system from within. Use popular culture and new forms of media to get the word out, but don't forget older techniques like lobbying and grassroots organizing. Deploy public spectacle and mass demonstrations to bring women (and men) into public spaces, while simultaneously creating instantly recognizable symbols and slogans to support their demands. Be intersectional: mobilize coalitions and alliances that cross race, class, and other boundaries and draw on the energies of multiple, overlapping generations. Remember that feminism is a cumulative effort, not a one-off event, and it will always be necessary. All of these observations are as relevant today as they were at the height of suffrage mobilization in the 1910s. History can be both a guide and an inspiration.

Gertrude Stein and Virgil Thomson grasped that dual legacy when they collaborated on *The Mother of Us All*, an operatic pageant that premiered in 1947. Following on the heels of their groundbreaking opera *Four Saints in Three Acts* (1934), *The Mother of Us All* tells the story of the winning of political rights for women in the United States through the life of Susan B. Anthony. The cast of characters includes historical figures such as Daniel Webster, John Adams, and Ulysses S. Grant, as well as some unusual additions such as the actress Lillian Russell and the anti-vice crusader Anthony Comstock. The opera culminates in a scene at the US Capitol, where a statue honoring Susan B. Anthony is unveiled.

As befits its creator, Gertrude Stein's playful but pointed libretto contains many whimsical moments, but its overall thrust is clear. *The Mother of Us All* is an operatic assault on the patriarchy. One of Susan B. Anthony's lines has special resonance: "I speak as loudly as I can.... I even speak louder than I can."[10] The powerful voices that suffragists raised to win the vote echo in the activism of the generations of women who followed and still speak loudly today.

NOTES

ACKNOWLEDGMENTS

INDEX

Notes

Prologue

1. Peter D. Shaver, "National Register of Historic Places Registration: Carrie Chapman Catt House," New York State Office of Parks, Recreation and Historic Preservation (October 2003). Carrie Chapman Catt later confirmed that there was a link between buying the property and the onset of Prohibition: "I know that the juniper is useful in making liquor, and that is why I bought the place— so that no one else would have opportunity to use the trees for that purpose." "Mrs. Catt Receives Women Picnickers," *New York Times*, June 26, 1921, 14.

2. The rationale for the placement of the plaques is described in Clara Hyde to Mary Gray Peck, September 29, 1919, Edna Lamprey Stantial Papers, Schlesinger Library, Radcliffe Institute, Harvard University.

3. At some point after Catt sold the property, the plaques were taken off the trees. They eventually came to the Schlesinger Library as part of the Edna Lamprey Stantial Papers. Along the way, the plaques for Susan B. Anthony, Aletta Jacobs, Minna Cauer, and Lucy Stone went missing.

4. The *New York Times* article on June 26, 1921, mentions two additional plaques— to Wyoming suffragist Esther Morris and NAWSA lobbyist Maud Wood Park— but there is no further documentation of their existence.

5. See Neil MacGregor, *A History of the World in 100 Objects* (New York: Penguin, 2010) and Laurel Thatcher Ulrich, Evan Gaskell, Sara J. Schechner, and Sarah Anne Carter, *Tangible Things: Making History through Objects* (New York: Oxford University Press, 2015).

6. Laurel Thatcher Ulrich, *Well-Behaved Women Seldom Make History* (New York: Knopf, 2007). Often the slogan is rendered as "well-behaved women rarely make history," but I follow her original formulation.

7. Winnifred Harper Cooley, "The Younger Suffragists," *Harper's Weekly* 58 (September 27, 1913), 7–8, quoted in Nancy F. Cott, *The Grounding of Modern Feminism* (New Haven: Yale University Press, 1987), 15; Estelle B. Freedman,

No Turning Back: The History of Feminism and the Future of Women (New York: Ballantine Books, 2002), 7.

8. Cott, *Grounding of Modern Feminism*, 5. Cott's definition of feminism is more specific to the 1910s, and it is broader than just gender consciousness. It is discussed at greater length in the chapter on Charlotte Perkins Gilman.

9. Susan Ware, "The Book I Couldn't Write: Alice Paul and the Challenge of Feminist Biography," *Journal of Women's History* 24, no. 2 (Summer 2012): 27.

10. Oreola Williams Haskell, *Banner Bearers: Tales of the Suffrage Campaigns* (Geneva, NY: W. F. Humphrey, 1920), 3–4. Little is known about Haskell (1875–1957). She was president of the Brooklyn-based Kings County Political Equality League, served as head of the Press Bureau of the New York City Woman Suffrage Party from 1915 to 1917, and joined the League of Women Voters at its inception. Ida Husted Harper, ed., *History of Woman Suffrage: 1900–1920*, vol. 6 (New York: National American Woman Suffrage Association, 1922), 459.

11. Haskell, *Banner Bearers*, 3–4.

Chapter 1. The Trial of Susan B. Anthony and the "Rochester Fifteen"

1. Mari Jo Buhle and Paul Buhle, eds., *The Concise History of Woman Suffrage* (Urbana: University of Illinois Press, 2005), 91–98.

2. Martin Naparsteck, *The Trial of Susan B. Anthony: An Illegal Vote, a Courtroom Conviction, and a Step toward Women's Suffrage* (Jefferson, NC: McFarland, 2014), 57–58; Angela G. Ray, "The Rhetorical Ritual of Citizenship: Women's Voting as Public Performance, 1868–1875," *Quarterly Journal of Speech* 93, no. 1 (February 2007): 1–26.

3. Naparsteck, *The Trial of Susan B. Anthony*, 51.

4. Ibid., 52.

5. Faye E. Dudden, *Fighting Chance: The Struggle over Woman Suffrage and Black Suffrage in Reconstruction America* (New York: Oxford University Press, 2011) and Laura E. Free, *Suffrage Reconstructed: Gender, Race, and Voting Rights in the Civil War Era* (Ithaca: Cornell University Press, 2015).

6. Lynn Sherr, *The Trial of Susan B. Anthony* (Amherst, NY: Humanity Books, 2003), xi.

7. Ibid., xv.

8. Voters did not technically vote for the president, casting ballots instead for delegates to the electoral college. Direct election of US senators did not happen until 1913, but there was no senatorial candidate on the 1872 ballot.

9. Naparsteck, *The Trial of Susan B. Anthony*, 100.

10. Ibid., 185.

11. Sherr, *The Trial of Susan B. Anthony*, 66; Naparsteck, *The Trial of Susan B. Anthony*, 185.

12. Sherr, *The Trial of Susan B. Anthony*, 82, 84.

13. *County Post*, June 27, 1873, quoted in *History of Woman Suffrage*, vol. 2, ed. Susan B. Anthony, Elizabeth Cady Stanton, and Matilda Joslyn Gage (Rochester, NY: Susan B. Anthony, 1887), 944.

14. Angela G. Ray and Cindy Koenig Richards, "Inventing Citizens, Imagining Gender Justice: The Suffrage Rhetoric of Virginia and Francis Minor," *Quarterly Journal of Speech* 93, no. 4 (November 2007): 375–402.

15. Naparsteck, *The Trial of Susan B. Anthony*, 206.

16. Ellen Carol DuBois, "Outgrowing the Compact of the Fathers: Equal Rights, Woman Suffrage, and the United States Constitution, 1820–1878" and "Taking the Law into Our Own Hands: Bradwell, Minor, and Suffrage Militance in the 1870s," both reprinted in *Woman Suffrage and Women's Rights*, ed. Ellen Carol DuBois (New York: New York University Press, 1998); Sherr, *The Trial of Susan B. Anthony*, xxiv.

17. Naparsteck, *The Trial of Susan B. Anthony*, 173.

Chapter 2. Sojourner Truth Speaks Truth to Power

1. Margaret Washington, *Sojourner Truth's America* (Urbana: University of Illinois Press, 2009), 366.

2. Nell Irvin Painter, *Sojourner Truth: A Life, a Symbol* (New York: Norton, 1996), 198–199.

3. For an excellent overview of Sojourner Truth's cartes de visite, see Darcy Grimaldo Grigsby, *Enduring Truths: Sojourner's Shadows and Substance* (Chicago: University of Chicago Press, 2015). I have relied on her research and chronology to date the various versions. For general background on cartes de visite, see Kenneth Florey, *Women's Suffrage Memorabilia: An Illustrated Historical Study* (Jefferson, NC: McFarland, 2013), 61–65.

4. Grigsby, *Enduring Truths*, 29.

5. Ibid., 15, 123–142.

6. Ibid., 15; Allison Lange, "Images of Change: Picturing Woman's Rights from American Independence through the Nineteenth Amendment" (PhD diss., Brandeis University, 2014), 145–146.

7. There is some uncertainty about Truth's actual date of freedom. Between 1826 and 1828, she had negotiated an exit date with her penultimate owner, but he reneged when she injured herself.

8. Painter, *Sojourner Truth*, 125, 139. Painter discusses the implications of the competing renditions of "Ar'n't I a Woman" on pages 258–287. She forcefully rejects Gage's version as historically inaccurate and demeaning.

9. Washington, *Sojourner Truth's America*, 334. The quote is from 1866.

10. Ibid., 337; Painter, *Sojourner Truth*, 220.

11. Painter, *Sojourner Truth*, 233.

12. Lange, "Images of Change," 186, 197.

Chapter 3. Sister-Wives and Suffragists

1. Ladies of the Church of Jesus Christ of Latter-day Saints, *"Mormon" Women's Protest: An Appeal for Freedom, Justice and Equal Rights* (Salt Lake City: Deseret News Print, 1886), iii.

2. It's even more complicated when the story of Utah's organized antipolygamy groups are factored in. They actually opposed woman suffrage because they saw women's votes as upholding the power of the Mormon Church on public life. See Lola Van Wagenen, *Sister-Wives and Suffragists: Polygamy and the Politics of Woman Suffrage, 1870–1896* (Provo, UT: Joseph Fielding Smith Institute for Latter-day Saint History and Brigham Young University Studies, 2003); and Carol Cornwall Madsen, ed., *Battle for the Ballot: Essays on Woman Suffrage in Utah, 1870–1896* (Logan: Utah State University Press, 1997).

3. Lola Van Wagenen, "In Their Own Behalf: The Politicization of Mormon Women and the 1870 Franchise," in *Battle for the Ballot*, ed. Madsen, 60–74.

4. Sarah Barringer Gordon, *The Mormon Question: Polygamy and Constitutional Conflict in Nineteenth-Century America* (Chapel Hill: University of North Carolina Press, 2002), 54. See also Nancy F. Cott, *Public Vows: A History of Marriage and the Nation* (Cambridge: Harvard University Press, 2000).

5. Twelve out of fifteen of the women who spoke were plural wives, as well as at least eight out of the nine additional speakers whose remarks were only included in the printed manifesto. Every participant was married or widowed, reflecting the total absence of single Mormon women, a sharp contrast to women's groups elsewhere in nineteenth-century America.

6. Laurel Thatcher Ulrich, *A House Full of Females: Plural Marriage and Women's Rights in Early Mormonism, 1835–1870* (New York: Knopf, 2017).

7. Ladies of the Church of Jesus Christ of Latter-day Saints, *"Mormon" Women's Protest*, 37–38, 54.

8. Ibid., 14.

9. Ibid., 87.

10. Ibid., 76.

11. Carol Cornwall Madsen, *An Advocate for Women: The Public Life of Emmeline B. Wells, 1870–1920* (Provo, UT: Brigham Young University Press, 2006) and Madsen, *Emmeline B. Wells: An Intimate History* (Salt Lake City: University of Utah Press, 2017).

12. Leonard J. Arrington, "Emmeline B. Wells: Mormon Feminist and Journalist," in *Forgotten Heroes: Inspiring American Portraits from Our Leading Historians*, ed. Susan Ware (New York: Free Press, 1998), 125.

13. Another example was Stanton and Anthony's short-lived but controversial association with the free-love advocate Victoria Woodhull. See Helen Lefkowitz Horowitz, "Victoria Woodhull: Free Love in the Feminine, First-Person Singular," *Forgotten Heroes*, ed. Ware, 111–120, and Horowitz, *Rereading Sex: Battles over Sexual Knowledge and Suppression in Nineteenth-Century America* (New York: Knopf, 2002).

14. Van Wagenen, *Sister-Wives and Suffragists*, 137.

15. Ibid., 135; Madsen, *An Advocate for Women*, 248.

16. Madsen, *An Advocate for Women*, 332.

Chapter 4. Alice Stone Blackwell and the Armenian Crisis of the 1890s

1. Agnes E. Ryan, *The Torchbearer: A Look Forward and Back at the Woman's Journal, the Organ of the Woman's Movement* (Boston: Woman's Journal and Suffrage News, 1916).

2. Peter Balakian, *The Burning Tigris: The Armenian Genocide and America's Response* (New York: HarperCollins, 2003), preface.

3. Ibid., xix.

4. There is no biography of Alice Stone Blackwell. For information about her life, see Edward T. James, Janet Wilson James, and Paul Boyer, eds., *Notable American Women: 1607–1950* (Cambridge: Harvard University Press, 1971) as well as the extensive documentation in the Blackwell Family Papers at the Schlesinger Library, Radcliffe Institute, Harvard University and the Library of Congress. Marlene Deahl Merrill, *Growing Up in Boston's Gilded Age: The Journal of Alice Stone Blackwell, 1872–1874* (New Haven: Yale University Press, 1990) introduces a younger Alice. See also Sally G. McMillen, *Lucy Stone: An Unapologetic Life* (New York: Oxford University Press, 2015).

5. Diary entry, December 31, 1873, quoted in Merrill, *Growing Up in Boston's Gilded Age*, 216.

6. For background, see Susan Schultz Huxman, "The *Woman's Journal*, 1870–1890: The Torchbearer for Suffrage," in *A Voice of Their Own: The Woman Suffrage Press, 1840–1910*, ed. Martha M. Solomon (Tuscaloosa: University of Alabama Press, 1991).

7. Merrill, *Growing Up in Boston's Gilded Age*, 237.

8. McMillen, *Lucy Stone*, 215; Marsha Vanderford, "The *Woman's Column*, 1888–1904: Extending the Suffrage Community," in Solomon, *A Voice of Their Own*.

9. Alice Stone Blackwell, "Some Reminiscences," *New Armenia* 5, no. 2 (February 1918): 20–21.

10. Alice Stone Blackwell to Professor Peabody, September 29, 1893, Ohannes Chatschumian student file, Harvard University Archives; Alice Stone Blackwell to Isabel Barrows, September 8, 1893, Barrows Family Papers, Houghton Library, Harvard University.

11. Isabel Barrows to Professor Everett, March 1, 1893 and Alice Stone Blackwell to Professor F. G. Peabody, September 29, 1893, Ohannes Chatschumian student file, Harvard University Archives; Alice Stone Blackwell to Henry Browne Blackwell, May 30, 1896, Alice Stone Blackwell Papers, Schlesinger Library.

12. My thanks to Hayk Demoyan, director of the Armenian Genocide Museum-Institute and a visiting fellow at the Davis Center at Harvard University, and Harvard Professor James Russell for their help in deciphering the coat of arms.

13. Alice Stone Blackwell, *Armenian Poems* (Boston: Roberts Brothers, 1896), ii. Blackwell retained the copyright to the volume. Extensive documentation of the preparation of the translations is found in the Blackwell Family Papers, Library of Congress.

14. Blackwell, *Armenian Poems*, i.

15. The *Woman's Journal* announced his death on the first page of the May 30, 1896 issue. "Some Reminiscences" tells the story of his death from Isabel Barrows's point of view, without mentioning that Alice was there too. Alice's letters to family from onboard ship and after they received the telegram focus much more on Isabel Barrows and her grief, saying hardly anything about her own feelings. She certainly didn't act like someone who had just lost her life mate.

16. "Editor's note" by Edna Stantial, found in "Chatschumian, Ohannes" file, Blackwell Family Papers, Library of Congress.

17. See Merrill, *Growing Up in Boston's Gilded Age* for a discussion of the importance of Alice's relationship with Kitty Barry.

18. *Woman's Journal*, May 11, 1896.

19. "The Women of Armenia," *Woman's Journal*, July 14 and July 28, 1894. The quote is from July 28.

20. Balakian, *The Burning Tigris*, 66–67, 97–98, 126–132.

21. Rebecca Jinks, "'Marks Hard to Erase': The Troubled Reclamation of 'Absorbed' Armenian Women, 1919–1927," *American Historical Review* 123, no. 1 (February 2018): 86–123.

22. Ohannes Chatschumian to Isabel Barrows, June 8, 1894, Barrows Family Papers, Houghton Library; *Woman's Journal*, March 14, 1896. This article, written from Germany, had originally been published in *Nor-Dar* (New Age), an Armenian paper published at Tufts University.

23. Alice Stone Blackwell to Isabel Barrows, June 17, 1894, Barrows Family Papers, Houghton Library.

24. Carrie Chapman Catt wrote, "Mrs. Park told me he was an Armenian." See Catt to Mrs. La Rue Brown, April 18, 1935. For a reference to the "Gulesian mess," see Ida Porter Boyer to Maud Wood Park, July 25, 1935. Both documents are included in Melanie Gustafson, ed., *Maud Wood Park Archive: The Power of Organization, Part Two: Maud Wood Park in a Nation of Women Voters* (Alexandria, VA: Alexander Street, 2014).

25. Merrill, *Growing Up in Boston's Gilded Age*, 237–238; Alice Stone Blackwell to Barrows, June 17, 1894, Barrows Family Papers, Houghton Library.

Chapter 5. Charlotte Perkins Gilman Finds Her Voice

1. This soon became Trans World Airlines (TWA). Cynthia J. Davis, *Charlotte Perkins Gilman: A Biography* (Stanford: Stanford University Press, 2010), 383.

2. Charlotte Perkins Gilman, *The Living of Charlotte Perkins Gilman: An Autobiography* (New York: Appleton-Century, 1935; New York: Harper, 1975), 333, 334. All references are to the 1975 Harper edition.

3. Iris I. J. M. Gibson, "Death Masks Unlimited," *British Medical Journal* 291, no. 6511 (December 21–28, 1985): 1785–1787.

4. Davis, *Charlotte Perkins Gilman*, 395; Jill Bergman, *Charlotte Perkins Gilman and a Woman's Place in America* (Tuscaloosa: University of Alabama Press, 2017), 63.

5. Ann Lane made this point in "The Fictional World of Charlotte Perkins Gilman," in *The Charlotte Perkins Gilman Reader*, ed. Ann J. Lane (New York: Pantheon, 1980), ix. For Gilman's use of the word *living*, see Davis, *Charlotte Perkins Gilman*, xv.

6. The best introduction to Gilman's feminism is Judith A. Allen, *The Feminism of Charlotte Perkins Gilman: Sexualities, Histories, Progressivism* (Chicago: University of Chicago Press, 2009).

7. Gilman, *Living*, 8; Davis, *Charlotte Perkins Gilman*, 61.

8. Davis, *Charlotte Perkins Gilman*, 89, 96–97. See also Helen Lefkowitz Horowitz, *Wild Unrest: Charlotte Perkins Gilman and the Making of "The Yellow Wall-Paper"* (New York: Oxford University Press, 2010).

9. Gilman, *Living*, 110, 165.

10. Ibid., 165; Susan Ware, "Charlotte Perkins Gilman: The Early Lectures, 1890–1893," unpublished seminar paper, May 29, 1973.

11. Gilman, *Living*, 294.

12. Charlotte Perkins Gilman, *Women and Economics: The Economic Factor between Men and Women as a Factor in Social Evolution* (New York: Harper, 1966), 149, 340. The book was originally published under the name of Charlotte Perkins Stetson.

13. Gilman, *Living*, 281.

14. Davis, *Charlotte Perkins Gilman*, 266.

15. Gilman, *Living*, 198.

16. The tally is from Davis, *Charlotte Perkins Gilman*, xii.

17. Ibid., 289.

18. Allen, *The Feminism of Charlotte Perkins Gilman*, 156.

19. "Something to Vote For" is included in *On to Victory: Propaganda Plays of the Woman Suffrage Movement*, ed. Bettina Friedl (Boston: Northeastern University Press, 1987), 143–161. The quotes are from p. 161.

20. Davis, *Charlotte Perkins Gilman*, 290, 287.

21. Allen, *The Feminism of Charlotte Perkins Gilman*, ix, 1. The quotation is from unpublished notes, c. 1908, found in the Charlotte Perkins Gilman Papers at the Schlesinger Library, Radcliffe Institute, Harvard University. That date suggests that the term was circulating before the 1910s.

22. See Nancy Cott, *The Grounding of Modern Feminism* (New Haven: Yale University Press, 1987), especially the introduction and chapter 1. The term gets even more slippery when it is appropriated by the National Woman's Party to describe supporters of the Equal Rights Amendment, first introduced in 1923. Because many women we would now call feminists disavowed the ERA because of its impact on protective legislation for women, they shunned the term, even though they all would have agreed with Eleanor Roosevelt's straightforward definition in 1935: "Fundamentally, the purpose of Feminism is that a woman should have an equal opportunity and Equal Rights with any other citizen of the country." Quoted in Ruby A. Black, "Is Mrs. Roosevelt a Feminist?," *Equal Rights* (July 27, 1935), 163.

23. Davis, *Charlotte Perkins Gilman*, 339. Cott, *The Grounding of Modern Feminism* also discusses Heterodoxy extensively.

24. This title was inspired by a suffrage cartoon by Lou Rogers. See the chapter on Nina Allender and suffrage cartoonists.

25. Allen, *The Feminism of Charlotte Perkins Gilman*, 169.

26. Ibid., 191, 183–84. Note the reference to menstruation ("curse").

27. Judith Allen talks about Gilman's shifting reputation in *The Feminism of Charlotte Perkins Gilman*. See especially Susan S. Lanser, "Feminist Criticism, 'The Yellow Wallpaper,' and the Politics of Color in America," *Feminist Studies* 15 (Fall 1989): 415–441.

28. Allen, *The Feminism of Charlotte Perkins Gilman*, 193.

29. Charlotte Perkins Gilman, *Suffrage Songs and Verses* (New York: The Charlton Company, 1911), 33.

Part Two. The Personal Is Political

1. Oreola Williams Haskell, *Banner Bearers: Tales of the Suffrage Campaigns* (Geneva, NY: Humphrey, 1920), 218.

Chapter 6. The Shadow of the Confederacy

1. Mary Johnston, *Hagar* (Boston and New York: Houghton Mifflin, 1913), 314–315, 316.

2. Ibid., 318.

3. Marjorie Spruill Wheeler, "Mary Johnston, Suffragist," *The Virginia Magazine of History and Biography* 100, no. 1 (January 1992): 103; Wallace Hettle, "Mary Johnston and 'Stonewall' Jackson: A Virginia Feminist and the Politics of Historical Fiction," *Journal of Historical Biography* 3 (Spring 2008): 46.

4. Marjorie Spruill Wheeler, *New Women of the New South: The Leaders of the Woman Suffrage Movement in the Southern States* (New York: Oxford University Press, 1993), xiii; Wheeler, "Mary Johnston, Suffragist," 100; Clayton McClure Brooks, Samuel P. Menefee, and Brenda Wolfe, "Mary Johnston (1870–1936)," *Encyclopedia Virginia*, ed. Brendan Wolfe, Virginia Humanities and Library of Virginia, www.encyclopediavirginia.org/Johnston_Mary_1870 -1936.

5. C. Ronald Cella, *Mary Johnston* (Boston: Twayne, 1981), 21.

6. Annie Kedrick Walker, "Mary Johnston in Her Home," *New York Times*, March 24, 1900.

7. "Miss Mary Johnston: A Suffrage Worker," *New York Times*, June 11, 1911. For a general introduction to the history of suffrage in Virginia, see Wheeler, *New Women of the New South*, and Suzanne Lebsock, "Woman Suffrage and White Supremacy: A Virginia Case Study," in *Visible Women: New Essays on American*

Activism, ed. Nancy A. Hewitt and Suzanne Lebsock (Urbana: University of Illinois Press, 1993), 62–100.

8. Mary Johnston, "The Woman's War," *The Atlantic Monthly* (April 1910), 568, 570.

9. For discussions of *Hagar* by literary scholars, see Cella, *Mary Johnston*; Martha Patterson, *Beyond the Gibson Girl: Reimagining the American New Woman, 1895–1915* (Urbana: University of Illinois Press, 2005); and Anne Goodwyn Jones, *Tomorrow Is Another Day: The Woman Writer in the South, 1859–1936* (Baton Rouge: Louisiana State University Press, 1981).

10. Patterson, *Beyond the Gibson Girl*, 134.

11. Mary Chapman and Angela Mills, eds., *Treacherous Texts: US Suffrage Literature, 1846–1946* (New Brunswick: Rutgers University Press, 2012); Leslie Petty, *Romancing the Vote: Feminist Activism in American Fiction, 1870–1920* (Athens: University of Georgia Press, 2006).

12. Jones, *Tomorrow Is Another Day*, 186, 187–188.

13. Helen Bullis, "A Feminist Novel: Miss Johnston's 'Hagar' a Tale and a Theory," *New York Times*, November 2, 1913.

14. This summary of the southern suffrage movement draws heavily on Wheeler, *New Woman of the New South*. See also Anne Firor Scott, *The Southern Lady: From Pedestal to Politics, 1830–1930* (Chicago: University of Chicago Press, 1970) and Elna C. Green, *Southern Strategies: Southern Women and the Woman Suffrage Question* (Chapel Hill: University of North Carolina Press, 1997).

15. Wheeler, "Mary Johnston, Suffragist," 104.

16. In addition to Wheeler and Green, see also Paul E. Fuller, *Laura Clay and the Woman's Rights Movement* (Lexington: University Press of Kentucky, 1975).

17. A short story called "Nemesis" published in *Century* magazine in 1923 spoke out against lynching (earning her praise from the NAACP), and the novel *Slave Ship* (1924) tackled the issue of slavery. See Wheeler, "Mary Johnston, Suffragist," 108.

18. Ibid., 109.

19. "Miss Mary Johnston: A Suffrage Worker," *New York Times*, June 11, 1911; Wheeler, "Mary Johnston, Suffragist," 118, quoting a speech entitled "The Woman Movement in the South."

Chapter 7. Ida Wells-Barnett and the Alpha Suffrage Club

1. "Vote Yes" flier, Mary Earhart Dillon Collection, Schlesinger Library, Radcliffe Institute, Harvard University.

2. Alfreda M. Duster, ed., *Crusade for Justice: The Autobiography of Ida B. Wells* (Chicago: University of Chicago Press, 1970), 345.

3. Wanda A. Hendricks, "Ida B. Wells-Barnett and the Alpha Suffrage Club of Chicago," in *One Woman, One Vote: Rediscovering the Woman Suffrage Movement*, ed. Marjorie Spruill Wheeler (Troutdale, OR: New Sage Press, 1995), 267; Duster, *Crusade for Justice*, 345.

4. Paula J. Giddings, *Ida: A Sword among Lions: Ida B. Wells and the Campaign against Lynching* (New York: Amistad, 2008), 516.

5. Hendricks, "Ida B. Wells-Barnett and the Alpha Suffrage Club of Chicago," 269.

6. Giddings, *Ida: A Sword among Lions*, 516, 517; Hendricks, "Ida B. Wells-Barnett and the Alpha Suffrage Club of Chicago," 269; "Illinois Women Feature Parade; Delegation from the State Wins High Praise by Order in Marching; Cheered by Big Crowd; Question of Color Line Threatens for While to Make Trouble in Ranks," *Chicago Daily Tribune*, March 4, 1913. To the newspaper's credit, it did not duck the racial issue in its headline, even though its readership was predominantly white.

7. "Illinois Women Feature Parade," *Chicago Daily Tribune*, March 4, 1913; "Illinois Women Participants in Suffrage Parade; This State Was Well Represented in Washington," *Chicago Daily Tribune*, March 5, 1913.

8. Ida Wells-Barnett to Catherine Waugh McCullough, March 15, 1913, Mary Earhart Dillon Collection, Schlesinger Library.

9. In addition to Giddings, see Patricia A. Schecter, *Ida B. Wells-Barnett and American Reform, 1880–1930* (Chapel Hill: University of North Carolina Press, 2001); and Mia Bay, *To Tell the Truth Freely: The Life of Ida B. Wells* (New York: Hill and Wang, 2009).

10. Giddings, *Ida: A Sword among Lions*, 489.

11. For an overview, see Lisa G. Materson, *For the Freedom of Her Race: Black Women and Electoral Politics in Illinois, 1877–1932* (Chapel Hill: University of North Carolina Press, 2009).

12. Duster, *Crusade for Freedom*, 346.

13. Giddings, *Ida: A Sword among Lions*, 534.

14. Lisa Materson makes this point in *For the Freedom of Her Race*, which also reproduces the cartoon from *The Crisis*.

15. Ibid., 80.

16. Rosalyn Terborg-Penn, "African American Women and the Vote: An Overview," in *African American Women and the Vote, 1837–1965*, ed. Ann D. Gordon and Bettye Collier-Thomas (Amherst: University of Massachusetts Press, 1997), 21.

17. Duster, *Crusade for Justice*, xxxix.

18. Her daughter Alfreda Duster was instrumental in guiding the manuscript to print, almost four decades later, as part of a series of black autobiographies published by the University of Chicago Press under the general editorship of John Hope Franklin. It appeared in 1970 and quickly became an influential text on early women's history syllabi.

Chapter 8. Two Sisters

1. Kenneth Florey, *Women's Suffrage Memorabilia: An Illustrated Historical Study* (Jefferson, NC: McFarland, 2013), 31.

2. Florey, *Women's Suffrage Memorabilia*, 32. The Alice Park Papers are housed at the Huntington Library in San Marino, California.

3. Biographical material is found in their two (competing) autobiographies: Maud Nathan, *Once upon a Time and Today* (New York: Putnam, 1933), and Annie Nathan Meyer, *It's Been Fun* (New York: Henry Schuman, 1951). See also Robert Cross, "Maud Nathan," in *Notable American Women: 1607–1950*, ed. Edward T. James, Janet Wilson James, and Paul Boyer (Cambridge: Harvard University Press, 1971) and Linda Kerber, "Annie Nathan Meyer," in *Notable American Women: The Modern Period*, ed. Barbara Sicherman and Carol Hurd Green (Cambridge: Harvard University Press, 1980). The quotation is from Meyer, *It's Been Fun*, 11.

4. Meyer, *It's Been Fun*, 121, 120.

5. See Lynn D. Gordon, "Annie Nathan Meyer and Barnard College: Mission and Identity in Women's Higher Education, 1889–1950," *History of Education Quarterly* 26, no. 4 (Winter 1986): 503–522; and Rosalind Rosenberg, *Changing the Subject: How the Women of Columbia Shaped the Way We Think about Sex and Politics* (New York: Columbia University Press, 2004).

6. Nathan, *Once upon a Time*, 94–95, 42.

7. Meyer, *It's Been Fun*, 188; Carla Kaplan, *Miss Anne in Harlem: The White Women of the Black Renaissance* (New York: HarperCollins, 2013), 170. Kaplan found the captioned picture in the Barnard archives.

8. Nathan, *Once upon a Time*, 178.

9. Kaplan, *Miss Anne in Harlem*, 177; Nathan, *Once upon a Time*, 112–113.

10. Nathan, *Once upon a Time*, 181–182. In 1911 she beat out 27,452 entrants to win a contest for the best letter supporting woman suffrage, which is quoted above.

11. "In all the work that I did for the cause, my husband was at my side aiding and abetting me" (Nathan, *Once upon a Time*, 179). In the summer of 1912,

the Nathans embarked on a cross-country automobile trip to speak for suffrage. Frederick Nathan attended the first International Men's League for Woman Suffrage gathering in Stockholm in 1911, as well as the meeting of the International Woman Suffrage Alliance in Budapest in 1913. Gravely ill by the time of the November 1917 referendum, he insisted upon being wheeled to the polls so he could vote in its favor. It was the last vote he cast.

12. Clipping, May 12, 1911, scrapbook, Maud Nathan Papers, Schlesinger Library, Radcliffe Institute, Harvard University.

13. Joyce Antler, *The Journey Home: Jewish Women and the American Century* (New York: Free Press, 1997), 69.

14. Manuela Thurner, "Better Citizens without the Ballot," in *One Woman, One Vote: Rediscovering the Woman Suffrage Movement*, ed. Marjorie Spruill Wheeler (Troutdale, OR: New Sage Press, 1995); Meyer, *It's Been Fun*, 205. See also Annie Nathan Meyer, "Woman's Assumption of Sex Superiority," *North American Review* (January 1904).

15. The best source is Susan Goodier, *No Votes for Women: The New York State Anti-Suffrage Movement* (Urbana: University of Illinois Press, 2013).

16. Thurner, "Better Citizens without the Ballot," 209.

17. Ibid., 205–206.

18. Harriot Stanton Blatch and Alma Lutz, *Challenging Years: The Memoirs of Harriot Stanton Blatch* (New York: Putnam, 1940), 173.

19. Goodier, *No Votes for Women*, chapter 5.

20. Ibid., chapter 6. See also the discussion of the rightwing attack on Progressive women's politics in the 1920s in Nancy Cott, *The Grounding of Modern Feminism* (New Haven: Yale University Press, 1987).

21. Annie Nathan Meyer, "The Anti-Suffragist Replies," *The New Republic* (December 1, 1917): 124–125; Meyer, *It's Been Fun*, 207.

Chapter 9. Claiborne Catlin's Suffrage Pilgrimage

1. Linda J. Lumsden, *Inez: The Life and Times of Inez Milholland* (Bloomington: Indiana University Press, 2004).

2. Harriot Stanton Blatch and Alma Lutz, *Challenging Years: The Memoirs of Harriot Stanton Blatch* (New York: G. P. Putnam's Sons, 1940), 132–133.

3. Claiborne Catlin Elliman, "Stirrup Cups," 2, 4, Claiborne Catlin Elliman Papers, Schlesinger Library, Radcliffe Institute, Harvard University. By the time Claiborne Catlin Elliman wrote this account from notes and clippings she kept

at the time, she had remarried; however, in this account, I refer to her by the name she was known by in 1914.

4. Ibid., 3.

5. Sharon Hartman Strom, "Leadership and Tactics in the American Woman Suffrage Movement: A New Perspective from Massachusetts," *Journal of American History* 62, no. 2 (September 1975): 296–315. See also Barbara F. Berenson, *Massachusetts in the Woman Suffrage Movement: Revolutionary Reformers* (Charleston, SC: The History Press, 2018).

6. Elliman, "Stirrup Cups," 4.

7. Ibid., 3.

8. Clippings, *Boston Journal*, June 30, 1914, and *Boston Herald*, June 30, 1914, Claiborne Catlin Elliman Papers, Schlesinger Library; Elliman, "Stirrup Cups," 9.

9. Elliman, "Stirrup Cups," 9.

10. Note the use of the somewhat derogatory term *suffragette* here and in later newspaper coverage. See the discussion of the term in Chapter 10 on Raymond and Gertrude Foster Brown.

11. Elliman, "Stirrup Cups," 18.

12. Ibid., 25.

13. Clipping, *Fall River Daily Globe*, July 7, 1914, Claiborne Catlin Elliman Papers, Schlesinger Library.

14. Clipping, *New Bedford Evening Standard*, July 5, 1914, Claiborne Catlin Elliman Papers, Schlesinger Library.

15. Clipping, *Boston Daily Advertiser*, September 19, 1914, Claiborne Catlin Elliman Papers, Schlesinger Library; Elliman, "Stirrup Cups," 93.

16. Carrie Chase Sheridan to Mrs. Carson, July 25, 1914, reproduced in Elliman, "Stirrup Cups," [111].

17. Elliman, "Stirrup Cups," 78, 87.

18. Ibid., 54, 81.

19. Ibid., 95–96.

20. Ibid., 31, 37.

21. Ibid., 90.

22. Clipping, *Boston Evening Record*, September 19, 1914, Claiborne Catlin Elliman Papers, Schlesinger Library; Elliman, "Stirrup Cups," 93. She had lost thirteen pounds over the past eleven weeks.

23. Clipping from a Fitchburg newspaper [title illegible], October 23, 1914, Claiborne Catlin Elliman Papers, Schlesinger Library.

24. Clipping, *Worcester Daily Telegram*, October 26, 1914, Claiborne Catlin Elliman Papers, Schlesinger Library. See also "Mrs. Catlin's Horse Killed; Tour Ends,"

Boston Evening Record, October 27, 1914, Claiborne Catlin Elliman Papers, Schlesinger Library.

25. Elliman, "Stirrup Cups," 5.

26. Ibid., 3, 69.

27. Ibid., postscript, 120.

Chapter 10. "How It Feels to Be the Husband of a Suffragette"

1. Jill Lepore, *The Secret History of Wonder Woman* (New York: Knopf, 2014), 11.

2. Brooke Kroeger, *The Suffragents: How Women Used Men to Get the Vote* (Albany: State University of New York Press, 2017), 101, 241.

3. Arthur Raymond Brown [Him, pseud.], *How It Feels to Be the Husband of a Suffragette* (New York: George H. Doran, 1915), 7–8.

4. Mary Chapman's and Angela Mills's *Treacherous Texts: US Suffrage Literature, 1846–1946* (New Brunswick, NJ: Rutgers University Press, 2011) includes an excerpt which it says "probably" (231) was written by Arthur Brown. (His full name was Arthur Raymond Brown, but he was always known as Ray.) Conclusive confirmation is found in the Gertrude Foster Brown Papers at the Schlesinger Library, Radcliffe Institute, Harvard University.

5. Material about Ray Brown, especially his distinguished New England lineage, is found in the Gertrude Foster Brown Papers, Schlesinger Library.

6. Gertrude Foster Brown, "Suffrage and Music—My First Eighty Years," draft manuscript, 42, Gertrude Foster Brown Papers, Schlesinger Library. The manuscript includes some editorial additions by Mildred Adams, Brown's niece.

7. Ibid., 71, 97.

8. Ibid., 103.

9. Gertrude Foster Brown to Ray Brown, November 20, 1904, Gertrude Foster Brown Papers, Schlesinger Library; Brown, "Suffrage and Music," 111.

10. Brown, "Suffrage and Music," 119; Ray Brown to Gertrude Foster Brown [undated, but probably 1905], Gertrude Foster Brown Papers, Schlesinger Library. In the original, the order of the two sentences is reversed.

11. Brown, "Suffrage and Music," 128–129. Brown, *How It Feels to Be the Husband of a Suffragette* has practically a verbatim version (22).

12. Brown, "Suffrage and Music," 129; Brown, *How It Feels to Be the Husband of a Suffragette*, 20; Brown, "Suffrage and Music," 129a.

13. Brown, "Suffrage and Music," 129a.

14. Ibid., 136.

15. Ibid., 158–159.

16. See Johanna Neuman, *Gilded Suffragists: The New York Socialites Who Fought for Women's Right to Vote* (New York: New York University Press, 2017).

17. Mrs. Raymond Brown, *Your Vote and How to Use It* (New York: Harper, 1918).

18. Kroeger, *The Suffragents*, provides thumbnail photos of 157 male suffragists as chapter openers. Ray Brown is not included.

19. Brown, "Suffrage and Music," 210–211; Brown, *How It Feels to Be the Husband of a Suffragette*, 9, 39.

20. Ray Brown to Gertrude Foster Brown, April 16, 1910, Gertrude Foster Brown Papers, Schlesinger Library.

21. Brown, *How It Feels to Be the Husband of a Suffragette*, 51; Ray Brown to Gertrude Foster Brown, March 1, 1913 and March 13, 1914, Gertrude Foster Brown Papers, Schlesinger Library.

22. Brown, *How It Feels to Be the Husband of a Suffragette*, 63.

Chapter 11. The Farmer-Suffragettes

1. Henry David Thoreau, entry for April 3, 1852, *The Writings of Henry David Thoreau: Journal*, vol. 3, ed. Bradford Torrpy (New York: Houghton Mifflin, 1906), 386, available online as *The Journal of Henry David Thoreau*, Walden Woods Project, www.walden.org/collection/journals/; Laurel Thatcher Ulrich, Ivan Gaskell, Sara J. Schechner, and Sarah Anne Carter, *Tangible Things: Making History through Objects* (New York: Oxford University Press, 2015), 141–148.

2. I am using the term in its modern usage as "outside of properly normative behavior." Stina Soderling, "Queer Rurality and the Materiality of Time," in *Queering the Countryside: New Frontiers in Rural Queer Studies*, ed. Mary L. Gray, Colin R. Johnson, and Brian J. Gilley (New York: New York University Press, 2016), 339.

3. Moss Acre scrapbook, in possession of Virginia Bourne, Castine, Maine. Unless otherwise noted, all material is drawn from Susan Ware, *Partner and I: Molly Dewson, Feminism, and New Deal Politics* (New Haven: Yale University Press, 1987).

4. *Wellesley '97 Classbook* (1910), found in Molly Dewson Papers, Schlesinger Library, Radcliffe Institute, Harvard University.

5. Molly Dewson, Suffrage Scrapbook, Woman's Rights Collection, Schlesinger Library.

6. Ibid.

7. Molly Dewson to Helen Gahagan Douglas, February 23, 1944, Papers of Mary W. Dewson, Franklin D. Roosevelt Library, Hyde Park, New York; Dewson, note on letter from Carrie Chapman Catt to Molly Dewson, July 26, 1934, in possession of Virginia Bourne, Castine, Maine.

8. Molly Dewson to Lucy Stebbins, September 1917, letter in possession of Virginia Bourne.

9. Molly Dewson to Lucy Stebbins, October 15, 1917, letter in possession of Virginia Bourne.

10. Molly Dewson to Lucy Stebbins, November 18, 1917, and Molly Dewson to William D. Porter, Jr., December 3, 1917, letters in possession of Virginia Bourne.

11. Queer theory sits at the intersection of gender studies and gay history. See Sharon Marcus, "Queer Theory for Everyone: A Review Essay," *Signs: Journal of Women in Culture and Society* 31, no. 1 (2005): 191–218; Annamarie Jagose, *Queer Theory: An Introduction* (New York: New York University Press, 1996); and Nikki Sullivan, *A Critical Introduction to Queer Theory* (New York: New York University Press, 2003). Foundational texts include Judith Butler, *Gender Trouble: Feminism and the Subversion of Identity* (New York: Routledge, 1990) and Eve Kosofsky Sedgwick, *Epistemology of the Closet* (Berkeley: University of California Press, 1990).

12. Biographical material on Catt is found in Jacqueline Van Voris, *Carrie Chapman Catt: A Public Life* (New York: Feminist Press, 1987) and Robert Booth Fowler, *Carrie Catt: Feminist Politician* (Boston: Northeastern University Press, 1986). The monument quotation is found in Van Voris, *Carrie Chapman Catt*, 219.

13. Jean H. Baker, *Sisters: The Lives of America's Suffragists* (New York: Hill and Wang, 2005), 61, 89.

14. Susan Ware, "The Book I Couldn't Write: Alice Paul and the Challenge of Feminist Biography," *Journal of Women's History* 24, no. 2 (Summer 2012): 13–36.

15. For more on Stevens and her active sex life, see Mary K. Trigg, *Feminism as Life's Work* (New Brunswick, NJ: Rutgers University Press, 2014).

16. Molly Dewson to Herbert Kahn, December 4, 1958, Molly Dewson Papers, Schlesinger Library.

Chapter 12. Suffragists Abroad

1. Leila J. Rupp, *Worlds of Women: The Making of an International Women's Movement* (Princeton, NJ: Princeton University Press, 1997), 22.

2. Jacqueline Van Voris, *Carrie Chapman Catt: A Public Life* (New York: Feminist Press, 1987), 110.

3. Mary Church Terrell, *A Colored Woman in a White World* (Washington, DC: Ransdell, 1940; Amherst, NY: Humanity Books, 2005), 237–238.

4. Ibid., 239.

5. Rupp, *Worlds of Women*, 71; Terrell, *A Colored Woman*, 241. In 1896 the H. J. Heinz Company in Pittsburgh, Pennsylvania introduced "57 Varieties of Pickles" as

an advertising slogan to highlight the range of products it offered. Soon after it was shortened to "Heinz 57 Varieties." That slogan was likely the inspiration for the comment.

6. Mary Church Terrell, "The International Congress of Women," *Voice of the Negro* (December 1904), 460, quoted in Alison M. Parker, *Mary Church Terrell: Woman Suffrage and Civil Rights Pioneer* (Alexandria, VA: Alexander Street, 2015); Terrell, *A Colored Woman*, 244. Sources refer to it both as congress and council, but International Council of Women is the correct term.

7. Terrell, *A Colored Woman*, 243–244. In the official proceedings, her talk was titled "*Die Fortschritte der Farbigen Frauen*," but when it was later translated back into English, the translator used the phrase "white crow."

8. Mary Church Terrell, "The Progress of Colored Women," June 13, 1904, in Parker, *Mary Church Terrell.*

9. Regine Deutsch, *The International Woman Suffrage Alliance: Its History from 1904 to 1929* (London: Stephen Austin and Sons, 1929), 14.

10. Rupp, *Worlds of Women*, 75.

11. Biographical information is found in Terrell's autobiography and the Alexander Street documents collection curated by Alison Parker, who is writing a biography of Terrell. See also Joan Quigley, *Just Another Southern Town: Mary Church Terrell and the Struggle for Racial Justice in the Nation's Capital* (New York: Oxford University Press, 2016).

12. Terrell, *A Colored Woman*, 132.

13. Ibid., 137.

14. Alison Parker, "'The Picture of Health': The Public Life and Private Ailments of Mary Church Terrell," *Journal of Historical Biography* 13 (Spring 2013): 164–207; Treva B. Lindsey, *Colored No More: Reinventing Black Womanhood in Washington, DC* (Urbana: University of Illinois Press, 2017), especially chapter 3.

15. Mary Church Terrell, "Woman Suffrage and the 15th Amendment," *Crisis* (August 1915): 191.

16. For general background, see Deborah Gray White, *Too Heavy a Load: Black Women in Defense of Themselves, 1894–1994* (New York: Norton, 1999); and Paula J. Giddings, *When and Where I Enter: The Impact of Black Women on Race and Sex in America* (New York: William Morrow, 1985). See also Stephanie J. Shaw, "Black Club Women and the Creation of the National Association of Colored Women," *Journal of Women's History* 3, no. 2 (Fall 1991): 11–25.

17. Rosalyn Terborg-Penn, *African American Women in the Struggle for the Vote, 1850–1920* (Bloomington: Indiana University Press, 1998), 65–66.

18. Terrell, *A Colored Woman*, 29, 349.

19. Alison Parker, *Mary Church Terrell*, 2; Terrell, *A Colored Woman*, 471–472.

20. Terborg-Penn, *African American Women in the Struggle for the Vote*, 123.

21. Terrell, *A Colored Woman*, 371–372.

22. Ibid., 375.

Part Three. Winning Strategies

1. Willa Cather, *Not under Forty* (New York: Knopf, 1936), preface.

Chapter 13. Mountaineering for Suffrage

1. *Washington Women's Cook Book* (Seattle: Washington Equal Suffrage Association, 1909), frontispiece and preface; Jennifer M. Ross-Nazzal, *Winning the West for Women: The Life of Suffragist Emma Smith Devoe* (Seattle: University of Washington Press, 2011), 130.

2. Acknowledgements, *Washington Women's Cook Book*. For an overview of suffrage cookbooks, see Kenneth Florey, *Women's Suffrage Memorabilia: An Illustrated Historical Study* (Jefferson, NC: McFarland, 2013).

3. Paula Becker, "Alaska-Yukon-Pacific Exposition in Seattle Celebrates Suffrage Day on July 7, 1909," *HistoryLink.org: Online Encyclopedia of Washington State History*, May 3, 2008, www.historylink.org/file/8574.

4. Paula Becker, "Alaska-Yukon-Pacific Exposition (1909): Woman Suffrage," *HistoryLink.org*, May 6, 2008, www.historylink.org/file/8578.

5. Rebecca Brown, *Women on High: Pioneers of Mountaineering* (Boston: Appalachian Mountain Club, 2002), 121; Rachel da Silva, Jill Lawrenz, and Wendy Roberts, "A Brief History of Women Climbing in the Coast and Cascade Ranges," in *Leading Out: Women Climbers Reaching for the Top*, ed. Rachel da Silva (Seattle: Seal Press, 1992), 69–70. For more background on early women climbers and explorers, see Bill Birkett and Bill Peascod, *Women Climbing: 200 Years of Achievement* (Seattle: Mountaineers Books, 1990); and Elizabeth Flagg Olds, *Women of the Four Winds* (Boston: Mariner Books, 1985).

6. Da Silva, Lawrenz, and Roberts, "A Brief History," 78; Anne Foster, "Suffragettes in Yellowstone: Dr. Cora Smith Eaton," *Yellowstone*, June 10, 2014 (Washington, DC: National Park Service, US Department of the Interior), www.nps.gov/yell/blogs/suffragettes-in-yellowstone-dr-cora-smith-eaton.htm.

7. Paula Becker, "Suffragists Join the Mountaineers Outing to Mount Rainier and Plant an A-Y-P Exposition Flag and a 'Votes for Women' Banner at the Summit of

Columbia Crest on July 30, 1909," *Historylink.org*, April 25, 2008, www.historylink .org/file/8578.

8. Biographical material on Eaton is found in da Silva, Lawrenz, and Roberts, "A Brief History," and Ross-Nazzal, *Winning the West for Women*. See also Judy Bentley, Joan Burton, Lace Thornber, and Carla Firey, "The First Ladies," *Washington Trails* (March–April 2011): 22.

9. Ross-Nazzal, *Winning the West for Women*, 213, 126.

10. Ibid., 124; Eaton to Carrie Chapman Catt, October 24, 1909, Emma Smith Devoe Collection, Washington State Library, Tumwater, WA, quoted in Ross-Nazzal, *Winning the West for Women*, 124.

11. Cora Smith Eaton to Mrs. M. A. Hutton, June 17, 1909, Emma Smith Devoe Collection, Washington State Library; Rebecca J. Mead, *How the Vote Was Won: Woman Suffrage in the Western United States, 1868–1914* (New York: New York University Press, 2004), 111. According to a handwritten note on the top, this letter was crafted with the advice of three lawyers.

12. Eaton to Hutton, June 17, 1909, Emma Smith Devoe Collection, Washington State Library; Mead, *How the Vote Was Won*, 111.

13. Ross-Nazzal, *Winning the West for Women*, 128.

14. Ida Husted Harper, ed., *History of Woman Suffrage, Volume 6: 1900–1920* (New York: National American Woman Suffrage Association, 1922), 676.

15. Ross-Nazzal, *Winning the West for Women*, 143; J. D. Zahniser and Amelia R. Fry, *Alice Paul: Claiming Power* (New York: Oxford University Press, 2014), 269–270, 285.

16. Hannah Kimberley, *A Woman's Place Is at the Top: A Biography of Annie Smith Peck, Queen of the Climbers* (New York: St. Martin's Press, 2017), 277; Brown, *Women on High*, 184, 198. Smith was noted for her intense rivalry with fellow American climber Fanny Bullock Workman. Perhaps not to be outdone by Smith's feat, Workman included a photograph of herself reading a newspaper at twenty-one thousand feet in the eastern Karakoran that clearly showed the headline "Votes for Women."

17. Brown, *Women on High*, 192.

Chapter 14. Hazel MacKaye and the "Allegory" of Woman Suffrage

1. Hazel MacKaye, "Pioneering in Pageantry," 7, MacKaye Family Papers, Rauner Special Collections Library, Dartmouth College, Hanover, NH.

2. Rebecca Coleman Hewett, "Progressive Compromises: Performing Gender, Race and Class in Historical Pageants of 1913" (PhD diss., University of Texas-Austin,

2010), 79; Annelise K. Madsen, "Columbia and Her Foot Soldiers: Civic Art and the Demand for Change at the 1913 Suffrage Pageant-Procession," *Winterthur Portfolio* 48, no. 4 (2014): 303.

3. MacKaye, "Pioneering in Pageantry," 7.

4. Ibid.

5. Sarah J. Moore, "Making a Spectacle of Suffrage: The National Woman Suffrage Pageant, 1913," *Journal of American Culture* 20, no. 1 (March 1997): 93; MacKaye, "Pioneering in Pageantry," 8.

6. MacKaye, "Pioneering in Pageantry," 8.

7. Karen J. Blair, "Pageantry for Women's Rights: The Career of Hazel MacKaye, 1913–1923," *Theatre Survey* 31 (May 1990): 37; *Woman's Journal*, March 8, 1913.

8. Harriet Connor Brown, ed., *Official Program of the Woman's Suffrage Procession, Washington, DC, March 3, 1913* (Washington, DC: National American Woman Suffrage Association, 1913).

9. Karen J. Blair, *The Torchbearers: Women and their Amateur Arts Associations in America, 1890–1930* (Bloomington: Indiana University Press, 1994), 118; Blair, "Pageantry for Women's Rights," 43.

10. Hewett, "Progressive Compromises," 66.

11. Hazel MacKaye, "Pageants as a Means of Suffrage Propaganda," *The Suffragist* 2, no. 48 (November 28, 1914): 6.

12. MacKaye, "Pageants as a Means of Suffrage Propaganda," 7, 8; Hazel MacKaye, "Campaigning with Pageantry," *Equal Rights* 1, no. 39 (November 10, 1923): 309. MacKaye was specifically referring to the Seneca Falls commemoration.

13. Blair, "Pageantry for Women's Rights," 30; Mary Simonson, *Body Knowledge: Performance, Intermediality, and American Entertainment at the Turn of the Twentieth Century* (New York: Oxford University Press, 2013), 66; Percy MacKaye, "Art and the Woman's Movement," *Forum* 49, no. 6 (June 1913): 683.

14. Hewett, "Progressive Compromises," 50.

15. "Real Beauty Show in League Pageant," *New York Times*, April 18, 1914.

16. *Six Periods of American Life: A Woman Suffrage Program* (1914) and "Program: Pageant and Ball, April 17th, 1914" in MacKaye Family Papers, Rauner Special Collections Library.

17. "Program: Pageant and Ball, April 17th, 1914." Recently married, she was now known as Inez Milholland Boissevain.

18. MacKaye, "Pioneering in Pageantry," preface, 10. MacKaye estimated that a budget of $600 would be adequate to mount a production, provided organizers could secure local contributions and gifts in kind. Blair, *Torchbearers*, 141.

19. MacKaye, "Pioneering in Pageantry," 14–16. For the place of Seneca Falls in women's history, see Lisa Tetrault, *The Myth of Seneca Falls: Memory and the Women's Suffrage Movement, 1848–1898* (Chapel Hill: University of North Carolina Press, 2014).

20. Hazel MacKaye, "Confessions of a Convert," *Equal Rights* 1, no. 14 (May 19, 1923): 109–110.

Chapter 15. "Bread and Roses" and Votes for Women Too

1. Florence H. Luscomb, "Brief Biographical Sketch" (1945), Women's Rights Collection, Schlesinger Library, Radcliffe Institute, Harvard University.

2. Rose Schneiderman with Lucy Goldwaithe, *All for One* (New York: Paul Eriksson, 1967), 100–101.

3. Biographical information drawn from Nancy Schrom Dye, "Rose Schneiderman," in *Notable American Women: The Modern Period*, ed. Barbara Sicherman and Carol Hurd Green (Cambridge: Harvard University Press, 1980); Schneiderman, *All for One*; Joyce Antler, *The Journey Home: Jewish Women and the American Century* (New York: Free Press, 1997); and Annelise Orleck, *Common Sense and a Little Fire: Women and Working-Class Politics in the United States, 1900–1965* (Chapel Hill: University of North Carolina Press, 1995). See also Rose Schneiderman, "A Cap Maker's Story," *The Independent* (April 27, 1905).

4. See Orleck, *Common Sense and a Little Fire*. Another person who butted heads with a middle-class ally was Clara Lemlich, who had a falling out with Mary Beard.

5. Ellen Carol DuBois, *Harriot Stanton Blatch and the Winning of Woman Suffrage* (New Haven: Yale University Press, 1997), 94.

6. Ellen Carol DuBois first made this point in her 1987 article "Working Women, Class Relations, and Suffrage Militance: Harriot Stanton Blatch and the New York Woman Suffrage Movement, 1894–1909," which is reprinted in Ellen Carol DuBois, *Woman Suffrage and Women's Rights* (New York: New York University Press, 1998).

7. Linda J. Lumsden, *Inez: The Life and Times of Inez Milholland* (Bloomington: Indiana University Press, 2004), 1–2.

8. Harriot Stanton Blatch and Alma Lutz, *Challenging Years: The Memoirs of Harriot Stanton Blatch* (New York: Putnam, 1940), 108.

9. Orleck, *Common Sense and a Little Fire*, 53; Johanna Newman, *Gilded Suffragists: The New York Socialites Who Fought for Women's Right to Vote* (New York: New York University Press, 2017).

10. Orleck, *Common Sense and a Little Fire*, 87, 104.

11. John Thomas McQuire, "From Socialism to Social Justice Feminism: Rose Schneiderman and the Quest for Urban Equity, 1911–1933," *Journal of Urban History* 35, no. 7 (2009): 1001; Orleck, *Common Sense and a Little Fire*, 105.

12. See Susan Goodier and Karen Pastorello, *Women Will Vote: Winning Suffrage in New York State* (Ithaca, NY: Cornell University Press, 2017).

13. Susan Ware, *Beyond Suffrage: Women in the New Deal* (Cambridge: Harvard University Press, 1981). Three of the women in this book (Schneiderman, Molly Dewson, and Sue Shelton White) belonged to the women's network in the New Deal.

14. Schneiderman, *All for One*, viii, 125. Annelise Orleck includes the "bread and roses" remark in her entry on Rose Schneiderman in the Jewish Women's Archive encyclopedia (https://jwa.org/encyclopedia/article/schneiderman-rose). The quote dates to 1911, and it likely inspired James Oppenheim's poem "Bread and Roses," published in December of that year in *The American Magazine*.

Chapter 16. Cartooning with a Feminist Twist

1. "Learning New Tricks," *Christian Science Monitor* (February 1, 1920), www.nationalwomansparty.org/womenwecelebrate/nina-allender/.

2. Alice Sheppard, *Cartooning for Suffrage* (Albuquerque: University of New Mexico Press, 1994), 53.

3. In addition to the three cartoonists discussed here, Sheppard also highlights Rose O'Neill (who invented the Kewpie Doll), Fredrikke Palmer, Mary Ellen Sigsbee, Nell Brinkley, and Ida Sedgwick Proper, among others.

4. For biographical information, see Sheppard, *Cartooning for Suffrage*, and Alice Sheppard, "Political and Social Consciousness in the Woman Suffrage Cartoons of Lou Rogers and Nina Allender," *Studies in American Humor* 4, no. 1–2 (Spring / Summer 1985): 39–50. Also of interest is Allender's anonymously published "Lightning Speed through Life," *Nation* 124 (April 13, 1927): 395–397, which is reprinted in Elaine Showalter, *These Modern Women* (New York: Feminist Press, 1978).

5. For more on the connections between Wonder Woman and the suffrage campaign, see Jill Lepore, *The Secret History of Wonder Woman* (New York: Knopf, 2014); the *Woman's Journal* quote is on 84.

6. "Meanwhile They Drown," *Woman's Journal*, June 5, 1915. For biographical information, see Anne Biller Clark, *My Dear Mrs. Ames: A Study of Suffragist Cartoonist Blanche Ames* (New York: Peter Lang, 2001).

7. Sheppard, *Cartooning for Suffrage*, 116; Sheppard, "Political and Social Consciousness in the Woman Suffrage Cartoons of Lou Rogers and Nina Allender," 39.

8. Inez Haynes Irwin, quoted in Sheppard, *Cartooning for Suffrage*, 116. See also J. D. Zahniser and Amelia R. Fry, *Alice Paul: Claiming Power* (New York: Oxford University Press, 2014), 127–128.

9. "The Summer Campaign," *The Suffragist*, June 6, 1914; "The Inspiration of the Suffrage Worker," *The Suffragist*, June 13, 1914; "Child Saving Is Woman's Work— Votes for Women," *The Suffragist*, July 25, 1914; "Woman's Place is the Home," *The Suffragist*, August 29, 1914.

10. Sheppard, "Political and Social Consciousness in the Woman Suffrage Cartoons of Lou Rogers and Nina Allender," 46; Sheppard, *Cartooning for Suffrage*, 196. Interesting, of course, that it is not "The Allender Woman."

11. Mary Chapman and Angela Mills, eds., *Treacherous Texts: US Suffrage Literature, 1846–1946* (New Brunswick, NJ: Rutgers University Press, 2012), 241; Kenneth Florey, *Women's Suffrage Memorabilia: An Illustrated Historical Study* (Jefferson, NC: McFarland, 2013), 197.

12. "President Wilson Says, 'Godspeed to the Cause,'" *The Suffragist*, November 3, 1917.

13. Sheppard, "Political and Social Consciousness in the Woman Suffrage Cartoons of Lou Rogers and Nina Allender," 47; Sheppard, *Cartooning for Suffrage*, 168, 169.

14. "Will You Make 1918 Safe for Democracy?" *The Suffragist*, January 5, 1918; "One Vote for Victory Women," *The Suffragist*, May 10, 1919; "Any Good Suffragist the Morning After," *The Suffragist*, September 1920.

15. "Judiciary Committee: 'Wha' Jer Goin' to Do Next?," *The Suffragist*, December 16, 1915.

16. Lou Rogers, "A Woman Destined," quoted in Sheppard, "Political and Social Consciousness in the Woman Suffrage Cartoons of Lou Rogers and Nina Allender," 42.

Chapter 17. Jailed for Freedom

1. Doris Stevens, *Jailed for Freedom: The Story of the Militant American Suffragist Movement* (New York: Boni and Liveright, 1920; New York: Schocken Books, 1976), 246. All page references are to the 1976 Schocken Books edition.

2. Ibid.

3. Kenneth Florey, *Women's Suffrage Memorabilia: An Illustrated Historical Study* (Jefferson, NC: McFarland and Company, 2013), 39; Katherine H. Adams and Michael L. Keene, *After the Vote Was Won: The Later Achievements of Fifteen Suffragists* (Jefferson, NC: McFarland and Company, 2010), 122.

4. Rosalind Rosenberg, *Jane Crow: The Life of Pauli Murray* (New York: Oxford University Press, 2017), 130–131, 290.

5. Hazel Hunkins-Hallinan, "Talk to Women's Press Club," August 23, 1977, Washington, DC, found in Hazel Hunkins-Hallinan Papers, Schlesinger Library, Radcliffe Institute for Advanced Study, Harvard University.

6. Ibid.

7. Ibid.; Christine Stansell, *The Feminist Promise: 1792 to the Present* (New York: Modern Library, 2010), 158.

8. Linda G. Ford, *Iron Jawed Angels: The Suffrage Militancy of the National Woman's Party, 1912–1920* (Lanham, MD: University Press of America, 1991), 103; Hazel Hunkins-Hallinan, "Speech Delivered July 24, 1977 at the Memorial Service for Alice Paul," Hazel Hunkins-Hallinan Papers, Schlesinger Library.

9. Hazel Hunkins, "Notes from Picketing," [1917] and "Vassar Suffrage Sentinel Tells What It Is to Picket the White House," *Washington Post*, January 29, 1917, both found in Hazel Hunkins-Hallinan Papers, Schlesinger Library.

10. Katherine H. Adams and Michael L. Keene, *Alice Paul and the American Suffrage Campaign* (Urbana: University of Illinois Press, 2008), 182; Hunkins, "Talk to Women's Press Club." For the larger context, see Julia L. Mickenberg, "Suffragettes and Soviets: American Feminists and the Specter of Revolutionary Russia," *Journal of American History* 100, no. 4 (March 2014): 1021–1051.

11. Hazel Hunkins to Mother, July 8, 1917, Hazel Hunkins-Hallinan Papers, Schlesinger Library.

12. Hazel Hunkins to "Dear little Mother of Mine," July 5, 1917, Hazel Hunkins-Hallinan Papers, Schlesinger Library. For Alice Paul's fraught communication with her mother, see J. D. Zahniser and Amelia R. Fry, *Alice Paul: Claiming Power* (New York: Oxford University Press, 2014), chapter 3.

13. Stevens, *Jailed for Freedom*.

14. Hazel Hunkins to Mother, December 6, 1918, Hazel Hunkins-Hallinan Papers, Schlesinger Library.

15. Stevens, *Jailed for Freedom*, 271–272. The newspaper reference is to the *New York Evening World*, August 13, 1918.

16. Stevens, *Jailed for Freedom*, 271–273; Zahniser and Fry, *Alice Paul: Claiming Power*, 305; Hazel Hunkins, telegram, August 15, 1918, Hazel Hunkins-Hallinan Papers, Schlesinger Library.

17. Hazel Hunkins, "Prison Described by the Prisoners," *The Suffragist*, August 31, 1918, 8–9.

18. Ibid.; Julia Emory, "Prison Described by the Prisoners," *The Suffragist*, August 31, 1918, 9.

19. Emory, "Prison Described by the Prisoners," 9.

20. Hazel Hunkins to "Muddy," September 16, 1918, Hazel Hunkins-Hallinan Papers, Schlesinger Library.

21. A scandal was avoided back home by Hazel's careful coaching of her mother about the "situation." Hunkins to "Dearest Wonderful Mother," November 10, 1920, Hazel Hunkins-Hallinan Papers, Schlesinger Library.

22. Cheryl Law, "Hazel Hunkins Hallinan," *Oxford Dictionary of National Biography*, online ed., Oxford University Press, doi:10.1093/ref:odnb/63871.

Chapter 18. Maud Wood Park and the Front Door Lobby

1. Maud Wood Park, *Front Door Lobby* (Boston: Beacon Press, 1960), 39. The book was edited by Edna Lamprey Stantial and published five years after Park's death.

2. Ibid., 42

3. Ibid., 1. Maud Wood Park did not receive a salary but was reimbursed for her living expenses and travel; other suffrage workers paid to live at Suffrage House. For an introduction to the colorful and sometimes sordid history of lobbying, see Kathryn Allamong Jacob, *King of the Lobby: The Life and Times of Sam Ward, Man-about-Washington in the Gilded Age* (Baltimore: John Hopkins Press, 2010).

4. Nancy F. Cott, "Across the Great Divide: Women in Politics before and after 1920," in *Women, Politics, and Change*, ed. Louise A. Tilly and Patricia Gurin (New York: Russell Sage Foundation, 1990), 161.

5. Sharon Hartman Strom, "Maud Wood Park," in *Notable American Women: The Modern Period*, ed. Barbara Sicherman and Carol Hurd Green (Cambridge: Harvard University Press, 1980); Maud Wood Park, supplemental notes to "Suffrage Reminiscences," January 1943, in *The Power of Organization, Part One: Maud Wood Park and the Woman Suffrage Movement*, ed. Melanie S. Gustafson (Alexandria, VA: Alexander Street, 2014).

6. Maud Wood Park, supplemental notes to "Alice Stone Blackwell," December 1942, in Gustafson, *The Power of Organization, Part One*; Melanie S. Gustafson, introduction to *The Power of Organization, Part Two: Maud Wood Park in a Nation of Women Voters* (Alexandria, VA: Alexander Street, 2014).

7. Park, supplemental notes, "Alice Stone Blackwell."

8. Maud Wood Park, "An Explanation as to Why Bob and I Were Not Publicly Married Is Probably Needed," June 1945, in Gustafson, *The Power of Organ-*

ization, Part One. See also Gustafson's introduction for a discussion of Park's personal life.

9. Park, supplemental notes to "Suffrage Reminiscences"; Park, *Front Door Lobby*, 35.

10. Park, *Front Door Lobby*, 17.

11. Ibid., 52, 62.

12. Ibid., 173–174, 70.

13. Ibid., 185–186.

14. *Woman Citizen*, October 5, 1918; Park, *Front Door Lobby*, 194, 210, 212.

15. Park, *Front Door Lobby*, 256.

16. Ibid., 259. This was a serious problem. During the sixty-fifth Congress, ten senate seats were vacant due to death; seven of those had been suffrage supporters.

17. Ibid., 263.

18. Ibid., 269.

19. Ibid., 270, 180.

Chapter 19. Tennessee's "Perfect 36"

1. Susan Ware, "The Book I Couldn't Write: Alice Paul and the Challenge of Feminist Biography," *Journal of Women's History* 24, no. 2 (Summer 2012): 23.

2. Ibid., 24–25.

3. Carol Lynn Yellin and Janann Sherman, *The Perfect 36: Tennessee Delivers Woman Suffrage* (Memphis, TN: VOTE 70, 1998), 139. "Rat" did not refer to a rodent, but to a popular cartoon which depicted an old woman with a broom, trying to catch the letters R-A-T and join them to the rest of RATIFICATION.

4. Katherine H. Adams and Michael L. Keene, *After the Vote Was Won: The Later Achievements of Fifteen Suffragists* (Jefferson, NC: McFarland, 2010), 147. Additional biographical information is found in Betty Sparks Huehls and Beverly Greene Bond, "Sue Shelton White (1887–1943): Lady Warrior," in *Tennessee Women: Their Lives and Times*, ed. Sarah Wilkerson Freeman (Athens: University of Georgia Press, 2009).

5. Sue Shelton White, "Mother's Daughter," in *These Modern Women: Autobiographical Essays from the Twenties*, ed. Elaine Showalter (New York: Feminist Press, 1978), 49.

6. Huehls and Bond, *Tennessee Women*, 157.

7. Marjorie Spruill Wheeler, *New Women of the New South: The Leaders of the Woman Suffrage Movement in the Southern States* (New York: Oxford University Press, 1993), 47.

8. James P. Louis, "Sue Shelton White and the Woman Suffrage Movement in Tennessee, 1913–1920," *Tennessee Historical Quarterly* 22, no. 2 (June 1963): 170–190.

9. Sue Shelton White to Carrie Chapman Catt, April 27, 1918, Sue Shelton White Papers, Schlesinger Library, Radcliffe Institute, Harvard University.

10. Adams and Keene, *After the Vote Was Won*, 145–146.

11. Carrie Chapman Catt to Mrs. Leslie Warner, April 24, 1918, Sue Shelton White Papers, Schlesinger Library.

12. Sue Shelton White to Carrie Chapman Catt, April 27, 1918; White to Catt, May 9, 1918; Catt to White, May 6, 1918, all in the Sue Shelton White Papers, Schlesinger Library.

13. Sue S. White, "'Militant' Suffragists and How They Won a Hopeless Cause," *Montgomery Times* [Alabama], August 1919, TS copy, Sue Shelton White Papers, Schlesinger Library.

14. Adams and Keene, *After the Vote Was Won*, 33, 146.

15. Huehls and Bond, *Tennessee Women*, 140; "The Prison Special," *The Suffragist* (February 1, 1919): 10; White, "Militant Suffragists and How They Won a Hopeless Cause," 13. See also the extensive coverage in *The Suffragist* throughout February and March 1919.

16. White, "Militant Suffragists and How They Won a Hopeless Cause," 14.

17. A full accounting of the ratification battle awaits a historian. Most accounts of the suffrage struggle end the story in June 1919 or skip directly from the senate passage to the final stages in Tennessee. Maud Wood Park, *Front Door Lobby* (Boston: Beacon Press, 1960) ends with only a short epilogue after the victory in the Senate. Doris Stevens, *Jailed for Freedom: The Story of the Militant American Suffragist Movement* (New York: Boni and Liveright, 1920) relegates the ratification fight to an appendix. Elaine Weiss, *The Woman's Hour: The Great Fight to Win the Vote* (New York: Viking, 2018) focuses primarily on the Tennessee story, not the preceding thirty-five state campaigns.

18. Betty Gram Swing, "A Brief Accolade to Sue S. White, the Intrepid Feminist," 1959, Sue Shelton White Papers, Schlesinger Library. Louis, "Sue Shelton White and the Woman Suffrage Movement in Tennessee, 1913–1920," covers the legal issues surrounding the special section.

19. Swing, "A Brief Accolade"; Florence Armstrong recollections, 1959, Sue Shelton White Papers, Schlesinger Library. Armstrong, a government economist, shared a home with White in Washington, DC, until White's death in 1943.

20. Wheeler, *New Women of the New South*, xix; Swing, "A Brief Accolade." See also the tribute by Florence Boeckel, "Sue Shelton White," *Equal Rights* (July–August 1943).

Epilogue

1. This inscribed volume is found in the collections of the Schlesinger Library, Radcliffe Institute for Advanced Study, Harvard University.

2. Susan Ware, *Beyond Suffrage: Women in the New Deal* (Cambridge: Harvard University Press, 1981), 31. The original quote is found in the reminiscences of Frances Perkins for the Oral History Collection, Columbia University.

3. Gertrude Foster Brown, "Suffrage and Music—My First Eighty Years," 192, draft manuscript, Gertrude Foster Brown Papers, Schlesinger Library; Carrie Chapman Catt and Nettie Rogers Shuler, *Woman Suffrage and Politics* (New York: Charles Scribner's Sons, 1923), 107–108.

4. Melanie Gustafson, Kristie Miller, and Elisabeth Perry, eds., *We Have Come to Stay: American Women and Political Parties, 1880–1960* (Albuquerque: University of New Mexico Press, 1999). See Nancy Cott, *The Grounding of Modern Feminism* (New Haven: Yale University Press, 1987) for a discussion of women's activism on either side of the "great divide" of 1920.

5. See Liette Gidlow, *Resistance after Ratification: The Nineteenth Amendment, African American Women, and the Problem of Female Disfranchisement after 1920* (Alexandria, VA: Alexander Street, 2017); Ann D. Gordon and Bettye Collier-Thomas, eds., *African American Women and the Vote, 1837–1965* (Amherst: University of Massachusetts Press, 1997); and Rosalyn Terborg-Penn, *African American Women in the Struggle for the Vote, 1850–1920* (Bloomington: Indiana University Press, 1999).

6. Alexander Keyssar, *The Right to Vote: The Contested History of Democracy in the United States* (New York: Basic Books, 2000; rev. ed., 2009), 132–134. Support for voting was far from universal in the Native American community, including among women activists, because it involved accepting the sovereignty of the United States over the claims of indigenous peoples for self-determination. See Joanne Barker, "Indigenous Feminisms," in *The Oxford Handbook of Indigenous People's Politics*, ed. Jose Antonio Lucero, Dale Turner, and Donn Lee VanCott, Oxford University Press, 2015, www.oxfordhandbooks.com/view/10.1093/oxfordhb/9780195386653.001.0001/oxfordhb-9780195386653-e-007.

7. Catt and Shuler, *Woman Suffrage and Politics*, 107–108; Oreola Williams Haskell, *Banner Bearers: Tales of the Suffrage Campaigns* (Geneva, NY: W. F. Humphrey, 1920), 43.

8. The Sophia Smith Collection at Smith College is another major archive whose history is linked to suffrage. Originally founded in 1942 to collect works by women writers, it quickly expanded its mission under Margaret Storrs Grierson to document women's history more broadly. Suffrage material also provided the bulk of women-related material deposited at established repositories such as the Library of Congress and the Huntington Library.

9. Mary Ritter Beard, *Woman as Force in History: A Study in Traditions and Realities* (New York: Macmillan, 1946).

10. Gertrude Stein and Virgil Thomson, *The Mother of Us All* (New York: Music Press, 1947), 23.

Acknowledgments

The genesis of this book was a Radcliffe conference in the spring of 2015 called "The University as Collector." As the interim faculty director of the Schlesinger Library, I was asked to speak for ten minutes about a specific document or artifact in our collections. When I surveyed the Schlesinger staff for their favorites, Maryléne Altieri, the curator of books and printed material, drew my attention to the Susan B. Anthony inscription in the fourth volume of the *History of Woman Suffrage* that would later supply the inspiration for my epilogue. That artifact struck a chord as a possible theme for a book, but it took a while to find the right balance between material culture and biography. At a brown-bag lunch with Schlesinger staff to gather suggestions of objects and people to include, Ellen Shea playfully suggested I aim for nineteen chapters in honor of the Nineteenth Amendment. As I tracked down manuscripts and followed leads, the wonderful reference staff, especially Sarah Hutcheon, guided my way. Diana Carey gets a special shout-out for her help securing images of all of the objects. The fingerprints of the Schlesinger Library are on practically every page of this book.

I have been mining the collections of the Schlesinger Library for more than four decades, and I offer this book as a heartfelt "thank you" for an institutional affiliation that has enriched my entire professional life. Not only did the library's holdings shape my scholarship and teaching, but the time I spent there offered myriad opportunities for friendship and collegiality. As a member of the library's advisory board in the 1980s and 1990s and the Schlesinger Library Council since 2011, and now as the Honorary Women's Suffrage Centennial Historian, I have also become a member of the larger Radcliffe community. My tenure spanned transition from Radcliffe College to the Radcliffe Institute for Advanced Study, where I had the chance to work with two fellow historians, Drew Gilpin Faust and Lizabeth Cohen, during their tenures as dean. Being part of the Radcliffe family, in combination with my involvement with the American Repertory Theater, in turn gave me access to the intellectual and scholarly resources of Harvard University, which I gratefully acknowledge.

I also want to acknowledge a hearty band of co-conspirators involved in commemorating the suffrage centennial. In tribute to Alice Paul's silent sentinels who picketed the White House starting in 1917, I call this group the Not-So-Silent Sentinels, because we not only refuse to stay silent, we speak as loudly as we can. Jane Kamensky, who came on board as the faculty director at the Schlesinger Library in 2015 just as the planning for the library's seventy-fifth anniversary and the suffrage centennial ramped up, has enthusiastically embraced the library's exploration of what we are calling "the long Nineteenth Amendment." Working with the historians Corinne Field, Lisa Tetrault, and Allison Lange on various suffrage-related projects at the library has been a real treat, as has been collaborating with my dear friend and Schlesinger colleague Kathy Jacob, who has been monitoring the centennial planning on the local, state, and national levels. And what fun to acknowledge not just scholars but also a range of artists and filmmakers who are bringing the suffrage story to modern audiences through music, film, and theater, including Sammi Cannold, Shaina Taub, Rachel Sussman, and Gene Tempest. If we ever convened a gathering of the Not-So-Silent Sentinels, nearly all of us could sport the bright pink pussy hats hand-knit by me while I worked on this project—my designated therapy for dealing with the current political climate, which has made my work as a feminist historian even more necessary.

I also have a wider network of cherished friends (many of whom have hand-knit pussy hats of their own) to thank for their support and encouragement. Joyce Antler and I have been each other's first readers since the 1980s. I can't imagine writing a book without her, and I know she feels the same way. That also goes for the friendships I have forged with Carla Kaplan, Carol Oja, Carol Bundy, and Kathleen Dalton over our shared writing projects. Thanks as well to Katherine Marino, who graduated (literally) from an undergraduate biography class I taught at Harvard to becoming a fine historian in her own right. Collaborating on a suffrage web exhibit with Lola Van Wagenen and Melanie Gustafson at Clio Visualizing History gave the three of us the chance to continue the strong connections we first formed at New York University in the 1980s. The book has also been enriched by conversations about history, writing, and so much more with Claire Bond Potter, another NYU connection. Joyce Seltzer and I have known each other for decades, and finally (just in time!) got to do a book together. I couldn't possibly have written this book without Rob Heinrich's steady presence as the research editor at *American National Biography*. And on the home front, Don Ware, a master himself when it comes to working hard and being successful, has helped provide an environment where I can pursue my passion for history and biography.

This book is dedicated to Anne Firor Scott, who, like so much else that is good, came into my life through the Schlesinger Library. The dedication honors our long friendship, Anne's pioneering role in the field of women's history, and her place in suffrage history. The math doesn't quite work out, but I fancy the idea that she was conceived on the very night in August 1920 that the Nineteenth Amendment formally became part of the US Constitution.

Index

Page numbers that refer to figures are noted with *f.*